UNIVERSITY OF NORTH CAROLINA
STUDIES IN THE ROMANCE LANGUAGES AND LITERATURES
Number 110

RAIMON VIDAL
POETRY AND PROSE

Volume II: Abril issia

RAIMON VIDAL

POETRY AND PROSE

Volume II: Abril issia

... Venir a perfeccio
de la art de trobar.

EDITED BY

W. H. W. FIELD

CHAPEL HILL
THE UNIVERSITY OF NORTH CAROLINA PRESS

DEPÓSITO LEGAL: V. 4.892 - 1971

ARTES GRÁFICAS SOLER, S. A. - JÁVEA, 28 - VALENCIA (8) - 1971

TABLE OF CONTENTS

Pages

PREFACE   9

ABRIL ISSIA

   Text 11

   Translation 61

   Notes 89

   Index of Names 129

BIBLIOGRAPHY 189

PREFACE

Abril issia, which with *So fo e · l temps* represents the extant totality of Raimon Vidal's poetic output, is contained in the single MS. R (Bib. nat. fr. 22543, ff. 136v-138v). It was first brought to the attention of the public by the synopsis given in the *Histoire littéraire des troubadours*, vol. II pp. 283-296. Raynouard presented extracts in his *Choix*, vol. V pp. 342-348. Both Millot and Raynouard ascribed the poem to Peire Vidal, in spite of the fact that the MS. gives Raimon as the author. The error was rectified by Diez in *Die Poesie der Troubadours* (1826), p. 225, who, in addition to mentioning the evidence of the MS., noted that Raimon Vidal, of Besalú, situated the action of the poem in his native town.

The first publication of the entire poem was that of Karl Bartsch, in his *Denkmäler der provenzalischen Litteratur* (1856), pp. 144-192.

Extracts were published by Mahn (*Werke der Troubadours im provenzalischer Sprache*, [1846], vol. I pp. 250-254), and by Milá y Fontanals (*De los Trovadores en España*, [1889], pp. 341-354), who enriched the text with copious notes and historical studies. The edition of Wilhelm Bohs, which appeared in *Romanische Forschungen* XV (1904), 204-316, was the first that could be called critical, and the only one made until the present. He offered a text markedly superior to Bartsch's in its reading of the MS., profited from Levy's observations on Bartsch's work (*Z. r. Ph.* XIII [1889], 310-315) in establishing his text, and accompanied it with a translation that is in the main accurate. It is a mark of the superiority of his work that I have not hesitated to quote from it on many occasions. I have in addition used the corrections and suggestions of Jeanroy and

Herzog, whose reviews of Bohs appeared in *Romania XXXIII* (1904) and *Z.r.Ph.* XXXI (1904) respectively.

The identification of Raimon Vidal's quotations from the works of other troubadours owes much to the investigations of Massó Torrents, whose article "La Cançо provençal en la literatura catalana," appeared in the *Miscel·lania Prat de la Riba* (Barcelona: Institut d'Estudis catalans, 1923), pp. 344-370; while the unpublished doctoral dissertation of A. Comas i Pujols (Barcelona, 1956) shed some new light on the patrons mentioned in *Abril issia*, utilizing some documents published since Milá y Fontanals' investigations. With the greatest generosity Mr. Comas furnished me with a microfilm of relevant parts of his work. L. T. Topsfield kindly made available to me page-proofs of his long-awaited edition of Raimon de Miraval.

The publication of the second volume of Raimon Vidal's poetry and prose has been made possible by a grant from the University of Washington, to which I would like to express my deep thanks. It is with the greatest gratitude and pleasure that I acknowledge the influence of my teacher and friend, John Corominas. It is impossible to measure adequately my indebtedness to him, for even by listing each and every suggestion of his, such a testimony would not indicate the extent of my obligation nor the depth of my gratitude.

W. H. W. FIELD

        Abril issi' e mays intrava,
        e cascus dels auzels chantava
        josta sa par, que autz que bas
        e car remanion atras
    5   vas totas partz neus e freidors,
        venion frugz, venion flors,
        e clar temps e dossa sazos.
        E yeu m'estava cossiros
        e per amor .l. pauc embroncz.
    10 Sove·m que fo mati adoncx
        en la plassa de Bezaudun,
        es anc ab me non ac negun,
        mas amor e mon pessamen
        avion m'aisi solamen;
    15 c'alhors no·m podia virar,
        ni yeu que non o volgra far
        s'autres no m'en fos ocaizos,
        mas vas Dieu dos e poderos.
        E sel que totz fizels adzora
    20 volc e·m donet que·n eysa ora
        que ieu m'estav' aisi pessatz
        venc vas mi vestitz e caussatz
        us joglaretz a fort del temps
        on hom trobava totz essems
    25 justa·ls baros valor e pretz.
        E si eu deman co fuy letz
        a son venir, ni com joyos,
        no m'en crezessetz en perdos,
        ni a mi no tanh que·us o jur.

(Note: all references are to the unique MS. R unless otherwise specified.)
1 issie   14 lolamen   18 vers

30 Mas aitan vos puesc dir segur
e ses tot cug, c'al saludar
venc josta me son cors pauzar.
E yeu rendey li sas salutz
e si be·m fuy aperceubutz
35 a son venir que fos joglars,
si·m volgui saber sos afars
per *lui* meteus, et el me dis:
 "Senher, yeu soy us hom aclis
a joglaria de cantar,
40 e say romans dir e contar,
e novas motas e salutz
e autres comtes espandutz
vas totas partz azautz e bos,
e d'en G*uiraut* vers e chansos
45 e d'en Ar*naut* de Maruelh mays,
e d'autres vers e d'autres lays
que ben deuri' en cort caber.
Mas er son vengut vil voler
e fraitz a far homes malvatz
50 que·n van per las cortz assermatz
a tolre pretz entre las gens.
Per qu'ieu ni nulhs hom avinens
ni savis non es aculhitz
ans on pus venc josta·ls chauzitz
55 on cujaria trobar loc;
ades truep mays qui·m torn en *joc*
e en soan so que vuelh dir.
E vey los jangladors venir,
e·ls homes hufaniers de sen
60 a penre solatz mantenen,
nessis e ses tot bon esgar.
Et yeu, c'om no·m vol escotar
ni vol entendre mon saber,
vau m'en ad una part sezer
65 aichi co homs desesperatz.
Aichi soi vengutz et anatz
per vos vezer entro aisi."

37 m̄l 44 dē .G. 45 dē ar̄ 56 t.e. loc

E yeu, per so car ora·n vi
e sazos me ofri coratje,
70 li dis: "Amicx, ses tot m*u*satje
vuelh que·ns anem ades disnar.
Apres, si res voletz comtar,
e tot o pauc o trop o mout,
ieu soi sel que sas cor estout
75 vos auzirai mot volontiers."
    Apres manjar en .l. vergiers
sobr'un prat josta .l. rivet
venguem abduy, e si no.y met
messonja, sotz .l. bruelh flurit.
80 Aqui seguem, e non petit
segon que comtar m'auziretz.
E·l temps fon clars e dos e quetz
e suaus e francx e cortes,
e yeu a pauc en solatz mes
85 per seluy c'aisi·m vi denan,
adreg e franc ab .l. semblan
aital com cove a saber.
E s'ie·us dizia c'al parer
fossan siey vestir maltalhat,
90 no m'en crezessetz, car tr*i*at
semblavan ad e*l a* doblier.
Aiso m'aduys .l. cossirier
aital com sol aver hom fis,
e membret mi qu'en Gaucelm dis
95 que tan se fes a totz prezar:
    "*Eu vi* per cortz *anar*
us joglaretz petitz
gen caussatz e vestitz
sol per donas lauzar."
100 E si·m fos natural de far
aisi·m volgra estar tostemps,
may sel que fon ab mi essems,
aital aisi co yeu vos dic,

---

70 messatje   90 No mē crezatz c. trait   91 ades del doblier
96 Veni .l. per corsa maniar·······

me dis: "Senher, a bon abric
105 vey que em *ena*isi vengut(z).
Per qu'ie·us prec, si dieu vos aiut
a far tot so que vos volres,
c'aisi puramen m'escotes,
com s'era messatje d'amor;
110 co'us sabetz ben que·l chauzidor,
cal que siam, o mal o bo,
an mes chauzir en tal tenso
c'apenas s'en sabon issir.
Li .l. an chauzitz c'ab mal dir
115 venson poestatz e baros;
e·ls autres son si amoros
e ben dizens vas totas res;
e n'i a que, car son cortes,
ses autrui saber son joglar.
120 Ieu no dic ges c'a ben estar
no·n torn .l. sol mestier per loc;
mas cascus pot saber que groc
ni vert non platz a totas jens,
per que·ls faitz e·ls captenemens
125 segon las jens deu hom camjar.
Aiso m'a fag man ben estar
apenr'e man divers saber;
e cuydava·n secret aver
entre·ls baros mant gazardo
130 a far mon cors azaut e bo
e de melhor captenemen.
Mas er conosc c'a perdemen
son tug vengut, estiers petitz;
per qu'ieu me'n fora tost partitz
135 per penr'un autre cossirier,
mas aventur'e siey mestier,
que mant homes fan benenans,
volgron qu'ieu fos a Monferrans
vengutz en Alvernh'al Dalfi.
140 E si fon .l. sapte mati
si co suy vengut de Riom;
e si anc genta cort vi hom

ni de bon solatz, si fo sela.
Non y ac dona ni donzela
145 ni cavayer ni donzelo
no fos pus francx d'un auzelo
c'om agues noirit en sa man.
Aqui trobey senher sertan,
[e] companha ben entenduda
150 per qu'ieu laisi dans una muda
a gran joys, si Dieu mi sal.
E si s'avenc entorn nadal,
c'om apela kalendas lay,
venguem e fom, ses tot esmay,
155 a Monferran sus e·l palaitz;
e s'anc vis homes essenhatz
ni ab baudor, so fom aqui.
E la nueg si fo, co yeu vi,
mot tenebrosa apres manjar,
160 e·l solatz gran, josta·l foc clar,
de cavayers e de joglars
adreitz e fis e dos e cars
e suaus ad homes cortes,
e no·y ac cridat ni pus mes
165 per pegueza sol de primier.
Aital solatz e pus entier
aguem aqui pus que no·us dic.
E·l cavayer ses tot prezic
a lur temps s'aneron jazer;
170 car mo senher volc remaner
ab .l. companho josta·l foc.
Per qu'ieu, can vi sazon ni loc
a demandar so que doptava,
vas luy mi trays sobr'una blava
175 tota cuberta de samit.
E s'anc trobey bon cor ardit
a ben parlar, si fis yeu lay.
Per que·l dis: "Senher, ab esmay
ai lonjamen estat ab vos.

146 aizelo   155 monferrat   165 per pergueseza

180 E dirai vos per cals razos,
si·eus play que·m escotetz ades.
Vos sabetz be que luenh ni pres
non es homs natz ni faitz ses paire;
per qu'ieu n'aic .l. mot de bon aire
185 e tal que·s saup far entre·ls pros.
Cantaire fo meravilhos
e comtaires azautz e ricx.
E yeu [lh'auzi] si com n'Enricx,
us reys d'Englaterra, donava
190 cavals e muls, e can sercava
vas Lombardia·l pros marques,
e de terras .ll. o .lll.
on trobava baros assatz,
adreitz e ben acostumatz
195 e donadors vas totas mas.
E auzic nomnar catalas
e proensals mot, e gascos,
vas donas francx et amoros;
e fazian guerras e plays.
200 Per c'a mi par' aital pertrays
ab vostres motz me fis joglars.
E ai sercat terras e mars
e vilas e castels assatz
vas totas partz, e poestatz
205 e baros que no·us dic .ll. tans.
Non truep d'aquels .ll. de semblans
mas mot petit, so·us dic de ver,
li .l. donon ab bo saber
e li autre nessiamen;
210 e li autre, privadamen
a sels que son acostumatz.
Aisi ai trobat, e pus fatz
que no·us auria dig d'un an;
e vos mezeus, si tot semblan
215 que es a tot bon fag cauzir,
non e*tz* aital com auzi.m dir

188 E yeu peytz s. c. n.   216 é

adoncx a la gen ni comtar.
Per qu'ie·us vuelh, senher, demandar,
si·eus platz, co es endevengut
220 d'aital mescap, c'aisi perdut
an pretz e valor li baro."
    Et el estet, si Dieu be·m do,
e·l cor .l. pauc totz empessatz,
e al respos far fon levatz
225 e sezens de jazens que era,
e dis, "Amicx, non es enquera
a mon semblan tot ton saber,
car demandat m'as a lezer;
es mot a mi e pauc als pros
230 per qu'ieu non cug aital respos
a far, co·s cove ni·s taisses.
Mas pero, car vengutz say es
e per solatz de mi meteus,
vuelh que t'emportz, si tot s'es greus
235 a contar, .l. pauc de mon sen.
Car saber deus c'ome valen
e savi — c'aisi com es caps
vers Dieus de tot cant es ni saps —
ni yeu meteys, que m'i esper —
240 son cap de pretz a mantener
nobles cors e sens e sabers.
E non es hom lials ni vers
vas pretz si aquestz .lll. non a.
    Noble cors fay home serta
245 e vassalh e larcx e cortes
e drechuriers vas totas res
e conqueredor de regnatjes,
e adutz abrivatz coratjes
e gentilez'a totas gens,
250 e fay far gran adzautimens
e desgrazir malvat cosselh.
    Saber, per qu'ieu lo·us aparelh,
iosta luy ven accidental

224 e alres pos   234 v. q. tē portz

  e fay conoisser ben e mal
255 en los lurs bels captenemens.
  E vieu n'om mielhs entre las gens,
  adreitz e francx e de solatz.
  E ja non er hom acabatz
  ses luy, per qu'ieu tostemps n'ay cura.
260 Sens aporta grans e mezura
  vas totz aquestz mestiers qu'ie·us toc,
  e fay cascu metr'en son loc
  segon que es ni tanh a far.
   Aquestz feron pretz gazanhar
265 e paratges nostres premiers
  e noms o faitz de cavayers
  e franqueza sobre las gens
  a far en totz captenemens
  e abrivatz en totz afars.
270 E ja non er hom de pretz clars
  ni bos, ses aquestz que yeu dic.
  En aquestz .lll. feiron n'Enric,
  un rey d'Englaterra, pujar;
  c'auzist a ton paire nomnar
275 segon que tu mezeis m'as dit, —
  e sos filhs .lll. que no·y oblit,
  n'Enric ni·n Richart ni·n Jaufre
  — car en lor ac .ll. tans de be
  c'om non poiria d'un an dir —
280 josta luy vic en cort venir
  e domneys e guerras menar.
  Et ac sazon sel que saup far
  noblezas ni valors ni sens,
  aisi com ac us conoyssens
285 sarrazi ric una sazo.
  E dirai te .l. comte bo
  ver, pus aisi m'as a ta man.
   En Espanha ac .l. soudan,
  valen segon sos ancessors;
290 e levet s'en us almassors

---

255 els lurs 274 c'auzit a ton p. n. 290 e levet ses u. a.

vas Marrocx, adretz e valens
e francx e larcx e conquerens
et abrivatz a totz coratges.
E·l reys, cuy plac sos vassalatjes
295 e d'aital home sos mestiers,
volc lo retener voluntiers
a sa cort servir et onrar.
E sel penset, que o saup far,
de son senhor a retenir
300 et a onrar et a servir
adrechamen e de bon grat,
aichi en son melhor estat
e en son mager pretz que·l vic.
A son senhor .l. jorn s'ofric,
305 co hom valens et ensenhatz.
Dis li, "Senher, yeu no suy natz
ni faitz mas per vos a servir
e a donar e a blandir
e ses tot genh a car tener;
310 e si no mi basta poder,
no mi sofranh cor ni bos sens.
Per qu'entre·l autres onramens
que m'avetz faitz, vos pregaria
per so que, si s'esdevenia
315 el mieus mescaps ni bayssamen,
c'us jorns vos fos remembramens
so qu'ie·us ai de ben dig ni fag."
E·l reys, cuy plagron tug be*fag*
e totz vetz, li dis, "Amicx
320 almassor, car e dos amicx,
si anc senher se de*c* lauzar
de son vassalh, si dey ieu far,
e de vos o fas *veraymen*.
Per que·l befait e·l onramen
325 vuelh que vos meteys lo preng*atz*."
E sel que fon apparelhatz
avia d'un temps .l. capel

318 illeg.   321 se des lauzar   323 illeg.   325 illeg.

vermelh, azaut, e gent e bel;
'*Almussa*' l'apelan payan
330 ... ey de vostra man
... ...
... qu'el a pauzetz sus el cap
que l'ay gazanhat per proeza
e per senhal de gentileza
335 e d'onramen a mon linhatje.
E c'autr'om non l'aus, per paratje
ni per poder, portar .l. jorn;
e si o fay, qu'el cap *no*·n torn
ses dan de perdre totz *sos* pre*tz*.
340 Aitals fo·l dos com vos auzetz
com el anc sol volc demandar.
   Adenan c'aiso fetz passar
hoblit, de temps e de sazo,
venc en la ter*r*a us baro
345 aitals o mielhors d'autras jens,
e·l rey fon autres eyssamens
apres seluy que vos ai dit.
E s'anc senher trobet ardit
son vassalh, ni cavalairos
350 ni dos ni francx ni amoros
ni valen, si fes seluy.
E·l bars atrobet ses enuy
son senher, e franc e cortes;
e qu'el fo sobre totas res
355 de sa terra cap e senhor.
E so fon .l. jorn en pascor
e·l temps sere e vert e clar,
que sel baro volc cavalcar
e fes venir sos palafres
360 e sos cavals e sos arnes
e sos companhos totz jostatz.
E aportet can fo pujatz
un'almussa d'aquel semblan

330-332 illeg.   338 q. c. lon torn   339 en d. d. p. ses totz precz
344 terrus

com sela que·l rey ac denan
365 donad'*al* almassor premier
e fetz la·s a *s*on cavayer
per se mezeus e·l cap pauzar.
Aiso fes gens maravilhar
per la terra, e paucx e grans,
370 car hom auzet d'aquel semblans
portar capel mes del linhatje
cuy fon donatz per vassalatje,
el linhatje que mant honor
e mant be e manta ricor
375 ac avuda per lo capel.
E·l rey venc ab lo temps novel
un jorn josta en sa maizo,
si com fero mant aut baro,
e mant onrat e mant valen
380 li dissero: "Senher, mot gen
e mot car nos avetz tengutz;
mas er nos es us mals cregutz
si doncas vos no·l castiatz.
Us vostre baros s'es levatz
385 ab almussa per si mezeys.
E non deu esser coms ni reys
ni *nu*lhs autr'oms tan poderos
que port l'almussa mas sol *v*os,
non deya·l cap perdre aqui.
390 Aissi s'es tengut, et aissi
o gazanhet us almassors
que crec ab vostres ancessors
e nos trastug, co hom valens."
E·l rey, aisi com conoissens
395 senher deu far, lur dis: "Li*n*hatjes
adreitz e cars, vostres uzatjes
non er us jorns baissatz per me;
ni ja non auretz tan de be
com yeu volria, so sapchatz.
400 Aquel baro, si vos a platz,

---

365 donadalmassor   366 la sazo cavayer   387 lunhs   388 nos
395 Liatjes

mandaray yeu, e si a fait
vas vos vilan tort ni mesfait
ni vas autruy, yeu ne faray
so que ma cort esgart; so say
405 c'aysi sera fayt lialmen."
    Mandatz fo·l baro veramen,
e la cort fon grans e pleneyra,
e·l rey co hom d'aital maneyra
savis e ricx, dis als baros:
410 "Vos sabetz qu'ieu sy poderos
no soy mas de tener drechura;
e rey que de dreg non a cura
ses regne vieu motas sazos.
Vos avetz fag .l. ergulhos
415 e sobrier fag, segon que·m par,
cau auzes l'almussa levar
contra·l mandamen que n'es faitz.
Per qu'ieu, si tot mi son atraitz
en vos onrar et obezir,
420 no vuelh mon poder tan aunir
que no·y fassa castic plenyer."
E·l baros, [cui] tot cossirier
foron leugier a departir,
estet en pes ses tot cossir,
425 d'on noble cors l'ac deslieurat,
e dis al rey: "Senher, *on*rat
m'avetz mantas vetz e yeu vos,
aisi com puesc mantas sazos,
e no·y esgarday be ni mal.
430 Per qu'ieu vos dic, si Dieu mi sal
ni·m don a far totz faitz onratz,
qu'el mon non es homs vieu ni natz
tan vuelha vostre pro co yeu.
Per c'a vos non deu esser grieu
435 s'ieu puesc l'almussa gazanhar
ses autruy tort, que no vuelh far,
a llinhatge petit ni gran.

410 poderos sy   422 an t. c.   426 aurat   437 al linhatge

Vers es c'us almassors antan,
aisi son ben .C. ans passatz,
440 per so car ac .l. cor auratz
e per servir vostr'ansessor,
per far a son linhatj'onor
volc gazanhar aquest senhal.
Per qu'ieu, que m'ay fait atretal
445 o mielhs, lo vuelh tot atressi.
E s'ieu per nulh erguelh o fi,
no mi laisses cap remaner
e faitz n'a tot vostre plazer
ni·m fassatz be vas nulha part."
450   Aisi et ab aital esgart
de valor gazanhet aquist
so que no fera si fos trist
ni flacx ni malvatz per aver,
per paratge ni per poder,
455 ni per autra cauza del mon.
Adoncx eran en pretz preon
tug li baro, car poestatz
avian noble cors onratz
a gazardonar las valors
460 e a far dos e bels secors
azautz e cars e ben estans,
be fazians so que·n Bertrans
del Born dis en .l. sirventes
a far ricx homes pus cortes
465 e pus francx e pus donadors, ...
que sian ses tortz faire, elitz,
et adretz e francx e chauzitz:
   "Ad aiso fon pretz establitz
c'om guerrejes, e so fortmens
470 e*t* a caresma et avens
e fezes soudadiers manens."
   Aquist avian cors valens
a far guerras e messios
e a bastir cortz ab ricx dos

470 el a c. e. avens

475 per esforsar joys e solatz.
E no·y era fols remembratz
ni malvatz homs ni recrezens,
mas emperaires valens
e reys e coms et autz baros,
480 a metre cor per c'om fos pros
e de major auctoritat.
Mas eras son tug retornat
silh que solian premier far
e car vas pretz non an cor clar
485 e maystrejon las proezas,
per que donas e gentilezas
vas bas e ses cap entre lor.
E ven saber sols ses valor
e creys vil cor flac a cascu
490 a tolre el pretz a negu;
no vey far mas captenh vilan.
Per que·ls baros fan tornar van
e desesperat de senhor
car aissi·l falh bes del major.
495 Car noble cors aver solian
a far proezas, don venian
adzautimens e joy e pretz.
A Dieus, cuy anc non plac engres
ni malvatz homs ni recrezens,
500 per so car ilh son de valens
aisi tornat trist e ses sen,
volra s'en far aital prezen
com als [Marabetis] d'Espanha;
cuy, car foro bona conpanha
505 e nobles gens, lur fon donatz
paratjes e locx e regnatz
de Marroc e·n totz los pays.
Aquestz foron Marabetis
e d'aquetz fetz hom caps e reys
510 per menar guerras e plaideys
....

500 desvalens   502 voltan   503 Maruu d'e.   508 feron

adenan, ses autruy forfay*tz*
c'om non lur fes mas lur paren,
torneron flac e recrezen
515 e fals, e mantengro gran tort;
per c'un linhatge ric e fort
—so fo Mal mut— s'emparatic
sobr'aquels per so car castic
e noble cors volgron aver.
520 E las gens, cuy venc a plazer
so qu'ilh fero, donero lor
per las terras loc de senhor,
e abatero totz aquels.
Aisi·s perdet linhatje dels,
525 e decazet adoncx paratjes.
Car aisi cay tost fals linhatjes
e malvat cor ses retener,
e aisi perdet son poder;
e car aital em devengut
530 ses noble cors e recrezut.
Per que donars es pauc grazitz
e apres pretz, qu'er aculhitz,
non es hom empres ses donar,
....
535 ni ven bos noms a nulha gens.
Donars adutz pretz veramens
vas totas partz, e lutz e lums,
c'adutz als sieus terras e flums
e senhoria, ses desman.
540 E noble cors fay, ses enjan
per conquerre, lo sobre pus;
adutz donar e ten tot sus,
va*l* e fay valen so senhor.
E sol esser que .l. donador,
545 adreit e de faitz avinens,
avian pretz contra las jens,
e sobre totz autres baros
s'esforsavon ad esser pros

532 q̄ra culhitz   539 deman   543 vay

silh per cuy crec aisi valors.
550 Mas er, per so car als majors,
si com yeu t'ay d'amor contat,
son fait mot noble cor onrat
e al mays d'autres atressi
ven us mendicx saber aqui,
555 sestz senhors tug en son tornat
avaros e flac e malvat,
per que no·y es le pretz que sol
enans son tug cazug e·l sol:
per que paratjes fon bastitz.
560 E si trop pueys emparatgitz,
veyras per nobles cors autrus
—car non es dreitz mas grans enutz—
e'nversat ses tota bontat;
com se servir tenh'al sendat
565 a far proezas e bos faitz.
    Paratges fon donatz als faitz
e als nobles cors barnatjos
per que los mendicx nualhos
ses noble cor no·n an razo.
570 Sobr'aiso fon fag man sermo
per lo mon, e man proamen:
cossi dechay vils faitz fazen.
E si tot son amantz viltat
nessiamen, yeu vi·n Lobat
575 per noble cor aitan prezat
com baron qu'en la terra fos.
E vi estar mant paratjos
vencutz e las vas una part.
E sel que vol aver esgart,
580 en Mercadier o pot comtar,
e Margarit que fes per mar,
ses paratje, manta nobleza
e mant fait e manta proeza,
per que hom quer pretz natural.
585 Paratjes, so per que tan val,

560 Es si   564 com ses   570 mon   573 amatz   584 q̄l p.

es car adutz als sieus honor
e de pretz enans e temor
per qu'entre las gens son onratz
mas ses valor no son prezatz
590 ni ses saber grazitz for be;
ni valor ses ric cor no ve,
ni sabers, si hom non l'apren.
A far faitz onratz pretz-valen
venon per cor e per saber,
595 non per parens ni per poder;
e per bon cor venon li loc,
non per paratje ni per joc,
e·l ris e·l jocx e·l plazers;
per que·ls pros conqueron poders
600 a far proezas e faitz fis
si com n'Arnaut de Maruelh dis
ad enans de totz mestier:
"Que vers es que huey e ier
que totz prozoms conquier
605 ab sen et ab saber
et ab bon pretz poder."
Malvatz reman ab son dever
e·ls pros son ric e conoissen.
Huey may si·n vols aver sen
610 ni bon coratje retengut,
per que·ls baro son recrezut
a far proezas per toz locx,
aisi·ns partam; e si·n vols flocx,
enqueras *as* per remaner."
615 E anem nos tantost jazer
cossiran so qu'ieu aic auzit;
e conuc que·l Dalfi m'ac dit
ver en secret al foc canutz.
E lo mati, vezen de tutz
620 .l. dijous qu'ieu prezi comjat.
E s'anc vis home ben pessat
e de senhor, ieu ben o fuey.

592 la pren   602 totz mestiers   614 enqueras per r.   615 non

Per Alvernhe e per lo Puey
m'en vinc en Proensa de sai,
625 on atrobey mant baro gai
e·l bon comte e la comtessa.
E si be fon grans l'esdemessa,
d'aqui m'en aney en Tolzan
on atrobey ab cor certan
630 mo senher lo comte premier,
e mant avinen cavayer
que son ab luy, e n'ayc arnes,
per qu'ieu m'en vinc en Savartes.
E a Foys non trobey negu,
635 que·l coms era ad Alberu,
on nos an*em* vas Castilho.
E Dieus, car yeu ai*c* cor tan bo
c'aisi y tengues ma via plana,
fes me venir a Mataplana
640 aquel dilus que es passatz.
Aqui trobey, si a vos platz,
mo senher n'Ugo avinen
e franc e dos e conoissen
ad escotar tot bo saber.
645 E trobey lay donas per ver
que fero remembrar mon paire
e·l segle bo que a fag traire
mal, qu'er es vilan, pauc cortes.
Auzit avetz cossi m'es pres
650 ni com son anatz ni vengutz
ni com ai estat esperdutz
ni per que ni per cal razo.
E si no fos, car en sazo
m'a tornat mo senhe·l Dalfi,
655 jamay no fora jays vas si
ni al segle nulh be volens.
Aisi son vengut en *f*orsens
que·l segle volgra *r*emenar

636 on nos an be v. c.   637 yeu ai cor   657 en .ll. sens   658 volgra menar

  e no say com, car no say far
660 so que s'atanh a la manieira."
  Et yeu, cuy voluntat leugeira
no·m aduys anc nulh pessamen,
estiey .l. petit en mon sen
aisi co hom savi deu far,
665 e car sabers m'ac fag pensar,
e sens e cor, de mon cosselh.
Ieu li dis ses tot apparelh:
  "Amicx, vos es vas mi vengut,
segon que dizetz, esperdutz
670 e fors issitz de vostre sen,
per so car no sabetz comen
ni per que es aisi camjatz
le segles e fina bontatz
e [bos] pretz c'avia poder;
675 e per c'amors voles saber
s'es aisi perdud'e baissada,
que sol esser riqu'e prezada
a far mant home pros e bos,
vos non o vis, mas la sazos
680 auzis ja dir a vostre paire,
e qu'enqueras neys non a gaire
c'aissi·s tenian tres baros.
E faitz vos en meravilhos
per so car avetz mout sercat
685 e non trobatz mas per dintat
a far vostre cor jauzion,
ni no·n sabetz com ni per on
s'es tot anat aisi ensems;
pareys que fos mostrat a temps
690 e que sia rendut huey mays.
E si·l Dalfi fis e verays
no vos agues aital sen mes,
vos foratz tornatz descortes
e fis vilas, lunhatz dels pros.
695 Assatz semblera mi razos,

674 e de pretz 684 anetz 687 ni hō

a vertat fina, ses tenso,
c'om non degues al sieu sermo
ni als sieus ditz metre mai re;
ni ieu no fera, per ma fe,
700 si als no·y aguessetz mesclat.
Mas per so que disses que·n fat
vos es tals segles a menar,
e car no·y podetz atrobar
art ni manieira ni semblan,
705 avetz mon cor mes en afan
e mays, car me queretz cosselh.
    Ieu non dic ges, si tot no velh
mantas sazos en esgardar,
qu'entre totz homes, ses doptar,
710 no·n venhan de sen natural,
e que no·y puesc'om ben o mal
aver tot jorn en son coman
cascus—ja no venha ni an
ni·n fassa lonc ni breu estatje
715 car sen ven e nais en coratje
tantost com es natz e noiritz;
*m*ais sabers, per c'om es grazitz
e pus onratz e pus temsutz
e may amatz e may volgutz,
720 e que fay homes captener,
non pot venir ses mout vezer
e ses mot auzir e proar.
Per qu'ieu no·us *n*'aus poder donar,
car res non ai vist ni auzit
725 a jutjar so que·m avetz dit
ni a departir tan gran fait
aisi del tot, mas, car retrait
cug que·n fos per sol jutjador
a mermatz de se*n*, m'er onor
730 qu'ie'us en dia so que·n enten
ni que·n conosc segon mon sen
ni que m'en sembla ni me'n par.

707 novelh   717 nais   723 nous aus   729 se mer o.

Vers es qu'ieu, per mon cor pagar
e car soven m'en mes en sen
735 mais que per autr'issernimen
ni per autre mon pro qu'y fos,
vinc en la cort del rey n'Anfos
del paire nostre rey cortes
que tan valc e servic e mes
740 *ai*tan d'onor a totas gens.
Lay vi faitz e captenemens
adretz e bos, azautz e cars,
per qu'er val mays en totz afars
e·n suy pus sertz en totas res.
745 E s'ieu fos tant com er apres—
si tot no suy mot entendutz—
aqui era mos sens saubutz
e, pus qu'er non es, escampatz.
E vos, si·eus y fossetz, assatz
750 viratz .l. pauc de segle bo
e del temps e de la sazo
que vostre paire dis l'autr'an,
hon foron tug li fin aman
e·l donador valen e fi;
755 e auziratz, si com yeu fi,
als trobadors dir e comtar
si com vivion per anar
e per sercar terras e locx;
e viras *lay* selas ab flocx
760 e tans autres valens arnes
e fres daURatz, e palafres;
meravilheratz vos en fort.
Li un venian d'otra·l port
e li autre d'Espanha say.
765 Aqui trobavon cuend'e gay
e donador lo rey n'Anfos,
e·n Diego que tan fo pros,
e Guidrefe de Gamberes,
e·l comte Ferran lo cortes

740 e tan   759 luy

770 e sos fraires tan ben apres
    qu'ieu no·n poiria dir lo cart.
    E p*u*is trobavon d'autra part
    vas Lombardia·l pros marques
    e d'autres baros .ll. o .lll.
775 e .llll. e .V. e mays de .C.,
    que en la terra veramen
    s'es mantengutz tostemps donars.
    E en Proensa homs avars
    non trobavon, ni *e*ran lot
780 als contes que tostemps an *d*ot
    de pretz mantengut ab donar.
    En Blacas no·y fai a laissar
    ni del Baus en *Guillem* lo blon,
    ni d'Alvernhe·l senher *Guion*
785 ni·l comte Dalfi que tan valc;
    ni sai en Gasto a cuy calc
    may de pretz c'om non li conoys.
    E silh que venion per Foys,
    aqui trobavon .l. senhor
790 adreg e plazen donador
    si com dizian totz le mons
    ....
    e al Vernet .l. Ponson gay.
    I trobaretz pros e veray
795 n'Arn*au*t de Castel Nou tostemps.
    Aqui trobaretz totz essemps
    so c'a cortes baro se tanh;
    E·n *R*aim*on* Gaucer*an* d'Estanh,
    de tot Malfait *tro* a Pinos
800 *i* trobaretz e bautz e pros;
    a Cardona·n *G*uillem lo ric,
    e en *U*rgelh; per qu'ieu vos dic:
    assatz baros pros e espertz!
    E al Castel Vielh fo n'Albertz,
805 us cavayers mot coratjos,

772 Apilhs t.   779 ni anclot   780 āclot   784 Dunun   793 e alv/nhet   795 nār   798 En .R. Gaucelm ad estanh   799 mal fait a P.   800 e t.   802 erguelh

e entorn luy d'autres baros
a totz bes far francx et arditz.
E si non aguess*etz* auzit
cals fo·n G*uillems,* sel de Montcade,
810 pogratz far tal matinade,
mot fora corteza d'auzir.
Mas vos non poiriatz sofrir,
a mon semblan, tan lonc sermo,
e trop parlar met en tenso
815 so que mezura fay grazir;
per qu'ieu vuelh a·*n* Miquel venir
en Arago, et a·n Garssia
Romieu que tanta cortezia
fetz; e *en* En*t*ensa·n Berenguier
820 que manten*c* pretz fin et entier,
adreg e complit e verai.
E pueys de say tornar vos ai
*a*l comte qu'es a Castilho,
en Pos bo, e so filh n'Ugo,
825 a mantener pretz e valor;
e a Rocaberti senhor
en Jaufre que tan fo prezatz
per mans locx e per mans regnatz
on foron per pretz enserratz,
830 e lur oncle trobar pogratz
a Vila de Mul, en R*aimon*,
atal baro qu'en tot lo mon
no·n ac ab dos tans de poder
que mielhs saupes pretz mantener,
835 car anc .1. sol jorn no fon las.
Trobaretz savi e de solas,
demest nos, en Pos de Serveira,
valen e de bona manieyra,
a totz faitz valens et ysnels.
840 A Maurelhas et a Monelhs
e per d'autres locx que no·us dic

808 aguesson 809 Montade 816 ami q̄l grazir venir 819 f. ē
dēiēsā 820 manten 823 lo comte 830 pogratz trobar

i foron man*t* baro tan ric
qu'en nulha terra·n troberatz
vas part ni tan non sercaratz
845 a nulhs bos faitz pus avinens,
e d'autras terras eyssamens
que no·us ai ditas atretal.
Mas per so car a so no·m val
....
850 mas ad obrar! via, del*s* faitz!
    Al vostre pair'e al Dalfi
vos ai desdig so que *e*n vi
ni qu'en auzi dir a la gen.
Apres dirai vos solamen
855 so qu'en auz*i* si m'escotatz.
Vers Dieus que per nos fon penatz,
si com crezem, e fes cant es,
volc qu'en Alamanha vengues
us emperaires Fredericx
860 et *en* Englelterra n'Enricx
si com auzis dir al Dalfi,
e mays de sos filhs atressi,
n'Enricx e·n Richartz e·n Jofres,
e en Tolza us coms cortes,
865 en *R*aimon, que tan fo prezatz.
E si ja no·us enamoratz
aisi o deuriatz saber,
per mot auzir e per parer,
cals fo·l pros coms de Barsalona
870 e sos fils n'Amfos que tan bona
valor saup aver totz sos jorns.
E aquestz fetz saber sos torns
e conoissens' en son coratje.
Aquist conogron per paratje
875 los mals e·ls bos segon qu'ilh s'ero.
Et e·l temps d'aquestz se levero,
qu'ieu vos ai dig, li trobador

842 baro m̄ā t̄ā   843 non trob/atz   850 del f.   852 q̄n vi
855 auz si   860 et ēglelterra   865 en .R.

e soudadier e·l contador,
e pro baro vas Astarac,
880 si com en Bernatz d'Armalhac,
en Arnautz Guillems de Marsa,
en Berenguier de Robian,
e de Cumeng'en Bernados
e vas Monpeslier us baros
885 en Guillems, adreg e membratz,
e tals que fon apparelhatz
a conoisser totz bos mestiers;
e sai us cortes cavayers,
Bertrans de Saissac l'apelavon.
890 Aquist venian et anavon,
e per aquest eran refait
joglar, e cavayer desfait,
e mantengut li dreiturier.
E qui avia son mestier
895 ni son saber azaut ni car
ad els l'anavon prezentar;
e ilh en la cort dels majors
on trobavon los guizardos
e las poestatz barnatjozas
900 adreitas e cavalairozas
e conegudas e onradas,
co foro pros totas vegadas!
Ni ja sol non demanderatz
mas a totz jorns la troberatz
905 aital com agratz sol pessatz.
Aquist foron enamoratz
e bastion torneys e guerras
per mans locx e per mantas terras,
e volgro las donas cortezas
910 e conogudas et entezas
si com'e ja lo pares vostres.
E no portavan pater nostres
ni autre senhal ab bel'onha

880 en .B. 881 en aR̄ .G. 885 en .G. 889 .B. 896 a dels
905 aura

mas per ma dona n'Escarronha
915 e per na Matieus del Palars
e per la dona d'en Gelmars,
la contessa d'Urgelh de lay
e per na Gensana de say,
que fo de selas bonas gens
920 ....
e fait'a Dieu onrar e creire.
Et establian mant preveire
e mant mostier a Dieu servir
ses que no volgro obezir
925 mas simplamen volian estar
sels que fan lo segle canjiar,
e·l segl'essems, mescladamens.
Per que·ls faitz e·ls captenemens
valc e duret ans e sazos.
930 Mas er es vengutz us perdos
e us sabers si com delieys.
E car trobon comtes et reys
e poestatz feblas e molas
an los tornatz en lurs escolas
935 e fan lur creire so que·s volon.
E sels, que per nien se dolon
e·s camjan soven e menut,
an o aisi tot resseubut,
que res non an assaborat.
940 Per c'aissi son de lor lunhat
azaut saber e conoissen,
e·l cavayer pros e valen
que solian vieure mest lor
son tornat apres bauzador,
945 si co·l Dalfi vos ar a dit;
mays yeu vos ai dig .l. petit
mays per que·s pert aisi valors,
joys e solatz, pretz et honors.
Er vos ai parlat dels baros,
950 per so que·n siatz pus ginhos

921 ōrat creaire   931 de lieys

per vos menar, e mielhs noiritz
e per mostrar si co hom ditz;
ni vos mezeys m'avetz pregat
per cal manieira son prezat
955 aitals homes ni mielh apres.
Saber devetz qu'el mon *non* es
sabers ni mestiers que tan valha
az adzaut hom, si tot si malha
vas fols, com joglaria *fay*.
960 Joglaria vol home gay
e franc e dos e conoissen,
e que sapcha far a la gen,
segon que cascus es, plazer.
Mas er venon, freg en saber,
965 us malvatz, fols desconoissen,
que·s cujan far, ses autruy sen
ab sol lur pec saber, doptar;
sabers, seluy que·l vol menar,
es lo melhor trezaur del mon,
970 mas *m*estiers li es que li son
ardimens, e sens e manieira
car ses questz non es leugieira
la dreita via per seguir.
Ardimens lo fay enantir
975 e abrivar entre·ls melhors
e manieyra·l dona secors
ad esgardar loc e sazso;
sens non l'aduy autra razo
mas que l'atempra si co·s tanh.
980 Ieu non dic ges c'om en estanh
non puesca maracde pauzar;
mas so*l*s ese*m*s es aur so*n* par,
aisi com de saber bos sens.
E sel qu'entre·ls desconoissens
985 vol ni cuyda saber trobar,
tot atretal *so* cuyda far

958 adzaut hon e si t. s. m.   959 vas fols com joglaria   970 mas estiers   976 dö s.   982 mas sos sēs esaur som par   986 se

c'anc Dieu no volc .l. jorn sofrir.
Saber vol homs ferms ses mentir,
adreg e franc e conoissen;
990 et el er aital eyssamen
e malvatz, entre·ls mals apres.
Que no·y a forfaitz homs cortes
ni pros si vos no·l conoissetz.
Aisi co·s tanh, an ilh lo pretz
995 e vos remanetz enganatz.
Homes de segle y a fatz
e desconoissens, c'al venir
cujan tantost home chauzir
e conoisser e·ls bos e·ls mals,
1000 menar en lurs solas cabals
e far aitals com ilh se son,
e saber com o fan li bon.
E silh que conoisson sabrer,
penson c'om ab mens de saber
1005 que puesc'om lo·s lunhar de lor;
e·ls marritz que non an paor,
—ni blasme non lur a que far—
volon los atressi lunhar,
aisi co·s tanh, vilanamen.
1010 E silh que son desconoissen
a maldir no·y gardon negu.
Atressi son dat a cascu
dels entendedors divers sens
per que n'i a de pus sabens
1015 e que s'enganon mantas vetz.
Aquels, segon que·ls trobaretz
vulhatz menar car, que per vos
no serian mas tensonos
e pec e de mal escuelh;
1020 per que·n dis n'Arnaut de Maruelh,
als desconoissens ensenhar,
    "Terra pot hom laissar
    a son filh eretar,

1003 saber   1055 luenh hom   1020 nArn.

mas pretz non aura ja
1025 si de son cor no·l tra."
      Natural cauza fay vila
      aisi com saber ensenhat.
      Aital son aquilh, e pus fat
      son mant autre malvat e pec,
1030 vilan cortes que, car son nec
      de saber, ja no·us sonaran
      ad una part, mas can veiran
      qu'entre donas seretz vengutz
      o pres d'autres; adoncx lur lutz
1035 al cor us pecx ensenhamens.
      E diran vos, c'als cays-sabens
      venon en grat aitals solatz,
      "En joglar, e vos, com calatz?
      Que non diretz una chanso?"
1040 E vos, si tot non an sazo
      lur dig, no vulhatz empeguir,
      car, ab .l. pauc que·ls sapchatz dir,
      seran lur van voler passatz.
      Aitan be son pro razonatz
1045 us autres que trobaretz motz,
      vilas e fatz coma us voutz
      que per so que·us puescon janglar
      volran auzir vostre cantar
      e son d'entendre vil e cau.
1050 Aquels vulhatz menar suau
      e gen, car a ren no son bo;
      e si·ls moviatz contenso
      serian vos vilan e fat.
      Joglar volpilh, mal acabat
1055 trist e d'apenre recrezen,
      ses que non an saber ni sen
      ni ren mas enueg e foldat,
      c'ades qu'ilh an .l. temps amat
      volran vos jutjar folamen;
1060 et ab .l. cantaret dolen

1036 dirai 1044 prezonatz 1055 trist: -ri- is difficult to read. 1058, 1059, 1063: The emendations supply letters that are illegible.

cujaran pagar mals e bos
e contra·ls cambis dels baros
aver cora*r*jes afortitz.
Per qu'ieu vos dic, per so car guitz
1065 vos er e·l segle gen menar,
c'al canjamen vulhatz canjar
vostre sen e vostre saber
e non sion contra plazer,
vilan, ni fat, ni mal estan
1070 ni com jutj'ar sels que faran
vas nulha part, mals fatz o bos,
novas d'amors e sas chansos
e autres chantars eyss*amens*;
e pagatz homens, trists e *gens*
1075 e totz autres, cals que tro*betz,*
e no·y gardetz mas que pag*uetz*
cascus segon que valens er
a far azautz l'us; com ...
e de terras captenemens
1080 adzautz e d'omes conoiss*ens*
vulhatz saber; e sobre tot
gardatz que li dig e li mot
vos venguan d'omes conoissens
per c'al contar entre las gens
1085 no·us en sia vils pretz donatz.
Per so car sos fa*i*tz e*s* mostratz
a cascun mestier propriamens,
e lors propris captenemens
per c'om conois cals es cascus,
1090 vos dic—e per so car es us
e pretz d'aital home com vos—
c'ades vulhatz bos saba*tos*
portar e caussas benestans,
cotel, borsas, coreg'e guans
1095 e capel, e·l captener gen

1073, 1074, 1075, 1076, 1078, 1080: illegible   1086 son fat e. m.
1088 captenenemens   1092 illeg.   1095 cap gentener

car aitals captenh son plaz*en*
adzaut e non trop may*strat.*
Vostre vestir sian talhat
e fait azaut e ben estan, ...
1100 e no sian lag ni tacos,
mays aisi fresc e fait ginhos
com si venian per orat—
adzautimens que *tan* en grat
venon a las gens mantas ves.
1105 No vulhatz aver ni portes
d'ome que pec captenemens,
ni tals arnes c'als conoissens
no semblon vostre tut ades;
car mal ten so mestier apres
1110 sel que dechay per captenh fat.
Vos non avetz semblan malv*at*
ni pec, ni paraulas perdudas,
per qu'ieu vos vuelh dir conogud*as*
razos e planas eyssamen
1115 a far conoisser per cal sen
ni com vieu aitals homs co*chos,*
ni com deu esser cabalos
a far onrat captenemen.
Per so car son valors e sens
1120 sobre totas autras vertutz,
e conoissensa s'i a*d*utz
et ab lo saber atretal,
vos dic—e car anc Dieus ta mal
home no fe ni tan vilan
1125 c'ades, si tot el no s'a plan
lo cor, ni franc ni conoissen,
no·l fasson gaug home valen
e gen noirit com que·us vulhatz—
entre fols o entre malvatz
1130 o entr'omes valens e pros,
que vostres ditz sian gen*hos*

1096, 1097 illeg.   1103 que cas en g.   1106 d'ome q̄ pecx   1109 mal tēso   1111, 1113 illeg.   1116 illeg.   1121 siaputz   1130 entro mes   1131 Illeg.

e vostre fag mesclat ab sen
e sobre tot azaut e gent
e per saber amezurat.
1135 Car anc home mal azaut, fat,
ni pec a re no foron bo.
Adzaut captenh fan hon pro
ades grazir en tot afar,
e azaut son saber menar.
1140 E val mays us *faducx azautz*
mantas vetz c'us oms *mal* azau*tz*.
E membre·us so c'us conoissens
trobaires dis, en Miravals
1145 a far azautz homens vassals
encontra mal esta*r ginhos*:
"C'oms mal azautz si *tot s'es pros*
non es gair'ad ops d'ama*r* bos."
Adzautimen fay grassi*os*
1150 mant home e plazer *a gen*;
per que·us deu membrar eyssamen
a far valens nostres *mestiers*
so que·us dis en P*eire* Rotgiers
a·n Raymbaut, c'ane*t vezer*:
1155 "Si voletz el segle caber
e*n* loc siatz fatz ab los fatz.
E aqui meteys vos sapchatz
ab los savis gen mantener;
c'aissi·s cove c'om los assay;
1160 l'us ab ira, l'autres ab jay,
ab mal los mals, ab be los bos."
Us homes y a nualhos
e ples d'erguelh e de no sen
que, can non an, se·n van dizen
1165 c'astruc no cal mati levar.
E vos, no·us o vulhatz pensar
ni en aitals cutz no *f*iatz;

1134 amezuratz   1140 saduey a ... (illeg.)   1141 c'us mals... (illeg.)
1146 estat gr ... (illeg.)   1147, 1148 illeg.   1149 grassis   1150 illeg.
1152 trob...   1153 ·p.   1154 illeg.   1156 e loc   1167 siatz

que tota res van a percas
e ab esfors de conquerer.
1170 Astre es apelatz esper
car hom no pot aver *per* sen
mas so c'om pot aver vezen
ni per plan saber acabatz
es sens e sabers apelatz,
1175 e esgart d'ome conoissens
don (hom) savis vieu ric e valens.
A bon esfors folh marrimen —
e·l pec mor *en* estranhamen
e·l mal-percassan ses poder.
1180 E per so c'a major plazer
vos vengan las razos qu'ieu trac,
aujatz so que·n dis a enac
us trobaires de manta gen:
"En amors a tals plazer sen
1185 que qui·lh en sabia traire,
cascus seria mielhs amaire
que·l fatz que en cochas pren.
Non venon joc *a* desplazen
ni a mal-percassan plazer."
1190 Per que·l fait e·l genh e·l saber
s'aizinon fort al percassan,
seluy que vol aver certan
josta·l baros nulh gazardo. ...
Ni bar non poc lonc mal aver,
1195 ni Dieu no fes segle tan ver
vas malvestatz, c'us homs curos,
adreitz e francx no·n traisses dos
a se pujar e far valer
si·n saup genh ni manieir'aver,
1200 ni l'art que se tanh, ni lo fait.
No·us metatz vos meteis en plait
ni en esperdemen de re
si tot si son failhit li be

1169 cōqrre   1171 av/sē   1177 folhs marrimens   1178 pec moron
estranhamens   1180 car m. p.   1185 quilhs   1187 quels faitz
1188 ioc desplazen   1190 faitz   1194 poc loc ṁl a.   1197 n̄ (n'en)

vas mantas partz als queredors;
1205 car tostemps er bes e secors
als conoissens e temps e locx
et als alegres ris e jocx
mays que non es al segles fatz;
et als percassans bos atraitz
1210 greu y pot per forssa caber.
Vostri fait e vostre saber
sian divers e ben estan,
car hom non troba d'un semblan
a nos segon que·ns es donat
1215 ... ...
no podem far homes novels.
Per so car hom, si tot s'es bels,
ses conoissensa res no val,
vos dic c'om, a saber aital
1220 com vos, deu esser angoyssos
e demandar locx e sazos
e dels baros captenemens
vas totas partz, car us dels sens
es de bruj'*e* de sos enans.
1225 E car no·us deu esser afans
mas gaug e bo saber adzaut,
aprendetz so que·n dis n'Arn*au*t
de Maruelh, que per melhurar
aquels que·n pretz volon pujar
1230 e per uzar gens ensenhadas:
"E las estranhas e privadas,
aprenda de las gens
fatz e captenemens;
e·n deman et enqueyra
1235 l'esser e la manieyra
dels avols e dels bos;
dels malvatz e dels pros
lo mal e·l be aprenda.
E·l mielhs gart e entenda
1240 per so mielhs a defendre

1208 "a" superscribed over the initial "m" of the verse. 1217 tot bels ses 1224 bruia 1227 AF

si hom lo vol reprendre"
sel que vol vieure mest las gens.
   Vos sabetz *quez* als conoissens
s'eschay a far entre·ls melhors,
1245 a lur pujar sens e valors
e a demostrar bos sabers.
   Per que vos dic — per so car vers
n'er vas totz locx totz vostres ditz
e vostre fag n'er pus complitz
1250 e vostre cors pus acabatz —
qu'entre totas vostras etatz
vulhatz homes joves triar,
sel cuy nobles cors fay far
so que s'atanh a pres-valen.
1255 Per so car non an sempre sen
volon ades far lur poder;
e·l malvat son larc per dever,
cuy aduy cors a tot joven.
   Aquist volon auzir soven
1260 chansos d'amors e sirventes
e totz chantars valens e fres,
cals que sian, e jocx partitz.
   E ja non er *ben* aculhitz
entre lor hom suau ni quetz.
1265 Estatz perfait, a cuy bon vetz
e noble cors es remazutz,
vulhatz, per so que siatz dutz
saber e sen soven vezer.
   Car silh que son a son poder
1270 volon ades homes suaus
e que sapchan dir los bos laus
e·l blasmamen si com cove.
   E aquilh volgron far ancse
valors e sens e conoissensas
1275 e totas bonas captenensas?
   Aisi co·*n* terra seca·l peys!
   D'aquels fa hom comtes e reys

1263 no er hom a   1265 per fait   1276 aisi com en terra secal p.

　　　　　　e arsivesques e prelatz
　　　　　　e dons e caps e poestatz
1280　　a mantener dretz e razos.
　　　　　　Sel on anc noble cor no fo,
　　　　　　ni jovens non lur es proans,
　　　　　　trobaretz flacx e fals enans
　　　　　　e de totz pretz vans e vilas.
1285　　Per que·us prec que ja no·ls siguas
　　　　　　volontiers propdas ni ve*zis*,
　　　　　　car de lor venon li fals ris
　　　　　　e·l soanamen dels joglars
　　　　　　ab us semblans, us jocx avars,
1290　　aisi de pretz desconoissens.
　　　　　　Aquist volon homes valens,
　　　　　　cal que sian, malvat o bo,
　　　　　　e tenon tot hom per bo
　　　　　　que per aver fay tota re.
1295　　Per que vivon trist, ses tot be,
　　　　　　sotz totas autras gens vencutz
　　　　　　a far solatz, si tot menutz,
　　　　　　s'ensembl'an mant homen ses sen.
　　　　　　Non agaretz entre la gen
1300　　totas sazos c'om vos apel;
　　　　　　car mantas vetz es bon e bel
　　　　　　a mant home, si tot s'estay
　　　　　　aisi suau ses semblan gay
　　　　　　qui·l solassava d'avinen.
1305　　Ni trop enujos eyssamen
　　　　　　no sias entr'els a sazos;
　　　　　　car us es us mantas sazos,
　　　　　　e·ls solatz, entre·ls conoissens
　　　　　　... ... ...
1310　　que fan lurs caps d'esquerns a dir
　　　　　　d'on fassa*n* home empeguir
　　　　　　ni blasmon volpilh a trescar.
　　　　　　Car hom que·s pot aissi camjar
　　　　　　no se tanh entre totas gens.

1284　e vās vilās　　1286　ni veus　　1304　qui la s.　　1311　fassa home
1312　volpilhatrescar

1315 Mant home son, que vens jovens,
ses noble cor, e cant son fait
sens lur adutz .l. tan lait fait
per que n'an cor valen e bo.
Aquels, per so car on pus so
1320 vas jorns volon ades mielhs far,
vulhatz soven vezer, e car
ades lur creys cor conoissens.
Homens paubres, d'erguelh manens
ses sen e ses far-ben i a
1325 que, car son pec, no volun ja
autruy solatz mas can lo lor;
aquist son tal c'a lo senhor
neys dirian viltatz e mals.
Per que vos dic qu'entre·ls aitals
1330 no vulhatz ses grans obs venir,
car nulh'etat no·ls fay chauzir
ni francx ni dos ni conoissens.
Aquist volon homes sufrens
a sostener lurs vas poder,
1335 qu'els s'empeguisson de plazer
ab us motz fals et avinens.
Estiers aquestz n'i a .V.C.
d'autres que son larcx e sotils
a totz sabers, mas tan son vils
1340 e vas pretz mal acostumat
c'un non podetz aver privat
ses gran maltrag; per qu'ieu vos dic
c'ap lor vulhatz .l. pauc d'abric
e de solatz aver soven,
1345 car greu er c'om d'ome saben
e larc non pot aver *bos* sens.
D'autres n'i a, humils saben,
que, cant non an cor abrivat,
volon ades homen privat
1350 a descobrir lur volontatz.
Aquels, si doncx no·ls trobatz

1321 e car vezer   1346 e lar ... los sens

ab autres gens, no·ls agaretz,
car anc us vas pretz res no fes.
Mas vergonh'*aver* d'autras gens
1355 es vaneza, qu'entre·ls valens
e entre·ls autres a son dan,
ven mantas vetz *en baralhan*:
als us car an enpessamen;
e als autres, car son valen
1360 ven mantas vetz per contenso
... ...
e de ric cor fait e noirit.
Volpilhatjes, qu'ieu no·y oblit,
adutz als autres pauc parlar,
1365 e car volun suau estar,
car lur natura s'es aitals.
Per qu'ieu vos dic, per so car als,
segon mon sen, non devetz far,
qu'entr'els vulhatz suau estar;
1370 e si no·ls trobatz en sazo
autra vetz n'auretz be e pro
que l'acsidens lur es partitz.
Als naturals, per so car guitz
lur es suaveza totz jorns,
1375 vulhatz venir ab cortes torns
eissamen ses semblan bru;
car silh non apelan negu
a solatz far, ni faran ja,
ni entr'els nulhas gens non a
1380 a nulh fag d'els pus conoissens.
Homen cuy falh valor e sens
e esser temens entre·ls pros
y a que, car son cabalos
entr'avols gens, cujan valer
1385 car sabon ajustar aver
o car cujan esser adzaut,
o car sabon far .l. bliaut
o autre vestir ben estan,

1357 per contenso   1358 After this verse the MS. repeats vs. 1357, expunctuated   1381 hom en c.

o car cujan aver cors gran
1390 e fait a plazer de la gen.
D'aital home no·us sia plazen
ni·ls vulhatz soven encontrar
car no sabon mas so que far
vezon a lur contravalens.
1395 Homes que donan a las jens
per so car sonan asermat
vulhatz, si tot no son prezat
ni lor cove aitals sabers,
aquel vezer; mas lors avers
1400 no·ls vos fassatz trop sopleyar;
car mespretz es sovendeyar
homen que saber non enten,
e grans plazers d'ome saben
qui·l pot trobar franc ni joyos.
1405 Per Dieu vos dic, per so car vos
aitals homens devetz sercar,
qu'entorn aquels vulhatz estar
e esser soven e menut
a refrescar vostra vertut
1410 qui s'espert entre l'avol gen.
Per Dieu e per vostre joven
vos conjur, e per totas res,
—e per so car saber non es
faitz mas per homens entendens—
1415 que vos entre·ls desconoissens
no vulhatz soven escampar
ni als pros ses razo comtar
que·s fan conoisser e grazir.
Car son saber fay escarnir
1420 comtaire pecx ses tempramen.
Us malvaitz son desconoissen
e d'azaut saber enemic,
avar e flac, trist e mendic,
e d'aver flac e familhos,
1425 escarnidors d'omes joyos

1392 nil v.   1395 donas   1401 mos precx   1410 la vol   1417 pro   1422 dazaut enemic de saber

e de tot autre ben estar.
E can volretz ab lor parlar
silh se metran a far deman.
Aquels per so car on pus an
1430 mays son malvat e pus dolen
vulhatz metr' ades o *so*ven
e*n* loc de tot vostre cossir.
Car aisi los volc Dieu bastir,
vils e ses tot melhuramen.
1435 Home que non an autre sen
mas voluntat e bo saber,
vulhatz ades estranhs aver
com *de* vostre solatz partitz,
car aisi par fatz e noiritz
1440 si com selh que lur es cossens.
Per so car anc Dieu a las gens
no volc donar engal captenh
ni engal *sen* ni engal genh
ni engalmen esser joyos.
1445 Vos dic qu'entre·ls valens e pros
n'i a que son ses tot esgart,
e que·us diran a una part
e mest autru*i* que lur cantes;
e no·y gardaran nulh vetz
1450 ni nulh temps ni nulha sazo,
e al ters de mot de la canso,
cal que digatz, ilh groniran
e josta vos cosselharan
o·s metran novas a comtar.
1455 Anc Dieus sen non lur volc donar
ni fara ja, mon essien.
Aquels si tot no son valen
menatz al pus gen que poiretz;
car aital hom can vos etz,
1460 cascu lo cuj'aver comprat
neus silh que son vilan e fat
e de malvatz captenemens.

1431 metre e de sove   1432 e loc   1438 com vostre   1440 com si selh   1443 ni ēgal ni e. g.   1448 mestz autrus

Vos sabetz be, per so car sens
als non adutz nulha sazo,
1465 qu'entre·ls baros n'i a que so,
on pus lor ven bes, ergulhos
e que·us cujaran far, si vos
lur voletz dir una chanso,
en l'escotar lo gazardo
1470 e car sol vos volran sonar.
Aquels vulhatz sovendeyar
si tot no s'an cor conoyssen,
car hom s'en fay a l'autra jen
ab lur privadesc esgrazir.
1475 Vi*l*an cortes qu'emperatgir
volon lurs faitz nessiamen,
ajatz privatz en lor joven
e mentr'aissi son empeguit
car greu er ca*n*, joven partit,
1480 non tornon paubr'e recrezen.
Mas paratje desconoissen
ni flac ni dig ni maistrit
no·us fassan gaug, car en oblit
an mes tot pretz ses recobrar;
1485 e can vos poiran esquern far
ilh se tenran per ereubut.
Homes cuy no son remazut
de paratje, mas sol l'endenh
e vils parlar e flac captenh,
1490 a*b* tot so qu'entre·ls pros mens val,
*fu*jatz car, can non poiran al,
o car non-lauzar es falhir,
car fan paratje escarnir;
per so fay mal qui·ls y cossen.
1495 Mendicx de cor, de dig valen
e de faitz bas, vos sian lonh,
per so car sies cascus sonh
ad esgardar home*s* ses sen,
sotz totz autres: son a la gen

1475 viran 1479 car 1490 a tot so 1491 ayatz car 1492 non
lauza res 1498 hoṁ 1499 sostz

1500 si com es dos e fastigos
e hufaniers e vils janglos.
E autres homes prezentiers
vulhatz trobar mest cavayers
e en autre loc vergonhos
1505 o se puescan fenher largos
e de cortes captenemens.
E s'i podetz ficar las dens
no·l doptetz a mordre calcat
car aital home mal fadat
1510 a greu atendon mas un mors.
Us homes son que non an cors
mas a manjar et a jazer
e a dormir e a sezer
e ad estar suau e gen;
1515 e no vos sufriran .l. ven
ni .l. freg ni una calor
ni neguna mala olor
ni res c'om afortitz sofris.
Aquilh son tals c'anc hom que·ls vis
1520 no·ls tenc per bos ni per adregz.
Per so vos dic, per so car feitz
e mendicx es totz lurs afars,
c'ab lor no·us sia bos l'estars
ni lor pan aver saboros
1525 car a totz jorns son usios
e lor torba·l cap cautz o vens.
Mais sel cuy cors e fis talens
ofron pretz a far lor poder
vulhatz anar soven vezer;
1530 e car hom lur deu far solatz
estiers comjat non atendatz
car sol no sabon que·s e*t*s vos.
Si tot non es entre·ls baros,
vas totas partz pretz ni valors,
1535 aisi com sol far secors
als trobadors ni als joglars —

1532 q̄ sēs nos

o car francx cors lur es avars
o car sens lor a castiatz
e can mespretz lur es donatz —
1540 vos non tornes desconoissens
a far grazir malvadas gens
ni al pros mens assolassieus;
car us sols bels ditz agradieus
vos er esmenda d'aital sen.
1545 E car hom per esgardamen
val may ades n'estatz membratz
qu'en Guiraut dis als acabatz
per esfortir lur bon captenh:
"Ni no tenh a dan si·m destrenh
1550 amors ni·m dechay;
c'una vetz n'auray
man bon esdevenh."
Aisi tanh c'om afortit tenh
a far sos faitz pus cabalos,
1555 vilan apres manjar joyos
o apres autr'esbaudimen
que no tanhon saber ni sen
adzaut; ni lur vulhatz fugir,
e us sapchatz ab lor esjauzir,
1560 vostre bo captenh retenen;
car a grat d'aital avol gen
no·s devon rendre trop curos.
Un home son flac, enujos,
amparador d'autruy mestier,...
1565 e·ls lors no sabon acabar;
e car son pec, volran blasmar
als conoissens so qu'es en lor.
Per qu'ieu·s dic aital jujador
no·us fassan vostre sen camjar,
1570 ni als cavaiers emparar
armas ni als clercx lurs prezic;
car mans mestiers, si tot s'es ric
ven s'esbefar als tensonos.

1540 ves   1547 .G.   1552 ben   1554 a sos faitz   1556 ho pres
1557 saber   1571 lu (illeg.) pzic   1573 vēses be far

Autru*i* joglars ni las chansos
1575 dels trobadors non reprendatz
qu'envejos e mal ensenhatz
sembla qui son semblan repren,
e cortes sel qu'en defenden
vol razonar sos companhos.
1580 Mant home son aisi com vos
e d'autre saber atretal,
que, car non an sen natural
adaut ni bo, van per lo mon
vagan, e no sabon per on
1585 s'en vay homs adretz ni cortes;
ni lur faitz ni lor sens non es
mas en apenre jocx partitz
e *casc*us motz estranh c'om ditz
als pecx que·ls teno*n* aut e car;
1590 e volran als pros ensenhar
per on s'en vay pretz ni plazers
e als savis cals es sabers
et als conoissens cals es sens;
e lors meteys captenemens
1595 faran conoisser qu'ilh son pec.
Per so vos dic, per so car *n*ec
son e malvat aital saber,
que cant volretz solatz aver
al venir qu'entre·ls pros faretz,
1600 si doncx ilh, ans que comensetz,
no·us an demandat et enquist,
lur vulhatz dir so c'aves vist
f*ors* per las terras ni auzit,
comensan petit a petit
1605 aisi co homs ven en solatz.
E dels baros, cals y trobatz
segon vostre sen pus cortes
no·y oblidetz ni y cales
segon auzida·ls pus valens.

1574 autrus   1576 que nuejos   1577 semblan qui son semblan reprenden   1582 ñ ā   1586 ñ es   1588 illeg.   1589 ten hom   1596 pec   1603 fo p   1608 cal ges

1610 E de las donas eyssamens
vulhatz contar las cals y so
a totz afars mielhs de sazo
per c'om deu dona mielhs prezar.
E si·ls vezetz ben comensar
1615 ad escotar vostre saber
novas per c'om pot mais valer
vas totz mestiers lay comensatz.
E apres aco, si·ls trobatz
adreitz ni prims ni entendens,
1620 valors e linhatje e sens
vos sian aman e chantars.
    Vostre semblan sian espars
e vostres ditz faitz autz e quetz
segon la razo que diretz;
1625 e·l cors aiatz ardit e bo
a ben formir vostre razo
e·l cors tenetz segur e dretz
e de vilan parlar estretz
e azaut e de bona faisso,
1630 e no·us metatz en tal sermo
per que·us venha nulhs torbamens.
E entre·ls *senhors* eyssamens
— si com ieu vos ai dat mon dit —
sian vostre saber partit
1635 vas que·ls trobaretz mals o bos.
Auzir e vezer fay a nos
saber so qu'es fag li premier
don nos sabem que·l cavayer
foron per home elegut
1640 a mantener pobol menut
et a far *barn*atjes e dos,
e que de lor feron chansos
e fon solatz fag e trobat.
E tug bon aip adreg onrat
1645 son mielhs en loc que·n autra gen.

1614 sil   1621 erā cars   1632 illeg.   1636 illeg.   1639 fo on
1640 illeg.   1641, 1642, 1648, 1649, 1650 illeg.

Mas ni·n volc far cominalmen
Dieus poderos, e no·y gardet
... ls atray can pujet
... als conoissens.
1650 *Per qu'ieu* vos dic, per so car sens
que vostre ... perdas dias
c'als conoissens, on que sias,
val *mais* ... *tug* solatz aver
per so qu'*en* puscatz *con*querer
1655 ... vos onra*mens* que lauzors
... (sin) ... dors
... iens
mos laus gen als co*no*issens
ni bo als pros la ... *en sazos*;
1660 *e, receubutz en lurs* mazos
vulhatz ades a pres tener
e lurs captenemens vezer,
per so que·n siatz pus cortes;
car lay son tug li ben-apres
1665 e l'ensenhamen fait e dit;
e lay venion li eyssarnit
e silh que·n pretz volon pujar.
E qui non a cor de donar
en autre loc, s'il n'a aqui.
1670 E aqui tornon li fals fi
e·l bo melhor e·l torbatz clar
e car Dieu res no volc laissar,
sembla qu'establimen sieu fos.
Un joglar son contrarios
1675 e lauzador de lor meteys,
e car son pecx, neys s'era·l reys,
se volran metre josta vos:
cays que semblan pus cabalos
e de major auctoritat.
1680 E on pus an en loc estat,
mens son prezat en totas res;

1651 illeg., dias perdas 1652 e als (?) fals (?) 1653, 1654, 1655,
1656, 1657, 1658, 1659 illeg. 1660, barely leg.

per qu'ieu vos dic, per so car es
vilas e fols aitals captenh*s*,
que, can venretz en loc, al men*h*s
1685 aiatz cor suau de premier,
e pueys faitz tan que·l dig entier
e·l saber menetz per razo,
que·us fassan enantit e bo,
e captene*n*s entre l*o*s pros.
1690 Vostre saber si tot s'es bos
ni cars, no lauzetz a las jens,
ni vostre cor als conoissens
ni als autres ples de ricor;
e s'eratz filh d'emperador
1695 no seriatz mas can joglar
mentr'aisi·eus sapcha bo l'anar
ni·l venir bos e saboros —
e, aprop, fag hom, si n'es pros
ni grazitz, pus sos mestiers es.
1700 E si tot s'es fort descortes
lo segles, per locx, ni vilas,
si trobaretz omes sertas
a conoisser vostre saber;
e vostre cor, si sap valer
1705 pro er qui·l lauzara ses vos.
Autz locx, e d'omes poderos,
e cortz vulhatz ades sercar,
car sel conve lay acostar
ses autruy saber *s*'es joglar
1710 entre las jens, neys al pus car
n'es sos solatz pus saboros,
Amarviment fay cabalos
a parlar mant home ses sen;
per qu'ieu vos dic c'ab aital gen
1715 no vulhatz parlan contrastar;
car tot lur fag es en parlar
aisi com en faitz d'omes pros.
Vilas blasmatz ni mal respos

1683 captenh   1684 mēs   1689 capteneus entrels   1709 nes

no·us aia volontat a ma;
1720 car silh que son trist ni vila,
ses vos, seran assatz blasmatz.
Ni trop lauzar, si tot li fatz
s'en empeguisson, no vulhatz;
car, .l. dels sabers mens prezatz,
1725 es atressi com trop blasmars.
E si·n voletz esser pus cars,
a.n Miraval venretz ades
que dis allunhat dels engres
que per entendre son cabal:
1730 "En que trop mays que no val
lauz si dona, fay parer
qu'esquern diga e non y es al."
Non lauzetz trop onra*t* capdelh;
trop eyssarnitz ni trop *d*'escuelh
1735 no vulhatz esser, ni trop trist
ni trop recrezen ni trop vist;
ni nulh trop no vulhatz aver,
car aisi con "trop" desplazer,
con mesura, plazers onratz.
1740 Per so car son trop daus totz latz
li sen, qu'ieu no·ls puesc totz contar,
e las manieyras que fan far
a las gens mans fagz dessemblatz
— si com avetz auzit assatz,
1745 que vos agues tan enansat —
vos dis c'ab home pec ni fat
ni otracujat no vulhatz
aver paria ni solatz
ni ren que torn a bon saber;
1750 car tug siey fag e siey saber
son atretal naturalmens.
Ni s'ieu vos dic qu'entre·ls valens
val may us aital homs com vos,
per so vos no·us rendatz als pros
1755 de tal manieyra que·n siatz

1733 nō lauzatz trop ōrar capduelh   1734 trop esvuelh

a los autres vils ni malvatz
ni de malvatz captenemens;
car mantas vetz ven aitals gens
o notz entre·ls pus cabalos.
1760 Mentr'es aisi fresc e joyos
ni aculhitz pe·ls avinens
vulhatz contar, qu'entre las gens
no se tanhon vielh ni floritz.
E membre·us c'om, entre nos, ditz
1765 a far home aperceubut
que can hom es reconogut
e hom es vielhs endevengutz;
astruc es sel vas cuy s'adutz
sens, mentre·l ven loc e sazos."
1770 E ab aitan, cor no·ns fo bos
lo partir, nos venguem
a l'ostal nostre, on mangem,
tro lo mati que s'en anet.
 E no say si·l segle trobet
1775 melhurat, car anc pueis no·l vi;
e Dieu m'aport a bona fi.

TRANSLATION

April was leaving and May entering, and every one of the birds was singing near his mate, some high, some low, and because [5] snow and cold lay far behind everywhere, fruit and flowers were coming, and clear weather and a gentle season. And I was troubled and rather morose because of love. [10] I remember that it was morning then, in the town square of Besalú, and there was no one with me, but Love and my thought had me thus alone. [15] For I could turn nowhere else (nor would I want to, if someone else were not the cause of it in me) except towards God, gentle and powerful. And He whom every believer adores, [20] willed and granted to me that at that time when I was thus downcast, there should come towards me a jongleur, dressed and shod after the fashion of the time in which [25] valor and worth were both found in the barons. And if I am asked how glad and happy I was at his coming, you would not completely believe me, and far be it from me to swear it to you. [30] But I can tell you this much definitely and for certain, that on greeting me he came up to me to rest. And I returned his greeting, and although I had realized [35] that he was a jongleur when he came, I wanted to know his affairs from him himself, and he said to me:

"Sir, I am a man inclined to the life of a jongleur, [40] and I know how to tell romances and many stories and greetings and other good and pleasing tales well-known everywhere, and verses and songs of en Guiraut (de Bornelh) [45] and more by en Arnaut de Maruelh, and other verses and lays, and should be able to find a place in some court. But now bad men have come to work their vile and ill desires, [50] who go through the courts ready to take worth away from people. So neither I nor any polite or wise person are welcomed, but instead I no longer get near the select people [55] where I would expect to find a place; I always find more people who make fun of me and despise what I have to say. And I see the chatterers and men puffed up with a sense of their own intelligence [60] who come at once to have a conversation which is silly and without any good judgment. And I, since no one wants to listen to me or hear my learning, go off and sit to one side [65] like a man in despair. And so I have come and walked as far as here to see you."

Because I saw that time and opportunity gave me the will, [70] I said to him:

"Friend, without any delay, I want us to go and dine now. Afterwards, if you want to tell me anything, all or little or much, I am he who, without a proud heart, [75] will hear you very willingly."

After dining in a meadow near a stream we both came into a leafy wood, if I am not wrong. [80] Here we sat down, and for not a little time, as you shall hear me tell. The weather was clear and soft and still, and gentle and agreeable, and I presently felt great pleasure [85] because of him whom I saw before me, courteous and noble, with an expression suited to learning. And if I told you that it looked as if his clothes were badly cut, [90] you might not believe me, because they seemed excellently chosen for him. That brought on a thought such as an accomplished man often has, and it reminded me of what en Giraut says [95] who made himself so highly esteemed by all:

"I saw a little jongleur, well dressed and shod, going around the courts only to praise ladies."

[100] And if it had been right for me, I would have liked to stay there always. But he who was with me, just as I am telling you, said to me:

"Sir, [105] I see that we have come to a good shelter. And so I beg you, if God grant that you may do all that you wish, that you should listen to me attentively, as though it were a message of love. [110] For you well know that those who debate, whoever we may be, good or bad, have caused debating to become so debatable that they scarcely know how to extricate themselves. Some have debated so that by slander [115] they overcome men of authority and the barons; others are so friendly and smooth-spoken towards all; and there are those who, because they are courteous, are jongleurs without any other knowledge. [120] I do not deny that knowing how to do only one thing may not result in perfection. But everyone knows that yellow and green do not please everybody, [*125*] so one should change one's conduct and actions according to people. That has caused me to learn many perfections and a great deal of varied knowledge; and I thought that I would privately have great reward among the barons [*130*] by making myself good and pleasing and of better conduct. But now I realize that they have come to ruin, except for a few; so I would have left quickly, [*135*] to get another opinion, but chance and its needs, which make many men happy, so willed it that I should come to the Dauphin at Montferrand in Auvergne. [*140*] And it was a Saturday morning that I came from Riom. And if ever anyone saw an agreeable court and good company, that was it. There was not a lady or damsel there, [*145*] knight nor squire, who was not more gentle than a bird fed in one's hand. Here I found a perfect lord and a very understanding company. [*150*] Which is why I left hardship for a while with great joy, so help me. And it happened that around Christmas, which is called the "Calends" in those parts, we came to and were at [*155*] Montferrand, with no trouble, up in the great hall. And if you ever saw well-bred and joyful men, that were we there.

"And the night, as I saw, was very dark after dinner [*160*] and next to the bright fire the company was large, knights and jongleurs, clever and accomplished and gentle and amiable and agreeable to courteous men. And there was not any outcry, nor [anything that could be] considered [*165*] foolishness, except at the beginning. Here we had such pleasure, and more whole-hearted, than I can tell you. And the knights, without any reminder, went to bed when they were ready, [*170*] for my lord wanted to remain with a companion near the fire. So I, when I saw the time and place [fit] to ask what I feared, I approached him, on a marble bench [*175*] all covered with samite. And if ever I found myself with a good heart eager to speak well, I did so then. So I said to him:

" 'Sir, I have been with you for a long time, and with discouragement. [*180*] And I will tell you why, if you will kindly listen to me now. You know that neither near nor far is there any man born or made without a father; I had one of a very good family, [*185*] and such that he knew how to conduct himself among worthy people. He was a wonderful singer and story-teller. And I heard from him how Henry, a king of England, used to give [*190*] horses and mules, and how much he [i.e., the father] used to make the rounds towards Lombardy, to the worthy marquis, and to two or three other lands where he found enough barons who were just and of good manners [*195*] and generous to everyone. And I heard many Catalans and Provençals named, and Gascons, gentle and loving toward ladies; and they used to make war and quarrel. [*200*] Because father described things to me thus, I became a jongleur [with] your verses. And I have gone over land and sea, many towns and castles in all directions, and visited lands [*205*] and barons, twice as many as I can tell. I did not find two among them who were like you; but very few, I tell you in truth, give with good judgment, and others foolishly, [*210*] others again to a small number of their followers, to whom they usually give. Thus I have found them, and more foolish than I could tell in a year; and you yourself, although seeming [*215*] to be ready to discern any good action, are not such as I have heard people tell and relate. So I have come to ask you, if you please, Sir, [*220*] how such a misfortune has come about, that the barons have thus lost merit and worth.'

"And, so help me, he remained with rather a heavy heart, and on replying, [*225*] he sat up, for he had been lying down before, and said:

" 'Friend, it seems to me that your knowledge is not yet complete; for you have asked me at length. It is difficult for me and easy for worthy men [*230*] because I do not think I can make an answer that is suitable nor which [on the other hand] would be becoming. However, because you have come here to talk with me, I want you to take with you [*235*] a little of my opinion, although it is difficult to relate. For you should know that, just as the true God is the head of all that you are and of what you know, [so] worthy and wise men—and I myself, as I put my trust in Him— [*240*] are not at all of such merit as to maintain noble hearts and wisdom and knowledge. And no man is loyal or true to merit unless he has these three.

" 'A noble heart makes a man perfect, [*245*] courageous, generous, courteous, just toward all things, a conqueror of kingdoms, and produces bold thoughts and gentleness toward all people, [*250*] and it makes him do honorable and courteous deeds and reject ill advice.

" 'Knowledge, as I can compare it for you, comes next to it in order, and enables one to know good and evil [255] in their fine manners. And one lives better among people [i.e., one gets on better with people], just, open and of pleasant society. And no man will be accomplished without it; so I am always careful about it.

" '[260] Understanding brings proportion and measure with respect to those matters which I have explained to you, and causes each one to put things in their place according to what they are and what is suitable. Those [three] enabled our forefathers to acquire merit and [265] nobility and the reputation for knightly deeds and openness toward the people, to conduct themselves honorably in every way and [to be] bold in all affairs. [270] And there will be no man who is of good and clear merit without those that I have mentioned. And these three caused Henry, a king of England, to increase in worth; for your father has heard tell [of him] [275] —as you yourself have told me— and of his three sons, Henry, Richard, and Geoffrey, let them not be forgotten—for in them was twice as much good as I could tell in a year. [280] I saw them appearing in court beside him, and making love and war. And he who knew how to do noble and worthy deeds, and was understanding, had the opportunity to do so, as once had a noble and [285] enlightened Saracen. And I'll tell you a good story which is true, since I am at your disposal.

"' There was a certain sultan in Spain, worthy of his ancestors. [290] And a certain high dignitary, just, worthy, frank, generous and valiant, became powerful in Morocco. And the king, who was pleased by the prowess [295] and service of such a man, would gladly have retained him to serve and honor his court. And the latter strove, for he knew how to do that, to protect his lord [300] and to honor and serve him well and willingly, and to keep him in his best state and the best renown that he saw him in. [305] One day he presented himself to him and like a worthy and well-bred man he said to him: "Lord, I was born and made only to serve you and to give [my service] and please you and hold you dear, with no deceit; [310] and if power is not enough for me, I am not lacking in heart or good sense. So that, among the other honors which you have bestowed on me, I would ask you, in case I suffer

[315] misfortune or abasement, that you remember what good things I have said and done for you."

"'And the king, who was always pleased by good deeds, said to him, "Friend *[320]* almassor, dear good friend, if ever a lord should congratulate himself on his vassal, I should, and I do so freely because of you. So I want you yourself to choose [take] *[325]* your honor and reward." And he, who was well-prepared for some time, had had a head-dress, attractive and becoming and of a fine red color, which the pagans call *almussa*. *[330]* [And he said to the king, "I would like you to place it on my head with your own hand, so that one may know without doubt that] I have won it through prowess and as a sign of nobility and honor to my lineage. *[335]* And let no one else dare wear it for a single day on account of his high birth or his might. And if anyone does so, let him not return except on pain of losing all his reputation." *[340]* The gift was, as you have heard, as he had always wanted to ask it.

"'Before that event had passed from memory, a baron came into the country, *[345]* as good or better than other people, and the king was another one too, after the one I told you about. And if ever a lord found his vassal bold, knightly, *[350]* gentle, open and amicable, the king found him to be so. And the baron found his lord to be unexacting, frank and courteous; and was *[355]* head and lord over everything in his [the king's] land. And so it was, one day in Spring when the season was serene and green and bright, that the baron wanted to go out riding and had his palfreys brought, *[360]* and his horses and harness and companions all assembled. And when he was mounted he bore an *almussa* just like that which the king had previously *[365]* given to the first almassor, and had his knight put it on his head for him. This caused people, high and low throughout the land, to wonder *[370]* that anyone who was not of the lineage dared in such a way to wear the head-dress that was given for service, the lineage that had had much honor and good and rank *[375]* because of the head-dress. And the king came one day in the Spring to his house, as did many high barons, and many honored and worthy men *[380]* said to him, "Sire, you have held us dear and in good esteem; but now an evil has arisen if you do not correct it. One of your barons has raised himself *[385]* to [the rank of wearing] the *almussa*. And there should be neither count nor king nor any other man so powerful as to wear the *almussa* except you who should not lose his head at once [if he does]. [*390*] Thus [the custom] has been kept, and thus an almassor won it, who grew with your ancestors and us all, like a worthy man." And the king, as a wise [*395*] lord should, said to them: "My dear noble kinsmen, your ancestors will never be cheapened by me; and know that you will never have as much good as I would like. [*400*] If you desire it, I shall summon that baron, and if he has done any wrong or misdeed toward you or anyone else, I shall do to him that which my court decides; I know this, [*405*] that thus it will be done legally."

" 'The baron was truly summoned, and the court was great and plenary, and the king, like a wise and noble man, said to the barons:

[*410*] " ' "You know that I am not powerful except as I uphold justice; and a king who has no respect for justice often lives to see himself deprived of his own kingdom. You have done a proud [*415*] and haughty deed, it seems to me, for you dare to wear the *almussa* contrary to the order that has been made concerning it. Therefore, although I have endeavored to honor you and grant your requests, [*420*] I do not wish to dishonor my authority by not reprimanding you to the full."

" 'And the baron, to whom all worries were easy to resolve, [*425*] from which a noble heart had freed him, remained standing and said to the king:

" ' "Lord, you have honored me many times, and I have done the same for you as well as I could for a long time, and I did not consider good or ill in it. [*430*] So I say to you, as God may save me and grant me to do every honorable deed, that there is not a man alive in this world who desires your enhancement as much as I. So it should not offend you [*435*] if I can gain the *almussa* without wrong to others, which I do not want to do, to any lineage high or low. It is true that formerly an almassor—well over a hundred years ago—wanted to gain this mark of recognition to do honor to his house [*440*] because he had a proud heart and served your ancestor. So I, who have done as much [*445*] or more, desire it in the same way. And if I did it through any pride, do not let me remain at all and do with me as you please, and do not do me any more good."

[*450*] Thus, and in such a way, did that man gain by valor what he would not have done if he had been downcast or weak or mean in [desirin] possessions or nobility or power [*455*] or anything else in the world.

" 'Then all the barons were held in deep respect, for great lords used to have noble and honored hearts to reward merit [*460*] and to rescue a man from danger sweetly and well, with grace and love and seemliness, such as Bertran de Born said in a *sirventes* so as to make powerful men more courteous, [*465*] frank and generous, so that they should be, without wrong-doing, distinguished, clever, frank and select:

" ' "And thus a prize was established, that one should make war, and vigorously, [*470*] and in Lent and Advent enrich soldiers of fortune." Those men had hearts worthy to make war and lavish expenditures and to found courts with rich presents [*475*] so as to increase joys and pleasures. And the foolish man was not remembered, nor the mean or cowardly man, but worthy emperors and kings and counts and high barons [*480*] so as to give heart to a man, to make him bold and of greater virtue. But now all those that used to be first have changed, and because they do not have a pure heart for merit [i.e., a pure desire for merit], [*485*] and they falsify prowess, so that generosity and goodness lose their position of esteem and lack prestige among them. And wisdom becomes without worth, and a low, weak heart grows in each of them, [*490*] to take merit away from everyone; I cannot see anything except bad conduct. For the lords have caused their barons to become vain and without hope, and in this way the good of the leader is lacking [from their conduct]. [*495*] For they used to have noble hearts for doing knightly deeds, from which came grace and joy and worth. And God, who is never pleased by bad or mean men [*500*] because, from being worthy men they have become sad and without feeling, will now want to do to them as He did to the Almoravides of Spain; [*505*] to whom, because they were of good company and noble people, were given nobility and lands and kingdoms of Morocco [and] in all countries. These were the Almoravides, and from them came captains and kings [*510*] to wage war and make treaties [and to do great deeds and fine actions]; from then on without guilt from anyone else except by their own people, they became weak and cowardly [*515*] and false, and they upheld great wrong; so that a noble and powerful lineage—that was the Almohade—was raised over them because they [the Almohade] wanted to have reform and noble ways. [*520*] And the people, who came to like what they did, gave them the lordship over the lands and overthrew all the others

[Almoravides]. Thus their lineage was lost [525] and their race driven out. For thus a false lineage quickly falls, and mean hearts without restraint [defence?], and thus it [lineage] lost its power; that is why we too have become like that, [530] recreant and without a noble heart. For giving is not held in great esteem, and a man does not pursue merit, which used to be sought after, unless he is generous, [535] nor does a good name come to anybody [without it]. For truly, giving brings merit and light and radiance to all sides, which it unfailingly brings to its lands and rivers and domain. [540] And a noble heart, without deceit in order to conquer, does the rest. It brings generosity with it and supports everything, is worth much and makes him who is generous worth much. And generous people, skillful [545] and attractive in their deeds, usually had high repute compared to [other] people, and more than all other barons, they whose worth increased in this way tried to be excellent. [550] But now, because many honorable hearts have become [this way, i.e., bad] the majority, as I have earnestly told you, and similarly because most of the others have only a beggarly knowledge [comes to the others], [555] these lords have all become miserly and weak and mean, so that the merit which used to be there is there no longer, and instead they have all fallen to the ground, so that nobility was just like a building; [560] and if later it will be seen to have climbed too high through the noble hearts of others—for such a thing is not right, but a great annoyance—it will also be seen to be overthrown, without any profit to anyone— [565] as if merit in the performance of great deeds and fine actions depended on wearing a silken gown.

" 'Worth was given to complete and noble, valiant hearts so that the lazy beggars without noble hearts should have no claim to it. [570] Many a discourse and many a demonstration have been made on this topic for the world: how it thus declines doing bad deeds. And although there are people foolishly loving lowness, I have seen en Lobat [575] held in esteem for his noble heart as much as any baron in the land. And I have seen many men of noble birth stand aside, beaten and tired. And he who wants to have consideration, [580] en Mercadier can tell it to him, and Margarit who, without being a nobleman, did many noble things, and many brave deeds and actions at sea, through which one seeks to acquire natural worth. [585] The reason why nobility is worth so much is because it brings honor to those who have it [i.e., prestige] and brings them the advantages and respect due to merit, so that they are honored among people, but without worth they are not prized [590] nor, without knowledge, are they very well received. And value does not come without a manly, noble heart, nor does wisdom unless one learned it. Praiseworthy people come to honorable deeds because of their heart and wisdom, [595] not from parentage or position; and the occasion [to do great deeds], and laughter, gaiety and pleasures come, not from noble birth or frivolity, but from a good heart, by which worthy men gain position, [600] by doing noble actions and fine deeds, as Arnaut de Maruelh said for the advancement of all good conduct:

" ' "For it is true that, today and yesterday, every worthy man wins position [605] by means of sense and wisdom and good merit."

" 'The mean man remains where he is, doing only what he must, and the worthy men are powerful and wise. And now, if you want to have a good understanding [610] without discouragement as to why the barons are recreant in doing deeds of prowess everywhere, let us part; and if you want just foolishness, you still have enough left to stay and talk.' [615] And so we went to bed immediately, thinking over what I had heard. And I realized that old, gray Dauphin had told me the truth, there in private by the fire.

"In the morning, [620] a Thursday it was, I took my leave in the sight of everybody. And if ever you saw a man well taken care of, and by a lord at that, I was he. By way of Auvergne and Le Puy I came to Provence in this direction [625] where I found many gay barons and the good count and the countess. And although the stage [of the journey] was great, from there I went to the county of Toulouse where I found, with a perfect heart, [630] my lord the first count, and many gracious knights who are with him, and I was given an outfit of clothes by him, and so I came to Savartès. And at Foix I found no one, [635] for the count was at Alberu, and I went on towards Castillon. And God—for my spirits were good enough so that I should make my way there directly—brought me to Mataplana [640] last Monday. Here I found, if it please you, my Lord Uc, gracious, frank, gentle, and a ready critic to listen to all good knowledge. [645] And there I found ladies who, in truth, reminded me of my father, and the good time that has brought on a bad time, for now it is despicable and of little courtesy.

"You have heard how things have gone with me, [650] and how I have traveled up and down, and how I have been bewildered, and why. And if it were not for my Lord Dauphin, for he put me on the right road at the right time, [655] I would never be kindly disposed towards it, nor would I think any good of the times in which we live. And so I have come bewildered, for I would like to shake up the world and I don't know how, for I don't know how [660] to do the things that are concerned with the proper procedure."

And I, to whom a light mind never would induce any thought, pondered for a moment as a wise man ought, [665] and because wisdom and sense and spirit made me think of my advice [that I would give], I said to him without any preparation:

"Friend, you have come to me, as you tell me, bewildered and [670] out of your mind because you don't know how or why the times and true goodness and good merit have changed, that used to hold sway; [675] and you want to know why love is thus lost and demeaned, which used to be honored and held in high regard [because it could] make many a man worthy and good. You have not seen it, but you [680] have heard your father tell of the time, and how there were not long ago still three barons that maintained themselves as they used to. And you begin to wonder at it because you have searched a great deal [traveled widely] [685] and you never find worth enough to make your heart joyful, and you do not know how or where everything has disappeared at once; it seems that it appeared for a while [690] and that henceforth it has been given up. And if the Dauphin, perfect and true, had not given you this idea, you would have become discourteous and a complete rogue, banished from worthy people. [695] For my part, it would seem reasonable, in real truth, and without discussion, that we should not add anything to his speech or to what he says. And I would not do so, by my faith, [700] if you had not raised another question; but because you said that, to accommodate yourself to the times you must act like a fool, and because you cannot find the manner or way of doing it, [705] you have upset me, and more, for you have asked me for advice.

"I do not say, although I don't spend many sleepless nights considering the matter, that among all men without question there are not some [710] with natural sense among whom one cannot have more or less easily everyone under one's control at all times regardless of whether he comes or goes or remains for a long or short time [*715*]—for sense arises and is born in the spirit as soon as it has grown and developed; but knowledge, through which one is welcomed and more honored and respected, and more liked and more sought after, [*720*] and which makes men behave correctly, cannot come without seeing and hearing much and trying hard. So perhaps I do not dare give you any [advice], for I have heard and seen nothing [*725*] by which to judge what you have told me, nor to entirely decide such a weighty point, but, because I think I should be shown up as a foolish arbiter of feeble intelligence, it will be an honor [*730*] for me to tell you what I think of the matter and what I know of it according to my understanding, and how it seems and appears to me.

"It is true that I, to fulfill a desire, and because I had often thought about it, [*735*] more than for any other consideration, and for the profit that might be there, came to the court of King Alfons, the father of our courteous king, who was so worthy and served so well, and did [*740*] such honor to everyone. There I saw deeds and actions that were good and well done, graceful and pleasing, so that now I am better in all forms of conduct and I am more sensible in all things. [*745*] And if I knew then what I know now —even though I am not very adept in these matters—there my learning would have been appreciated and more widespread than it is now. And you, if you had been there, [*750*] you would certainly have seen a little of the good old times that your father formerly spoke of, where all the fine lovers were, and generous men, worthy and fine; [*755*] and you would hear, as I did, the troubadours tell and relate how they lived by traveling and making the rounds of lands and places; and you would see there tasseled saddles [*760*] and much other costly harness, and gilded bridles and palfreys; you would marvel at it greatly. Some used to come from beyond the mountain passes, and others from Spain on this side. [*765*] Here they found, gracious and gay and generous, King Alfons, en Diego who was so worthy, and Guidrefe de Gamberes and the courteous Count Ferran [*770*] and his brothers, so gentlemanly that I couldn't tell you the half of it. Here they found from another direction towards Lombardy [Italy] the worthy marquis and two, three, [*775*] four, five—more than a hundred other barons, for truly in that country generosity has always been maintained. And in Provence they did not find stingy men, nor were they slow in coming to the counts, [780] who always have maintained the revenue of remuneration by generosity.

"En Blacas does not deserve to be left out, nor en William the Fair of Baux nor, from Auvergne, the Lord Guion [785] nor the Count Dauphin, who was so worthy; nor, closer to us, en Gaston, who cared more about merit than public recognition. And those who came by way of Foix have found a lord [790] who was courteous and a pleasant giver, as everyone said ... and in Vernet a gay Ponson. There you will still find, worthy and true, [795] n'Arnaut de Castelnou. There you will find all together everything that becomes a courteous baron; and en Raimon Gauseran at Estany; all the way from Malfet to Pinós [800] you will find bold and excellent men, and at Cardona the powerful en Guillem, and in Urgelh. So I tell you, there are plenty of distinguished and spirited barons. And at Castelvielh was n'Albert, [805] a very brave knight, and around him other barons, frank and eager to do good deeds. And if you had not heard about en Guillem, he of Montcada, [810] you could spend such a morning hearing about him as would be full of courtliness.

"But, it seems to me, you could not stand such a long speech, and talking too much makes disagreeable [815] that which restraint makes enjoyable; so I want to come now to en Miquel in Aragon and en Garcia Romieu who showed so much courtesy; and, at Entença, en Berenguier [820] who maintained merit, pure, entire, upright, complete and true. And furthermore, on this side I will bring you back to the Count who is at Castelo, en Pons and his son en Hugh, [825] both good at maintaining merit and valor; and at Rocaberti Lord Geoffrey who was so highly esteemed in many towns and kingdoms where they were surrounded by merit, [830] and at Vila de Mul you can find their uncle, en Raimon; there was not such a baron in the whole world with twice as much power who better knew how to maintain worth, [835] for he never tired for a single day. You will find en Pons de Cervera learned and of good company among us, worthy and of pleasing manners, strong and swift in all deeds. [840] At Maurellas and at Monells and in other towns that I do not mention there were many barons so noble that you [will] not find in any land, no matter where or how hard you search, [845] any more eager for good actions of any kind, and also in other lands which I have not told you about either. Yet, because it is not useful for this [my main purpose] [I do not want to stretch out that subject] [*850*] but let's get down to work and to the facts. I have contradicted your father and the Dauphin to you by what I saw and what I heard people say. Afterwards, I shall tell you only [*855*] what I heard, if you [will] listen to me.

"The true God, who was punished for us, as we believe, and made all that there is, willed that in Germany should come an Emperor Frederick, [*860*] and in England, Sir Henry, as you have heard the Dauphin tell, and his sons too, Henry, Richard, and Geoffrey, and in the Toulouse country a courteous count, [*865*] en Raimon, who was so highly esteemed. And if you are not excited by it, you should know too, by hearsay and appearance, what the worthy Count of Barcelona was like, [*870*] and his son n'Alfons, who knew how to have such good worth all his days. And the latter made knowledge and wisdom his heritage in his spirit. Through their nobility these men could estimate [*875*] bad people and good according to what they were. And in the time of those I have mentioned, there arose the troubadours and the paid [entertainers] and the story-tellers, and the worthy barons towards Astarac [*880*] such as en Bernart d'Armagnac, en Arnaut Guillem de Marsan, en Berenguer de Robian, and en Bernardon of Comminges, and towards Montpelier [*885*] en Guillem, a clever and prudent baron, and such that he was ready to recognize all good qualities; and on this side a courteous knight, Bertran de Saissac, he was called. [*890*] These came and went, and by them jongleurs and knights who were ruined were restored, and those who were in the right were supported. And he whose conduct [*895*] and knowledge were graceful and of good quality, went where he could present it to them. And they, in the court of the more influential people, where the rewards were to be found, and great and noble lords, [*900*] clever and knightly, well-known and honored, how noble they always were! And you would not even have to ask for it [the court] but would any day have found [*905*] such a one as you only could have imagined. They were great lovers, organized tournaments and started wars in many towns and lands, and they liked ladies to be courteous, [*910*] well-bred and sophisticated, as did your father. And they only carried rosaries or any other mark [of religion] with fine ointment because of Lady Escarronha, [*915*] Mahieu of Pallars, and en Gelmar's lady, the

Countess of Urgell on that side and Lady Gensana on this, who were of those good people [*920*] ... and accustomed to honor and believe in God. And they established many a priest and many a monastery to serve God; they didn't want to vow obedience, [*925*] but simply those who [are able to] change worldly life wanted to stay there [i.e., in monasteries], but still mixed with the world. That is how the deeds and the conduct were valid and lasted for ages [*930*]. But now a pardon and a [form of] knowledge has come that is like madness. And because they found counts, kings, and nobles to be feeble and weak, they have brought them back into their schools [*935*] and made them believe what they chose. And those who complain at trifles and change their opinion frequently have thus taken in all that [teaching], so that they found nothing palatable. [*940*] And for this reason, gay and sophisticated behavior [knowledge] have deserted them, and the noble and valiant knights that used to live among them have since become hypocrites, [*945*] just as the Dauphin told you. But I have told you a little more about why valor, joy and pleasant company, merit and honor, have thus been lost. I have now spoken to you of the barons, [*950*] so that you can be more adept in your behavior and more well-bred, and to show you how one speaks; and you yourself have asked me [*955*] why such men are esteemed and wherein their better learning lies. You should know that in the whole world there is no knowledge or behavior that is of so much value to a clever man, although he may protect himself against fools, as the art of the jongleur. [*960*] This art requires a man to be gay, open, gentle, and learned, and to know how to please people according to the nature of each. But now come, dull in understanding, [*965*] ungrateful, foolish, ignorant people, who think they can become formidable with only their foolish knowledge and without any assistance from the sense of others. Knowledge, to him who wishes to have it at his command, is the best treasure in the world. [*970*] But it must be aided by assurance and feeling and manner as well, for without these the right road to follow is not easy. Assurance brings it forward [*975*] and speeds it among the best people, and manner helps one to consider the [appropriate] time and place; feeling does not bring to it any other matter, but controls it as may be appropriate. [*980*] I do not say that a man cannot set an emerald in tin; but gold is its equal only, when they are together, just as good sense [sensibility] sets off knowledge. And he that [*985*] wants to, and believes that he can, find wisdom among the ignorant, exactly in the same way he thinks that he can do what God would never permit for a single day. Knowledge requires a man to be firm, without deceit, clever, open, and well-informed; [*990*] and if he is among unlearned people he will be such as they, and mean as well. For a courteous and worthy man is not to blame in that, if you do not recognize him as such; thus, as is fitting, they [who have learning] have the merit [*995*] and you remain deceived [because you have not recognized their merit]. There are worldly people, foolish and undiscriminating, who on the arrival [of a newcomer] think that they can judge a man and, distinguishing between good and bad men, [*1000*] admit them to their "superior" company and make them such as they are, and who think they know how good people behave. And those that can recognize taste think that [*1005*] they should reject a man with less learning than they; and they also want to reject, rudely, as is fitting, the bad people who are not afraid of it [i.e., of being rejected] and whom blame does not affect. [*1010*] And those who are undiscriminating in slander do not spare anyone.

"Likewise various intelligences are given to each of those that understand, so that there are some among the wise ones [*1015*] who are frequently in error. The latter, according as you will find them, you should treat with care, because they would only be troublesome to you, and stupid and ill-bred; [*1020*] for, as n'Arnaut de Maruelh says, instructing undiscriminating people, 'One can leave property for one's son to inherit, but he will not have merit [*1025*] unless he gets it from his own heart.' Natural cause[s] make a boor, just as education makes an informed man. Such are the former, and many other mean and stupid men are [even] more foolish, [*1030*] courtly boors who, because they are devoid of understanding, will not call you aside except when they see that you are among ladies or near other people [*1035*] and then their hearts are illumined with a foolish wisdom. And they will say to you, for such jokes delight these pseudo-scholars, 'You there, jongleur, why don't you sing us a song instead of sitting there saying nothing?' [*1040*] And, although their way of talking is out of place, you should not be put out with them, for their idle whim will have vanished however little you say to them. Just as reasonable [i.e., unreasonable] are

[1045] some others, of whom you will find many, who are boorish and stupid as a statue, who, because they can chatter to you, want to hear your song, and are low and empty of understanding. [1050] You should treat such people with discretion, for they are good for nothing; and if you get into an argument with them they will behave stupidly and foolishly toward you.

"Cowardly jongleurs, badly trained, [1055] gloomy and slow to learn, without knowledge or feeling or anything but boredom and foolishness, as soon as they have loved for a while, will want to judge you foolishly, [1060] and with a mournful ditty will think that they are paying both good and bad, and that they have fortified their courage against the charges of the barons. So I tell you, in order to be a guide to you toward gentle conduct in society [1065], you should change your way of feeling and knowledge. And let them not be considered contrary to [popular] taste, or low, foolish or unseemly [1070] nor such as I now judge those to be who will write, anywhere, well- or badly-written tales of love, tunes, songs and other verses as well. And you please sad and gentle men [1075] and all others as you find them. And do not refrain from it, but please each according as he is worth, according to whether he will be strong in making customs pleasant; you should know how one acquires pleasing conduct, both of lands [local customs] [1080] and from learned men. And above all be sure that your expressions and words come from learned men so that, when you tell stories to people [1085] a meager payment may not be given to you because of it. Because a man's action is clearly related to his profession, and in turn each profession has its own standards of conduct, so that one can tell what a man is, [1090] I tell you—and because it is customary and an excellent thing in a man like you—that you should wear good shoes and well-made hose, dagger, purses, belt and gloves [1095] and cap, and keep your hair well dressed. For such habits are a pleasure, gracious and not too affected. Let your clothes be cut and tailored tastefully and well, [1100] and let them not be dirty or stained, but as fresh and cleverly made as if they came [to you] as a distinction—attractive touches which often please people. [1105] Do not behave or dress like a man given to vice, but do not wear such an outfit that, to well-bred people, it does not immediately appear to belong to you; for he has badly learned his trade [1110] who fails because of foolish behavior. You do not have a mean or stupid appearance and you do not waste your words, so I will tell you well-known and clear reasons [*1115*] so that you may know how such an ardent [?] man lives, and how he should be a gentleman and conduct himself as such. Since worth and feeling are above [*1120*] all other virtues; and because knowledge leads to them, with skill as well, I tell you—and since God never made a man so badly or so low that at once, [*1125*] although he does not have a sincere heart nor one that is frank and learned, worthy and well brought up men may not be pleasant to him—be that as it may, among fools and mean people [*1130*] or among men who are worthy and valiant your speech should be courteous and your deeds imbued with feeling, and above all, gracious and gentle and tempered with wisdom. [*1135*] For never was anyone who is awkward, foolish or stupid, good for anything. Gracious deeds make a worthy man accepted in every undertaking, and to use his learning with grace. [*1140*] And a gracious fool is worth many times more than a man who is ungracious. And remember what a learned troubadour says, en Miraval, [*1145*] to make brave men well-mannered as opposed to unseemly behavior:

" 'For an awkward man, even though he is bold, is hardly any good at the business of love.'

"Gracefulness makes [*1150*] many men gracious and causes them to please people; and similarly, you should remember, in dignifying your profession, what Peire Rogier said to en Raimbaut when he went to see him: [*1155*]

" 'If you want to make your way in the world, be foolish in the appropriate place with fools, and you should know how to be well-behaved with wise people; for this is how one should deal with them, [*1160*] some with anger, others with joy, evilly with evil people, well with good people.'

"There are some idle men, full of pride and nonsense who, because they have no sense, go around saying [*1165*] that a fortunate man does not have to get up early in the morning. You should not believe that, nor trust in such ideas. For everything comes with striving and with an effort to succeed. [*1170*] Luck is called Hope because a man cannot have it by sensibility, but what a man can attain by seeing and by full and perfect knowledge is called wisdom and insight, [*1175*] and the regard of learned men, by which a man lives honored and worthy. 'To much effort, troubles seem trifling'—and the fool dies in exile and the unambitious man dies without attaining a position of authority. [*1180*] And so the reasons which I adduce may come to you with greater pleasure, hear what a troubadour says, to set many people straight:

" 'Feeling has such pleasures in love, [*1185*] that if everyone knew how to bring them to it, he would be a better lover than the fool who takes them (his pleasures) in haste. Gaiety does not come to an unpleasing person, nor pleasures to an unambitious man.'

[*1190*] "That is why deeds and ruses and knowledge reside in [i.e., are natural to] an ambitious man, who would like to get a reward from the barons. For a baron cannot be ill-disposed for so long, [*1195*] and God did not make this age so consistently bad, that an ambitious, clever and frank man could not get gifts out of it in order to rise and make himself noticed if he knew how to be clever and had the right manner [*1200*] and the knack of it, and had done things. Don't worry and get upset about a thing, even though good fortune is in many cases lacking to those that seek it; [*1205*] for there will always be good fortune and help at the right time and place for learned men, and he who is trying hard for something which is rightly attractive may be allotted a bad thing [*1210*] if force is used against him. Let your actions and knowledge be varied and sound, for one does not find anyone like us in proportion as is given to us [*1215*] ... we cannot make new men. And because a man, although he may be handsome, is worth nothing without knowledge, I tell you that a man who knows as much as you [*1220*] should be anxious and seek out the right occasions and ways of behaving from the barons on every side, for the use of sensitivity is preferable to noise and chatter. [*1225*] And since you should not cause worry [pain], but joy and good and gracious wisdom, learn what Arnaut de Maruelh says of the matter, that in order to make more prosperous those who want to increase in merit, [*1230*] and to make use of learned people, 'both foreign and native, he [who wants to live among people] may learn from them deeds and ways of behaving; and let him ask and inquire about [*1235*] the way of life and customs of the vile and the good from them; let him learn good and evil from the mean and the virtuous. And let him who wants to live in society consider and understand the best [*1240*] so as to defend himself better if anyone should reprove him.'

"You know that it falls to those who are learned to move among the best people [1245] and to increase sensitivity and valor among them, and to exhibit good learning. And so, in order that everything you say may be true everywhere and your deeds more accomplished [1250] and your heart more perfect, I tell you that among all the ages [of men] you should choose young men, those whose heart causes them to do what is fitting for a man of valiant merit. [1255] Because they do not always have forethought they immediately want to do what they can. Mean men are generous through a sense of obligation, but the heart leads young men to be generous. These often want to hear [1260] love-songs and *sirventes* and debates in verse, and all songs that are worthy and fresh, whatever they may be. And a gentle and quiet man will not be very welcome among them. [1265] You should desire a perfect condition, in which good qualities and a noble heart have remained, so that you may be led to see wisdom and knowledge often. For those who are at [the height of] their power always [1270] desire gentle men who know how to praise or blame as is necessary. And those people always want to act with boldness, feeling, and knowledge [1275] and behave in every good way? Like a fish on dry land! Counts and kings, bishops and prelates, lords, leaders and men in authority are made of such men, [1280] to maintain law and justice. Those in whom there never was a noble heart, and for whom youth offers no challenge, you will find on the contrary to be weak and false, vain of all worth and low. [1285] So I beg you not to follow them closely or near of your own will, because from them come the false laughter and contempt of the jongleurs, with barbed jokes and expressions [1290] that show that they cannot recognize merit. These want suitable men, whatever their nature may be, mean or good, and they consider any man good who does anything for gain. [1295] And so they dismally exist, without any benefit, looked down upon by all others, in order to give pleasure, although they are wretched if they have many men with no sense with them. Do not wait [1300] to be called on all the time when you are with people; for often many a man, even though he remains quiet and without a happy face, likes it when someone comforts him tactfully. [1305] Do not be too wearisome either, when you are sometimes with people, for there is often a [bad] habit among clever people that in conversations [instead of saying pleasant things], [*1310*] they follow their own bent by telling malicious jokes by which they provoke men to embarrassment and then blame them for being half-hearted in their performance. For a man who can thus change is not suitable for all kinds of society. [*1315*] Many men, because they succumb to the heedlessness of youth, are without nobility of heart, and when they are mature, wisdom brings such an ugly deed to them [to their conscience] that they have valiant and good hearts. You ought to see these people often, because [*1320*] the older they grow they want to achieve better things, and because then their learning and courage increases. There are plenty of men who are poor, without sense or the ability to accomplish anything, but who are rich in pride [*1325*] and who, because they are foolish, do not want any company but their own; these are those who would even say vile and evil things to [about?] their lord. So I say to you that [*1330*] you should not associate with such people unless it is absolutely necessary, for they do not become more discerning, frank, gentle or learned as they increase in age. These people need sycophants to support their empty authority, [*1335*] who make them speechless with pleasure with a few false and flattering words. In addition to these, there must be at least five hundred others who are liberal and well-versed in all learning, but they are so vile [*1340*] and so unfamiliar with merit that you cannot be intimate with a single one of them without suffering harm; so I tell you that with them you should try to have some protection and talk with them frequently, [*1345*] for it is seldom that one cannot get good sense from a man who is learned and generous. There are others, humble and wise, who, since they do not have a hasty temper, want a companion [*1350*] with whom they can talk things over. If therefore you do not find them with other people do not wait for them, for never has any one of them done anything worthwhile. But to be ashamed of other people [*1355*] is conceit, which in the valiant and in others who are opposed to it arises through quarreling: in some because they are of high rank; and in others, who are valiant, [*1360*] it often arises through quarreling, which shows them how brave, tough-hearted and well-trained they are. Let me not forget cowardice, which causes others to speak seldom, [*1365*] and because they want to be reserved because their nature is such. And so I tell you, because to my way of thinking you should not be otherwise, that you ought to be reserved with them; [*1370*] and if you do not find them at a good time, you will have goods and profit at any appropriate occasion later when their ill humor has worn off. Similarly, [*1375*] you should come, with marks of courtesy and with a face that is not overcast, to sincere people, because gentleness is always their guide; for these people do not summon anyone to divert them, and they never will, for there is no one in their group who knows more [*1380*] about anything than they do. There are men who lack valor and sense and who are timid when they are among worthy people and who, because they are superior among inferior people, think that they are worth something [*1385*] because they know how to amass property, or because they think they are graceful, or because they know how to cut a tunic [how a tunic should be cut?] or any other well-fitting garment, or because they think they have big, strong bodies [*1390*] that attract people's attention. You shouldn't admire such men, nor should you have very much to do with them, for they only know what to do by looking at what people like them are doing. [*1395*] You should see those men who give to people because they are prepared to do so, although they are not greatly esteemed nor suited to such sophistication; [*1400*] but you should not make yourself beg too much for their wealth, for it is contemptible to frequent a man who does not understand how things should be done; and it is a great pleasure to find a sophisticated man who is gay and sincere. [*1405*] I tell you, by God, because you should seek out such men, that you should be near them, and refresh your virtue frequently and often, [*1410*] which is dissipated among low people. By God and by your youth and by everything, I beseech you—and because wisdom does not exist except through men of understanding— [*1415*] that you should not often waste your time among ignorant people, nor without cause tell worthy people that they are known and liked. For a stupid storyteller, without moderation, [*1420*] lays his learning open to ridicule. Some mean people are ignorant and enemies of learning that graces the mind; they are weak and greedy, joyless and needy, and feeble and hungry for wealth, [*1425*] back-biters of merry men and of all other well-being. And when you want to speak to them they will start to cadge and wheedle. You should constantly, or as often as you can, keep such people under your eye, [*1430*] for the more they have the meaner and more miserable they become. For it pleased God to make them that way, vile and incapable of getting any better. [*1435*] You should keep your distance from men who have no other sense than desire and learning, as though they were no longer friends of yours, for he who is familiar with them appears [*1440*] as stupid and well-bred as they. Because God never intended people to be equal in conduct, sense or wit, nor to be equally good-humored, [*1445*] I tell you, that among the valiant and the worthy, there are those without any consideration, who will speak to you aside and ask you to sing in front of everyone else; and they will not observe good manners [*1450*] nor time nor occasion, and at the third word of the song, whatever you are singing, they will grumble and begin to mutter to someone else, or begin to tell a story. [*1455*] God never intended to give them any sense, nor will He, as far as I can see. Although such people are worthless you should treat them as gently as possible; [*1460*] for everyone thinks that he has hired a man such as yourself, even those who are low and foolish and of a mean disposition. You well know that, because sense never brings anything else, [*1465*] there are those among the barons who are haughty toward that from which they profit, and who think that you are sufficiently rewarded if they listen to you [*1470*] and condescend merely to address you. You should frequent such people although they do not have a grateful heart, because one is welcomed gladly on that account by others of their intimate acquaintance. [*1475*] Only when they are young and while they are stupid in this way should you be familiar with low, polite fellows who foolishly want to enhance the reputation of their deeds, for once their youth has vanished [*1480*] they can hardly avoid becoming poor and admitting themselves beaten. But do not be pleased by ignorant [ungrateful?], weak, affected aristocrats, for they have completely forgotten all merit, without any hope of recovering it; [*1485*] and when they can make fun of you they consider themselves supremely happy. There are men in whom remains no trace of their noble lineage, but only bad humor, vile speech, and weak manners, [*1490*] with everything that is of least account among worthy people. These you should shun, for when they cannot do otherwise, and because not to praise nobility is wrong, they at once disparage nobility, so that he who follows them in that acts very badly. [*1495*] Keep away from men who are mean at heart, valiant in words, and of small achievement, in order that every care should be taken to consider men without sense; they are in popular opinion below all others, [*1500*] such as fastidious or haughty men, and low gossips. And other men you should find to be well-mannered among the knights, but elsewhere they are ashamed, [*1505*] where they pretend to be generous and of courteous behavior. And if you can get your teeth into them, do not fear to bite hard, for such ill-starred men [*1510*] expect little else than a bite. There are some men who desire nothing else than eating and resting, sleeping and sitting and being comfortable at their ease. [*1515*] And they can't bear a draught, or heat or cold, or a bad smell, or anything that a hardened man can stand. [*1520*] These are such that no one who ever saw them would consider them good or capable. So I tell you, because all their dealings are miserable and foul, that staying with them should not seem good to you, nor should their bread taste good; [*1525*] for they are always idle, and either the heat or the wind gives them a headache. But you should often go and see those whose heart and good will stimulate them to do what lies in their power, [*1530*] and since one ought to talk to them, do not wait for any other permission, for they usually don't know that it is you [who are there]. Although merit and worth are not to be found everywhere among the barons [*1535*] as they used to be, who used to assist troubadours and jongleurs—either because the barons are lacking in generosity or because sense warns them against it or because they have been snubbed [by ungrateful people]— [*1540*] do not become ungrateful merely in order to curry favor with mean people, nor less amusing toward worthy men; for a single graceful compliment will recompense you for such a sensible thing. [*1545*] And since a man is worth more if he is thoughtful, you should always bear in mind what en Guiraut de Bornelh said to refined people in order to strengthen their good behavior:

" 'And I hold it to be no disadvantage if Love oppresses me [*1550*] or casts me down; for in the future I shall enjoy success in it.' "

"So I consider that it is fitting that a man who is sure of himself, in order to make his own achievements seem more knightly [should invite] to a gay dinner party or some such other amusement [*1555*] people of low degree [?] with whom neither taste [knowledge] nor refined minds have anything in common. You should not shun such people, in fact you should know how to enjoy yourself with them, [1560] provided that you watch your good behavior; for very careful people should not surrender to the tastes of such people. Some men are weak and tiresome, and critical of other men's technique, [1565] but are not masters of their own; and because they are stupid they want to blame on conoisseurs the fault that is in them. So I tell you that such judges should not make you change your mind, [1570] nor should you correct knights when talking of arms, nor priests concerning their sermons; for many professions, although honorable, are discouraged when confronted by quarrelsome people. Do not criticize the jongleurs of others or the songs [1575] of the troubadours, for he who criticizes his equal appears envious and uninformed, but he who, in defending his companions, excuses them, appears courteous.

[1580] "Many men are like you, of similar attainments [knowledge] who, because they do not have natural intelligence, lively and good, go wandering through the world, and they do not know where [1585] a clever and courteous man ought to go; and their only accomplishment and idea is to learn poetic debates and every wisecrack that one says to fools, who are impressed by them and like them. [1590] And they [will] want to show worthy men the road to merit and pleasure, and teach wisdom to the wise, and wit to those who are skilled in it; and their own behavior [1595] will reveal them to be fools. So I tell you, because such learning is fruitless and trivial, that when you want to have pleasant conversation when you come among worthy people, [1600] if therefore they, before you begin [your act], have not asked you and enquired, you should tell them what you have seen and heard away in [other] lands, beginning gradually, [1605] just as one would enter a conversation. And do not forget to mention those barons whom you find, in your opinion, to be most courteous, and do not omit those who, according to their renown, are most valiant. [1610] Similarly, you should tell which ladies are most mature in all things for which a man should esteem a lady most highly. And if you see them begin [1615] to listen to your information, then start to tell them stories in verse by which one can be worth more in any profession. And after that, if you find them clever and subtle and understanding, you should have at hand songs [1620] and [stories of] valor, noble birth, and cleverness.

"Your similes should be scattered [i.e., not consecutive or numerous] and your discourse should be elevated but quiet in style, according to the matter of which you are speaking; [1625] your heart should be inspired to express your subject well, and restrained in vulgar speech, and your body should be firm and upright and graceful and of good posture. [1630] And you should not use the sort of speech that will get you into trouble. And among the men also, as I have recommended, your skill should be divided [1635] according to whether you find them good or bad. Hearing and seeing make us know what it is that makes some men excel; from which we know that the knights were chosen as men [1640] to uphold lesser people and to do knightly deeds and to make gifts, and that they made up songs and entertainments about them, well-made and composed. And all good qualities that are honored and right [1645] are better in them than in other people. But [Almighty God] did not want to make them equally, and He did not take care that ... back when he climbed ... to those that are wise. [1650] So I say to you that, since intelligence ... that to intelligent men, wherever you may be, it is worth more ... to talk, to, so that you may be able to acquire some of it. [1655] ... my praises, gracious to the wise and good to the brave at appropriate times. [1660] [And when you are welcomed into their] houses, you should always esteem highly, and observe, their conduct, so that you may become more courtly; for all sophisticated people are there [1665] and instruction [received] by word and example; and distinguished people come there, and those that want to rise in merit. And he who is not of a generous nature elsewhere, is generous here. [1670] And here the false becomes fine and true, the good becomes better and the disturbed becomes clear; and since God did not want to omit anything, it seems as though it were established by Him.

"Some jongleurs are obstinate [1675] and sing their own praises, and because they are stupid they want to sit down beside you even if you were before the king, almost as if they were more knightly and of higher rank. [1680] And the longer they have been in a place the less highly are they considered in everything; so I tell you, because such conduct is vulgar and foolish, that when you come to a place, [1685] keep quiet at first at least, and then see to it that you lead the entire conversation, so that you may appear to advantage because of it, and behave yourself among worthy people.

[1690] Do not praise your skill to people, even though it may be good and choice, nor your mind to learned men or others full of honor. And if you were the son of an emperor [1695] you would still be no more than a jongleur as long as you enjoyed traveling back and forth and it was to your liking; and later, having become a man [in one's profession], one certainly is proficient in it and well received wherever one goes, since it is one's profession. [1700] And although [the manners of] the times we live in are very discourteous and vulgar in places, you will find experts who will recognize your learning; and if your spirit is able to impose itself on others, [1705] there will certainly be plenty of people who will praise it besides you. You should always visit courts and places of high society and of important people; for it is fitting for him, if he is a good jongleur, to visit such places without the [previous] knowledge of others; [1710] among the people, and even for one who is more reserved in judgment, his conversation is more piquant.

"Readiness makes many a senseless man an excellent talker; and so I tell you that with such people [1715] you should not oppose them in argument, for their only accomplishment is in words, just as that of a worthy man is in deeds. A wretch who is blameworthy and uncivil in his replies should not have a hold over your will [so that you answer in the same way] [1720] for those who are wretched and mean will be censured enough without you; nor, on the other hand, should you praise too highly, although fools may be embarrassed because of it, for, one of the least valuable forms of knowledge, [1725] it is just the same as too much slander. And if you want to be more high class, always refer to en Miraval, who said, being averse to those hot-headed people who excel in love:

[1730] "'And he who praises his lady beyond her worth makes it seem that he is making fun of her, and nothing else.'"

"Do not praise an honored patron too highly, and do not be too intelligent or pedantic [1735] nor too gloomy nor too backward nor too much in evidence; do not go to extremes in anything, for excess is just as displeasing as moderation is pleasing and highly considered.

[1740] "Because psychological types are so varied [minds are too much toward all sides] that I cannot enumerate them all, and because the manners [ways] that cause people to do many difficult deeds are also varied—since you have heard enough [1745] so that you have profited—I tell you that you should not keep company nor converse nor deal with questions of taste with stupid, foolish or conceited people, nor have anything to do with them; [*1750*] for all their deeds and knowledge are naturally like them. And if I have told you that a man like you is to better advantage among worthy people, you should not on that account devote yourself exclusively to people of merit [*1755*] so that you become low and mean and act unbecomingly toward the others; for such people often come among the most knightly men, where they can be harmful. [*1760*] You should tell your tales while you are fresh and gay and welcomed by gracious people, for old, gray-haired men are out of place in society. And remember that it is said among us, [*1765*] in order to make men clever, that when a man comes to repentance he has become old. Happy, indeed, is he whose knowledge increases while time and place are still opportune."

[*1770*] And then, since our parting was not easy for each other, we came to my home, where we ate, until the morning, when he went away.

And I do not know if he found the times [*1775*] improved, for I never saw him since that time. And may God bring me to a good end.

NOTES

1. "Abril": flex. -s omitted; a scribal error since "mays" shows -s.
13. "amor e mon pessamen": flex. -s omitted ("amors e mos pessamens"). Since the rhyme-word "solamen" can take a flex. -s (acc. to Raimon Vidal, *Razos*, ed. E. Stengel, p. 82) the omission may be an error or a hypercorrection (predicate subject of "ac").
18. "*vas*": (MS. "vers") Syntax and sense, continued from vs. 15, require the preposition "vas." Easily mistaken for an adjective (with incorrect -s) "vas" would be edited by a scribe to the conventional "vers." A N Fr. "vers" (< VERSUS) is quite unlikely.
23. "a fort del temps": ("a for del temps"?) Bohs: "nach der Weise der Zeit."
26. The verse of the MS. is a syllable short. "deman" is difficult to explain. A Catalanism "demanan" in the orig. instead of O. Occ. "demandan" would then be read by a scribe as a dittography with correction of "m" to "ieu".
37. "*lui*": (MS. "mi") Bohs emends to "li," Levy to "lui." Both are acceptable but "lui" better explained the scribal error mí for luí).
41. "salutz": Though not mentioned in the *Leis d'Amors*, the genre was recognized, as the present text shows. Arnaut de Mareuil wrote seven (Pierre Bec, *Les Saluts d'amour du troubadour Arnaut de Mareuil* [Toulouse: E. Privat, 1961]. Paul Meyer, "Le Salut d'amour dans les littératures provençale et française," *Bibliothèque de l'École des Chartes*, XXVIII (1867), 124 et seq., first defined the genre as "une épitre addressée à une dame par son amant ou par celui qui désire le devenir." Meyer quotes the present passage from which, with *Flamenca* 7061-074 he deduces that the "salut" was sometimes a public as well as a private message. Meyer's opinion is substantiated by E. Melli, "I salut e l'epistolografia medievale," *Convivium* IV (1962), 385-98, and by a passage in Denis Pyramus's *Vie Seint Edmund le rei* (ed. H. Kjellmann, Göteberg, 1935), vvs. 5-8:

> Kant courte hantey of les curteis
> Si fesei les serventeis,
> Chanceunettes, rymes, saluz,
> Entre les drues et les druz ...

and by the Lai d'Amours (ed. G. Paris, *Romania* VII [1878], 407-15). For Bec the "salut" was essentially a private message (p. 47). It is noteworthy, however, that the context in which "salutz" appears consists of narrative poems ("romans," "novas" and "comtes"). While other examples of the genre are lengthy, with an average of 165 verses, they are not narratives in the strict sense. In Catalan, however, the "salut," particularly in the use of proverbs (Amos Parducci, "'La lettera d'amore' nell' antico provenzale," *Studi Medievali*, New Series XV [1942], 69-110) developed into a vehicle for narrative used as "exempla." An example omitted by Parducci and Bec is found in P. Meyer's article "Nouvelles catalanes inédites, II," *Romania*, XX (1891), 193-209. Meyer attributes it to the beginning of the fourteenth century because of style and ideas, but according to the definitions of Bec and Parducci it falls within the canon of the genre. Hence it is possible that the genre as a narrative form was developed earlier than Meyer's example, and that it is to this type of "salut" that the jongleur is referring. While most examples are written in octosyllabic couplets (Bec, p. 21) as are "romans" and "novas," there are enough exceptions in other metres to justify the assumption that the jongleur is using content, not metrical structure, as the criterion.

49-50. MS. "e fraitz a far homes malvatz ... assermat": "malvatz: is indeclinable in O. Occ., but was replaced in O. Cat. by "malvat." Raimon Vidal's original "Malvat" has been subsequently corrected by an O. Occ. scribe, who also (incorrectly) modified "frait," "home," and "assermat."

74. "sas": in literary O. Occ. usually "ses," "sens." The form ABSENTIA, which is accepted to cover cases where derivation is impossible from SINE, cannot be accepted.

84. "a pauc": Levy, PSW, VI, 150, 11: "beinahe, fast," which does not fit the context. cf. Sp. "a poco," and Bohs's translation "bald."

89. "fossan": a rare form, but attested in the "Vida de Sant Honorat" and elsewhere (Ingegärd Suwe, ed., *La Vida de Sant Honorat: Poème provençal de Raimond Feraud* [Uppsala: Lundequistska, 1943], p. cxiii).

90-91. "triat semblavan ad *el a* doblier," MS. "trait semblavan ades del doblier": Bohs tr. "denn auserwählt erschienen sie mir jetzt, nach dem Wamms zu urteilen." Jeanroy (*Romania*, XXXIII, 614) proposes "empruntés à l'échiquier, c'est-à-dire bigarrés comme la surface d'un échiquier." Both versions are unsatisfactory. It seems better to assume an original "a doblier," cf. Levy, PSW, II, 261, 3: "reichlich, in Fülle, vortrefflich." The original "triat a doblier" might then have been misunderstood and emended to "triat del doblier" ("separated from the lining") which in turn would be emended to the MS. reading. The emendation of MS. "trait" to "triat" is necessitated because of the rhyme.

"ades" in the context can be understood as simply a scribal misreading of ſ for 1, or as an attempted emendation ("already separated from the lining").

96-99. Massó Torrents ("La Canço provençal," *Miscellania Prat de la Riba*, p. 367): "Quarta cobla de 'Per solatz revelhar' (Guiraut de Bornelh, *Sämmtliche Lieder*, ed. A. Kolsen [2 vols.; Berlin, 1910 and Halle, 1935], I, 416, No. LXV, vss. 31-34)." Kolsen notes quotations in *Abrils issia* as *B* (see also II, 116), also mentioned by Vincenzo Crescini (*Manuale per l'avviamento dell' antico provenzale* [3d ed. revised; Milan: E. Hoepli, 1926], p. 210). Bohs, p. 227, Karl Bartsch (*Denkmäler der provenzalischen Litteratur*, Vol. XXXIX of *Bibliothek des litterarischen Vereins* [Stuttgart, 1856], p. 147) both adopt the version of Raynouard's edition (*Choix*, IV, 291) which is that of MS. tradition CIKPQRc and U (Crescini, *Manualetto*, p. 210). The complete stanza according to Crescini's edition is a follows:

> E vi per cortz anar
> de joglaretz petitz
> gent caussatz e vestitz,
> sol per dompnas lauzar:
> or no n'auzem parlar;
> tant es lor pretz delitz.
>   Don es lo tortz issitz
> d'elas malrazonar?
> digatz de cals: d'elas o dels amans?
> Ieu dic de totz, qe·l pretz n'a traich l'engans

Variants: 96 E ui CKPQRc; Dui I; Ev ui U (adopted here); cort PQUc; arnar Q. 97 De] mainz IK; Us RV (adopted here); ioglaret c; iogaç perdiz Q; ioglars fromitz R. 98 Gens Q; chausat Uc; chausar Q. 99 lazar I; lauçars Q.

The form "veni .I." can best be explained by derivation from the U tradition "Ev ui." Separation of the marginal cap. E from -v followed by -u unclosed at the bottom then gives "e vni," a nonsense form emended to "E v̄ni" (-E nei) with a following .I. by homeoarcheon, or in an endeavor to make sense of a form which is neither Occ. nor Cat. ("veni .I."; "veni un"; "venion"?).

"per corsa māiar": "per cortz anar" interpreted as "per cors' anar," where "per cors"-"per corsa," "quickly." Assuming a hypothetical "i" introduced for the sake of scansion ("Eu vi per corsa i anar") a repetition by homeoteleuton would give "per corsanianiar" with a later attempted rectification to the present R form "per corsa maniar."

97. "us joglaretz": the error is found in U.

105. The verse is a syllable short. A stroke above the "v" of "vey" is probably not an abbreviation for "er." The reason for the missing syllable is to be found in a haplography of "ē ēaissi."

110. "chauzidor": Bohs (Ammerk.) "Teilnehmer an *jocx partitz*" based on Raynouard, *Lexique* II, 363. ("N'Ugo, gen faretz jocx partitz, si trobassetz bon chaussidor.") cf. "chauzir" vs. 112, "chauzitz" vs. 114.

115. "venson": Levy ("Anh," *Romanische Forschungen*, Vol. XV [1904]) proposes "venser."

116. "son si": Levy ("Anh.") emends to "si son."

120. Bobs tr. "(ich bestreite durchaus nicht) dass schon ein einziges Tun unter Umständen von Nutzen sein kann."

121. "un sol mestier": flex. -s omitted. "per loc": "occasionally," cf. "en loc."

122-123. "groc ... vert": flex. -s omitted.

137. "homes ... benenans": flex. -s unnecessary.

138. "Monferrans": i.e. Clermont-Ferrand. For the relations of Dauphin and Montferrand, see Teilhard de Chardin, "La première charte des coutumes de Montferrand," *Annales du Midi*, III (1891), 285-86. Dauphin probably gave Montferrand to his wife and son during his lifetime.

139. "al Dalfi": According to P. Fournier, "Le nom du troubadour Dauphin d'Auvergne," *Bibliothèque de l'École des Chartes*, XCI (1930), 66-99, and Alfred Jeanroy, *La Poésie lyrique des troubadours* (2 vols.; Paris, 1934), I, 158 and 358, "Dauphin" was a name and not a title. See, however, S. Stronski, "Recherches historiques sur quelques protecteurs des troubadours," *Annales du Midi*, XVIII (1906), 473-493, and S. C. Aston, "The

Name of the Troubadour Dalfin d'Alvernhe," *French and Provençal Lexicography*, ed. U. T. Holmes (Ohio U. P., 1964) pp. 140-163.

145-146. The verses are transposed in the MS. The similarity of "donzela" (vs. 144) with "donzelo" probably caused the omission of vs. 145, with correction.

148. "senher": The nom. is probably a scribal error.

149. The verse is a syllable short. Emendation by Bartsch.

157. "fom": could be "fon" (< FUIT), the error due to "fom" of vs. 154. On the other hand, "fom" may be a parallel with vs. 154, and as such it has been preserved here.

164. "y ac cridat" could be interpreted as a verb, "he had (not) invited there," and then "pus mes" is not "pus" with past participle but a form of "putnais" (-"stinking"), here "rogues, despicable people." The -es would then indicate a loan-word from O. Fr., in which by the thirteenth century [-ai-] was already [-ę-]. There may be some corruption in the MS. since the meaning as it stands is somewhat forced, but a form of "putnais" is unlikely, since examples of the word in O. Occ. attest a diphthong at the rhyme (PSW, VI, 602), and the proposed derivation from "putnais" leaves unexplained the "sol de primier" of the following verse. Also, there is no antecedent for the third sg. verb "ac cridat."

165. "per pegueza": Bartsch and Bohs read "peguezeza" only, whereas the MS. has an initial P as well. Because of the marginal sentence-marker it is impossible to read whether the P has a line through it (-per) or is expunctuated. The verse has one syllable too many.

"Peguezeza" is listed in PSW, VI, 177 with a query; the present case is the unique example, with Bohs's tr.: "Aber es wird nicht etwa gelärmt noch irgend welche *Torheit* getrieben, ausser zu Anfang." The form is a scribal error.

"Peguesso, pegueso, pegue" is listed by Mistral, II, 518, as "sottise, niaiserie, imbécilité, fadaise, futilité"; Levy (*Petit Dictionnaire* s.v.) lists "pegueza" as "sottise", probably because of Mistral. A. Alcover and F. de B. Moll list "peguesa, peguea" as "necedad" in *DCVB*, VIII, 378.

174. "blava": Du Cange: "Lapis caeruleus tegendis aedificiis aptus," i.e. "slate." Possibly a long bench of slate built into the chimney-corner. cf. OF "bloi" applied to marble, Tobler-Lommatsch I, 1004.

181. "Sieus": "si·eus" for "si·us" occurs in the present instance and in vss. 219, 749 and 1696. "eus" for "us" (unstressed) does not occur without preceding "si." In this case and in vs. 219 the solution may be found in vss. 400 and 641, where the full form is: "si a vos play (platz)." Unstressed [a] > [ə], written <e>. A conventional phrase of high frequency, "si·eus" may have replaced "si·us" in other contexts where the preposition "a" was not required, particularly since the reverse is true, i.e., "us" and "vos" for "a vos."

188. "peytz": *locus desperatus*.

200. "pertrays": PSW, VI, 279, 2 quotes vss. 186-201 (omitting vss. 188-195) as the unique example and translates as "Schilderung?" commenting as follows:

> Ubs. "Erzahlung." Die Hs. hat Z. 6 nach Angabe des Herausgebers *par* statt *plac*, das Anderung von Zenker ist. *Ab vostres motz*, übersetzt der Herausgeber "Eure Gedicht vortragend," was mir wenig zu passen scheint. Raynouard, der nur die letzten anderthalb Zeilen anfuhrt, liest *Per aitals pertrays* etc. und übersetzt "à cause

de pareil attirail avec vos mots je me fis jongleur." Ich habe Grobers Zs. 13, 311, unter Hinweis auf Mistral und auf Noulet Œuvres de Pierre Goudelin, Gloss. "pertraire" "représenter, dépeindre, gefragt, ob vielleicht *Per c'a mi fes aitals pertrays Ab d'autres motz,* etc. zu lesen und "weil er (mein Vater) mir solche Schilderungen machte, wurde ich mit vielen anderen Spielmann" zu deuten sei. *Ab d'autres motz* befriedigt allerdings nicht recht. Vielleicht ist *Motz* "Worte" und für *vostres* ein Adjectiv, das "schön rühmend" bedeutet, zu setzen; aber welches? Dann wäre natürlich nicht hinter *pertrays* sondern hinter *motz* zu interpungieren.

With the exception of the error in declension of "aital" for "aitals," vs. 200 is satisfactory and can stand.

"Ab vostres motz," which is clear in the MS., can stand only if it is assumed that the jongleur is acknowledging the inspiration and influence of Dauphin in the choice of his career. Since Dauphin must have been quite old when the action of the story took place (see Introduction, *Abrils issia*: Dating; Jeanroy, *Poésie lyrique,* I, 159) such an interpretation is not impossible. "Motz" must then be understood in the sense of "words," i.e., description (of the life of a jongleur) or else "verses" though, as Levy points out, "motz" in such a context is in opposition to "tune" ("Fetz Marcabrus los motz e·l so").

Several hypotheses are possible in addition to those already proposed. The explanation proposed by Corominas and accepted here is that "pertrays" is a verb (< PERTRAXIT); "par" (< PATER) is a Catalanism, "pare," as in vs. 911 (the usual O. Occ. "paire" is also found, vss. 183 and 851); "aital" is "thus," cf. Gasc. "atau."

An alternative explanation is that "ab d'autres motz" is to be understood according to PSW, V, 334, "gleich darauf," "aussitôt après." Cf. Godefroy, s.v.: "à un mot, aussitôt." But, immediately after what?

Or, "en aquest mot": "dans ces conditions" (Levy, *Pet. Dict.*), assuming a considerable alteration of the text.

211. "acostumatz": flex. -s unnecessary. However, "fatz," vs. 212 should have -s, so the error is Raimon Vidal's.

214-16. The joglar's monumental lack of tact is intended as a joke. Dauphin's stinginess was legendary in his later years, as Vida A shows (Boutière-Schutz, *Biographies,* p. 84).

215. Bohs emends to "Es que *sabetz* bon fag cauzir" without noting the reversal of the first two words, and tr.: "dass Ihr edle Handlungen auszuwählen versteht." The correction is unnecessary since the construction is clear: "Esser a" with the following infinitive, separated by "tot bon fag."

219. "sieus": see vs. 181, n.

226. Bohs emends to "non *sai* enquera," which was rejected by E. Herzog, "Besprechungen,", Z.r.Ph., XXXI, 379.

227. "Tot son saber": flex. -s omitted. (*mos*? see vs. 228, n.).

228. E. Herzog suggests "c'ar demandat," a possible reading that is rejected. Since the syntactic position of "ar" is variable the homophonous form "c'ar" would be avoided where possible. "lezer": PSW, IV, 391 quotes vss. 226-231 and notes "nicht klar," with trans. as follows: "weil du mich in Musse gefragt hast, so ist es schwer für mich, dir deine Fragen zu beantworten, wenn es auch für die Wackeren leich wäre." Tr. "a lezer": "at length"? The interpretation of the passage is as follows: "You have asked

me at length [and your question deserves an equally comprehensive reply]. It is difficult for me and easy for worthy men, because I do not think I can make a suitable answer; however, the question demands an answer."

In which case, emend "tot ton saber" to "tot *mon* saber," since Dauphin is excusing his own inability to answer. Otherwise his criticism of the jongleur is irrelevant.

229-31. The meaning is not clear. According to Corominas, vss. 229 and 230 may be reversed and the passage then interpreted: "This is why I do not think that such a [very difficult] answer is very [appropriate] for me to make and [little] appropriate for the proficient to make, as is becoming."

231-32. The rhyme is remarkable; "taisses" with [ę], "es" (2d sg.) with [ẹ] (cf. vs. 238).

236. "saber": Bartsch reads "sab"; Cornicelius (*So fo e·l temps c'om era jais*, p. 101) and Bohs emends to sab*er*. Their emendation is needless since the graphy b(er) is clear.

240. For the use of "cap" (- "not at all") see vss. 338-39, n.

252. "saber": flex. -s omitted. The usual form which Dauphin uses to address the jongleur is "tu," as is to be expected. However, in vss. 252, 261, 340 and 345 forms with "vos" are unmistakable. Since Raimon Vidal and the jongleur consistently use "vos" when talking to each other it seems likely that the jongleur slips into the "vos" form in telling his story to Raimon Vidal, forgetting for the moment that he is reproducing in direct speech what Dauphin said to him. Or else Raimon Vidal simply lost track.

253. "accidental": flex. -s omitted.

254. "ben e mal": Bohs suggests making the words plural, to re-establish by rhyme the missing flex. -s of the preceding verse. The emendation is justified only if one assumes that Raimon Vidal never made a mistake.

255. "lurs bels captenemens": Bohs emends to "*los* b. c. presumably because, as the phrase stood, "captenemens" was the attribute of "ben e mal," and evil cannot be exemplified by fine conduct. On the contrary, this is an example of dualistic morality. In this passage the three knightly virtues are contrasted with the three Christian virtues of Faith, Hope and Charity.

260. "grans e mezura": Jeanroy (*Romania*, XXXIII [1904], 614) "L'intelligence nous fait apprécier les choses selon leurs justes dimensions."

269. an infin. "esser" parallel to "gazanhar" must be assumed.

274. "auzi*st* a ton paire nomnar," MS. "auzit": the MS. has what appears to be the remnants of a ligature, "-itz." The form is unlikely to have appeared in the original since Raimon Vidal distinguishes carefully between sg. and pl. Two emendations are then possible. "c'auzit a*s* ton paire nomnar" is satisfactory with regard to sense. "c'auzist a ton paire nomnar" makes equally good sense, and the construction equivalent to a Spanish "que oíste nombrar *a* tu padre" would account for the scribal error if the scribe saw "a" as a verb and changed "auzist" to the past participle "auzit."

285. "sarazi ric": flex. -s omitted (Levy, "Anh.").

290. "levet s'e*n*": MS. "levet s'es." Confusion between the letter S and a nasal consonant, probably a bar of nasalisation in the exemplar, is found in vss. 615, 1086, 1103, and 1709.

299. "retenir": A Catalanism (O. Occ. "retener"), clearly attested by the rhyme. The correct O. Occ. form is used by Raimon Vidal in vs. 527 (: "poder").

303. "que·l vic": Bohs emends unnecessarily to "que·*s* vic."

NOTES 95

309-328. The last syllable and sometimes the last word of the verses in the MS. can be read, but with difficulty.

315. "bayssamen": flex. -s omitted.

319. "e totz vetz": According to the MS. the verse is a syllable short. "e totz *bos* vetz" is possible. Another possible reading, which solves the difficulty of the missing syllable but which does not make such good sense, is "e totas vetz"; in that case, however, it would be necessary to emend "e" to "*a*" or "e*n*".

320. "amicx": The repetition of the word as a rhyme, with no distinction either in meaning or grammatical function, is a rarity. Corominas suggests that "amicx" (vs. 339) is a scribal variant of "amis" < "ami(r)s," a Catalanism, and that its rhyme was "amis" < AMICUS (cf. vss. 339-340 for variants of -cx).

321. "des": Bohs emends to "dec." The lower curve of the -s is attenuated and unclear, so that "dec" may have been written.

322. "dey": Bartsch and Bohs read "deu." Levy ("Anh.") suggested emending to "dei."

329. "*almussa*": illeg., supplied by vs. 363; see DCEC, III, 466 "muceta."

330. The first part of the verse is illegible.

331. Omitted in the MS., indicated by a hiatus in sense and lack of a rhyme for "cap."

332. The first word is illegible. "vuelh" would fit the space. "que·l" can be read, followed by a letter that might be "a." The following letter or letters are illegible, but cannot constitute another syllable because of the demands of scansion; grammatically possible is "m" ("la·m").

329-33. Suggested readings:

> *Almussa* l'apelan payan.
> *E dis al rey*: 'De vostra man
> *vuelh* que la·*m* pauzetz sus el cap.
> *Aissi sabra om ses mescap*
> *que l'ay* gazanhat per proeza. . . .'

338-39. The passage can be interpreted in several ways. Bartsch (*Denkmäler*, p. 154, 1-2) wrote: "E si o fay quel cap lon torn / en dan de perdre sos totz pretz," emending in a note (p. 331) to "totz sos pretz." Bohs, p. 237, emended "lon" to "*lui*" and translated: "wenn er es aber doch tut, so möge sie ihm auf dem Kopfe alsbald zum Schaden ausschlagen derart, dass er sein ganzes Ansehn dadurch verliert." Both versions rest on an incorrect reading of the MS.; a correct reading yields: ". . . e si o fay, que·l cap lo·n torn / en dan de perdre ses totz precx" with "lo·n" to be emended to "*lui*" (easily explainable as a scribal error), following Bohs, and translating: "And if anyone does so, let him forfeit his head with no right of appeal." The rhyme "precx-auzetz" then is seen to be unusual. In any version "precx" or "pretz" has [ẹ] against the [ę] of "auzetz," but the corrected reading gave a -cx as being consonant with -tz.

Confirmation of this interpretation was seen in the fact that "tornar en . ." is well attested in PSW, VIII, 302-203, 10: "verwandeln, verkehren in," with an example from Raimon Vidal, *Razos* (Appel, *Provenzalische Chrestomathie*, p. 123, 6). Further confirmation was seen in vss. 446-49: "E si'eu per nulh erguelh o fi, / no mi laisses cap remaner / e faitz n'a tot vostre plazer / ni·m fassatz be vas nulha part." The translation would read: "And if I did it through any pride, do not leave my head [on my shoulders] and do with me as you please, and do not do me any more good. "

However, Corominas suggests that, since both sentences are negative, "cap" should be interpreted as a negative adverb of intensity (equivalent to Fr. "ne ... point"). "Cap" is found in this construction in NW Cat. (Andorra, Urgell, Pallars, Ribagorça, Vall d'Aran, Couserans and Comenge) from which is generalized the standard Mod. Cat. "cap" replacing "negun;" the earliest documentation dates from the sixteenth century. The use of "cap de" as a pronominal adjective, on the other hand, is more extensive, ranging from the Bearnese Pyrenees to Alacant. This, together with the archaizing nature of the dialects where "cap" is used as a negative adverb of intensity, leads to the conclusion that use as a pronominal adjective is secondary and derivative (J. Corominas, "De Gramática histórica catalana: A propòsit de dos llibres," *Studia Philologica et Literaria in honorem L. Spitzer* [Bern: Francke, 1958], pp. 138-39). A similar situation prevails in O. Occ., where another example beside the one here is to be found in PSW, I, 201, and where in Mod. Occ., in addition to the Couserans-Vall d'Aran-Cominges area, the form is used "un peu partout," according to Jules Ronjat, *Grammaire istorique des parlers provençaux modernes* (4 vols.; Montpellier: Société des Langues romanes, 1930-41), sec. 531. "Cap de," however, is found in Nîmes, Languedoc, Guyenne and Aquitaine. It would thus appear that the use of "cap" as a negative adverb of intensity is older than the sixteenth century, though confined to a relatively small area of Catalonia and Gascony, and that its rarity accounts for the misinterpretation of the scribe.

The original text would then read: "e si o fay, qu'el cap *no*.n torn / ses dan de perdre totz *sos* pre*t*z," to be translated: "and if [anyone] does so, let him not return except on pain of losing all his reputation." The MS. form is then seen to be the attempt of a scribe to edit a text that he had misunderstood, while keeping as close as possible to his exemplar; thus "no·n" becomes "lo·n," the scribal correction introducing an incorrect direct object for an indirect object; the meaningless "torn ses dan de perdre" is then emended to a familiar form "torn en dan de perdre," and "totz sos pretz," which can no longer be the direct object of "perdre," is emended to "sos totz precx," thereby introducing the defenctive rhyme with "auzetz."

Similarly, vss. 446-450 should be trans.: "And if I did it through any pride, do not let me remain at all [i.e., banish me], and do with me as you please, and do not do me any more good." This solution solves the slight difficulty in sense; otherwise it is difficult to see how the king could do his vassal any more good if he had been beheaded.

An even clearer case of "cap" as a negative adverb of intensity is found in vs. 240.

341. "anc sol": emend to "anc*se*.l"? Or possibly, according to Corominas, "anc so. l" (- co li).

342-43. Bohs trans." "Spater, als die Zeit diesen Vorfall bereits hatte vergessen lassen..." But Jeanroy trans. as: "'avant que l'oubli ait effacé le souvenir de cet événement — on voit par le vers 391 qu'on s'en souvenait encore."

344. "us baro": obl. sg. for nom. (Cornicelius, *So fo*, p. 69), confirmed by rhyme.

352. "bars": flex. -s unnecessary. According to Levy the rhyme "enuy" with "celuy" is a Catalanism (PSW, III, 13). Also in *So fo*, 535 rhyming with "abdui."

358. "sel baro": obl. sg. for nom. (Cornicelius, *So fo*, p. 69).

366. MS. "la sazō": a scribal emendation of an earlier "laz a son" where -z represents voiced -s of the pronoun "las."

376. "rey": flex. -s omitted.

377. "en sa maizo": that of the baron who assumed the "almussa"?

384. "us vostre baros": "vostre" with omission of flex. -s; "baros" (Cornicelius, *So fo*, p. 69) is a nominative with an incorrect flex. -s.

388. "vos": "nos" is clear in the MS., but is incorrect.

389. The MS. version is suspect because of "perdre aqui," where e and a should elide, and because scansion stress falls on the -e of "perdre," normally unstressed.

393. According to the text the barons are older men who remember from experience when the "almussa" was first given. Bohs, however, emends to "E. *Is* nost*res si* c. h. v.," thereby making the barons of the same generation as the king.

395. MS. "liatjes": the error is perhaps due to a scribe mistaking the "h" of the exemplar "linhatjes" for "lī," and omitting the "h."

397. "us jorns": flex. -s in obl. sig.

404. "ma cort": flex. -s omitted.

406. "baro": oblique form, although it is the subject of "fo." The form must be attributed to Raimon Vidal because of scansion.

408. "e. 1 rey": flex. -s omitted.

418. "son": 1st sg. pres. indic. "esser," a form condemned in the *Razos* but normal in O. Cat.

422. "baros": flex. -s unnecessary (Cornicelius, *So fo*, p. 69): "on": emendation by Levy ("Anhang").

425. "noble": flex. -s omitted.

426. "onrat": emendation by Bohs.

428. "puec": an abnormal form, but attested by Levy, PSW, III, 12 ("enuec, joc, loc, puec" in rhyme). Not mentioned as a variant by S. Aston (*Peirol* [Cambridge: Cambridge University Press, 1953], No. XIV, vs. 41).

437. MS. "al linhatge" is apparently an attempted scribal emendation to correct a Catalanizing exemplar reading "a llinhatge"; the def. art. is otherwise difficult to explain.

439. "ans passatz": flex. -s unnecessary.

440. "auratz": flex. -s unnecessary. Bohs emends to "onratz" although Levy (PSW I, 102) suggests "hochmütig" as well as the more usual "thöricht, närrisch (cf. Cat. "orat": "mad"). Mistral, I, 886: "exalté, monté, éventé, écervelé." See *DCEC*, III, 565, "orate" for geographic and semantic boundaries. The translation "proud" (i.e., "puffed up with foolish pride," where "pride" is inferred from vs. 442) may be bettered by "hasty, hot-tempered, wild."

447. See vss. 338-39, n.

451. "aquist": Though "aquestz" is found in vs. 264, "aquist" occurs here at the rhyme, indicating the form normal to Raimon Vidal, and is found again in vs. 472. The -i- is due to a following etymological long I which may also explain vs. 466 "elitz."

"Aquist" refers to the "almanzor"; he was not "trist ni flacx" but remained standing and asserted his own merit (vs. 424).

465. No rhyme, but no indication that a verse is missing.

466. "elitz": the normal reflex of ELĒCTUM is shown in "eleg" with the variant "eletz," both at the rhyme in Raim. de Vaqueiras, quoted by Raynouard, IV, 41. "elitz" is a re-formation based on a change of conjugation of "elire" to -ir (cf. "dire, dich") also attested by Raynouard: "Gardas cal deu la domna mais eslir?" or due to a treatment of e followed by -ī.

468. Massó Torrents (*Misc. Prat de la Riba*, p. 367) locates the passage in Thomas, *Bertran de Born*, p. 121, vss. 85-88 of "S'Abrils e folhas e flors." Another passage from the same poem is quoted in *So fo*, vss. 1372-75. According to Thomas and Stimming the passage is as follows:

>Qu'aissi fo pretz establitz
>qu'om guerrejes ab torneis
>e quaresmas e avens
>fezés soudadiers manens.

Discrepancies may be accounted for by the alteration of the length of the verses from seven syllables to eight, and "torneis" misread could yield "fort mens." There is no rhyme for "torneis" as it appears in the quotation; the alteration is therefore possibly due to a scribe.

The quotation appears irrelevant to the context. The first part of the stanza is more appropriate, and is as follows:

>Ric ome volh qu'ab amors
>sapchan cavaliers aver
>e quels sapchan retener
>ab befaitz et ab onors,
>e qu'om los trob sens tort faire,
>francx e cortes e chauzitz
>e larcx e bos donadors....
>   (ed. Thomas)

Many of the words and phrases occur in vss. 464-67 before the quotation begins.

473. "messios": "lavish display, expenditure" (Levy, PSW, V, 2), but cf. Cat. "fer messions," "to make great efforts."

476-79. There is confusion in these verses with respect to the use of flex. -s. The verb "era" is sg., and is qualified by several nouns (a frequent construction); "autz baros" is however plural and in the objective case.

478. One syllable missing; emendation to [mot] by Bartsch.

479. "baros": flex. -s unnecessary, attested by the rhyme.

485. "maystrejon": Levy's first ex. (PSW, V, 9-10) is the present passage. His interpretation follows Bohs's "unterdrücken"; it and Raynouard's "reprimer" (*Lexique*, IV, 118, present text) are not supported by other examples and should be corrected. "maystrejar" is well attested in O. Cat. ("maestrajar") with the meaning "to falsify"; cf. past participle as adjective in O. Occ.: "tricky, sly."

486. MS. "donas" makes sense, but "dona*r*s" (Cat. donas) is better, coming as the first of three abstract nouns (cf. vs. 531).

490. "el pretz." "el" as a form of the def. art. in the oblique case is extremely rare in O. Occ. Possibly a scribal error.

493. "de": Bohs' emendation to *li* supplies a subject for "fan"; however, "van" and "desesperat" (cf. vs. 492) do not have a flex. -s though they can only refer to the object of the sentence, although perhaps as a predicate of "tornar" these adjectives need no -s. "desesperat" means simply "very bad" and "desesperat de" is a normal construction. We could read "*v*an tornar van" in vs. 492, which could then be an O. Cat. periphrastic construction used as a vivid narrative present, altered by a scribe to whom the construction was unfamiliar. The scribe would also have emended ".ls baros" to ".lh baron." The meaning then would be: "so that barons are becoming boastful and very bad to their lord," a posible allusion to the disordered state during the minority of James I.

503. "Marabetis": emendation proposed by Jeanroy on the basis of vs. 508. The Marabetis are the Almoravides (DCEC, III, 429).

508. "A q u e s t z": "aqui*st*." "feron" due perhaps to homeoarcheon ("Aquetz fe-") with vs. 509.

510. "plaideys": Levy, *Pet. Dict.* "accord, traité," but cf. vs. 199 "fazian guerras e plays," vs. 281 "E domneys e guerras menar."

512. MS. "forfays" cannot rhyme with "plaideys" (wich already rhymes with "reys") and hence indicates the omission of a verse. Vs. 511: "*e far proezas e bos faitz*". "forfays" is a scribal attempt to supply a rhyme.

513. Bartsch and Bohs read "mal."

516. "c'un linhatge": flex. -s omitted.

517. "Mal mut": there is no trace of an Almohade Malmut or Mahmud. It is possible however that the name may be a corruption of Muhammad (ben Yakub ben Yusuf en-Nasir), 1198-1213. MS. "s'emparatic": probably a scribal error, cf. vs. 560 "emparagitz."

530. "cors": flex -s unnecessary.

534. Verse missing, to rhyme with "donar."

535. "nulha": flex. -s omitted.

540. "noble": flex. -s omitted.

543. "val": emendation by Bohs.

544. "sol" for "solc" appears consistently in the poem, cf. vss. 677, 1533, n. Levy, PSW, VII, 784: "Das Präsens von einem nicht der Gegenswart angehörigen Thun verwandt," although vs. 495 has Imp. "solian."

551. "d'amor": Bohs emended to "da*van*," an improvement in sense since Love has not been discussed so far. Perhaps "d'amor" is here a rare adverbial locution, found also in the *Libro de Buen Amor,* ed. J. Corominas (Madrid: Ed. Gredos, 1967), 1575d, and in the *Cid,* ed. R. Menéndez Pidal (Madrid; Bailly-Bailière, 1908-11), vs. 1139. On this account the MS. reading can be preserved, and trans. "earnestly."

555. "sestz senhors": flex. -s unnecessary. Perhaps due to scribe since "malvat," a qualifying adj., rhymes with past participle "tornat." "sestz senhors" is the subject of the sentence begun in vs. 550, and was probably the basis for Jeanroy's objection to Bohs's punctuation.

560-65. The sentence is complex, in Levy's opinion incomprehensible. Bohs makes sense of it only by reversing "trop" and "pueys" (vs. 560) and by emending vs. 561 "per" to "ses," vs. 562, "car to "Ges," with a period at the end of the verse, and vs. 563 "enversat ses" to "enversad'es," trans."

> Und wenn du dann siehst, dass Andere ohne adeligen Sinn sich in angesehenet Stellung befinden, so erscheint dies nicht recht, im Gegenteil, es bereitet grossen Verdruss. Alle Trefflichkeit ist umgekehrt worden, dass jemand, der nicht dient, das Seiden

gewand trägt, um Heldenthaten und auserlesene Handlungen zu verichten.

"autrus" for "autru*is*": cf. vs. 1574, where "autrus" appears for "autrui"; evidently a confusion between the letters s and i; see also vs. 274, "auzit" for "auzi*st*," vs. 562 "enutz" for "enuis": the same explanation is not valid. More likely a phenomenon related to the confusion of "fatz"-"faitz" where the affricate -ch with flexional -s gives -tz; cf. vs. 1071 n. Both sense and rhyme are preserved by assuming an original "autruis"-"enuis." "Es si" and vs. 564 "Com ses servir" for "E si" and "com se servir: repetition by anticipation of s at word boundary. "enversar": Levy, *Pet. Dict.* "enverser, tourner à l'envers," Levy, PSW, III, 107, "umkehren, verkehren." Mistral, I, 955, "changer les dispositions de quelqu'un par de faux rapports." *DCVB*, V (1), 103, "Capgirar; posar el revés. 'Lo cors de l'home és enversat com té los peus en amunt e'l cap a avall' Llull, Cont. 292, 12. 'Com hom és desobedient al vostre gloriós voler ... enversa hom son voler contra la final raó' Llull, Cont. 350, 14." Tobler-Lommatzsch, III, 108: " 'verkehren': 'entour les princes conversent / Et le bien et le pays enversent,' J. Cond. II, 169, 64 (*Dites et Contes de Baudouin de Condé*, ed. A. Schaler, Brussels; 1866-67)." Godefroy, III, 314 (fig.): " 'détruire': Cils trois murtriers nous mainent mainte guerre diverse, / Qui la paix de nos cuers tumbe, trouble et enverse.' (Jean de Meung, Test., 1417, Méon.)"

"bontat": Levy, *Pet. Dict.,* "valeur."

568. "los mendicx nualhos": Obj. for subj.

570. MS. "mon": scribal error because of "mon" (< MUNDUS), vs. 571.

573. "amatz": flex. -s unnecessary.

577. "mant": flex. -s omitted.

578. "vas una part": see Levy, PSW, VI, 92, 5.

584. "que*r*": emendation by Bohs.

585. The subject "paratje" of the causal sentence precedes the conjunction.

588. "onratz": flex. -s unnecessary.

589. "prezatz": flex. -s unnecessary. The fact that the flex. -s of this and the preceding verse occur at the rhyme does not mean that the error was by Raimon Vidal.

596. "loc": "village, feudal possession"? The meaning is current in Cat. and Gasc.

598. The verse is a syllable short. Emended by Bohs, to "l*i* plazers."

599. "que·l*s* pros": flex. -s unnecessary.

602. The verse is a syllable short. Emendation by Bohs to "tot *bo* mestier." The rhyme "-ier" of vs. 603, which cannot take a flex. -s, shows that "mestier," and hence "tot," should have one.

603. The text published by M. Eusebi ("L'*Ensenhamen* di Arnaut de Mareuil" in *Romania* XC 1969, 14-30) shows non-significant divergence for vs. 603 (corresponding to vs. 209) since Raimon Vidal's version is exceptional, but in vs., 606 R.V.'s version and that contained in R agree in showing "pretz" against "cor" of all other MSS.

603-06. Massó Torrents, *Misc. Prat de la Riba*: "De les noves rimades que comencen 'Rasons es e mesura.' "

609. The verse is a syllable short.

613. "flocx": Levy, PSW, III, 508, notes the passage as unclear, but cf. vs. 759, from which it can be inferred that the word means "(mere) adornments."

614. The verse is a syllable short. Bohs emends to "es." "as" is better since it continues the subject expressed in the protasis and can be explained as a scribal error.

618. Bohs emends to "li dutz," which Jeanroy rejects as unnecessary since at the time at which the jongleur met him Dauphin must have been very old.

620. "qu'ieu": Gascon declarative "que," cf. G. Rohlfs, *Le Gascon* (Halle: M. Niemeyer, 1935), § 440, according to which the limits of the feature extend eastward into Foix. Corominas notes that it is also heard in Ribagorçan Catalan, and has found examples in O. Cat. texts from Pallars dated 1230-57 and 1252-69.

622. "fuey": Cat. hypercorrection.

626. Raymond Berenguer V and Beatrice of Savoy.

636. "Castillo": probably Castillon-en-Couserans in the dept. of Ariège, 10 kil. southwest of Saint-Girons, on the right bank of the Lèze, sub-tributary of the Garonne. There is a chapel dating from the eleventh century. MS. "anē" mistaken for "an be." The use of the plural is not unusual in the context.

647. "traire mal": in the sense of "to suffer, endure" is amply attested (Levy, PSW, VIII, 363, 30), though here "fero" can only be causative: "that here caused to be endured ..." i.e., "brought on." Possibly "que m'a fag traire mal," with "quem," then "quē," finally "que."

650. "son": 1st. pers. sg. (cf. *Razos*, where such use is condemned). The form is also found in vs. 657.

654. "Dalfi": no flex. -s.

655. "vas si": assuming that the subject of "fora" is an unexpressed "ieu," the 3rd sig. reflex. pron. "si" should be emended to "mi." The sense of the protasis ("if it were not for the Dauphin") rules out the possibility of Dauphin as subject. If an impersonal is the subject ("there would be no joy toward oneself and no good will toward the present age") the construction is loose, especially with respect to what follows, which indicates that the jongleur had not returned from the present time altogether.

657-658. "son": a form condemned in the *Razos* (cf. vss. 418, 650). Vs. 658 is a syllable short. Several interpretations are possible.

In the interpretation accepted here, the emendation of MS. "en .II. sens" is made on the basis of vs. 670, "e fors issitz de vostre sen," thereby providing a repetition parallel to "esperdutz" of vss. 651 and 669; both refer to the state of mind of the jongleur. It can be accounted for by assuming that, at some previous point in the MS. tradition, the form "forsens" appeared in the Cat. reduced form "fossens," with subsequent misreading of initial for an attempted emendation. The "re-" of "remenar" was lost by haplography with the preceding "volgra."

Alternatively, vs. 657 can be assumed correct, and vs. 658 emended to "*de*menar." Such a scribal omission cannot be accounted for as a mechanical error. The trans. is then as follows: "And so I have come in two minds, for I would like to come to terms with the times. ..." The form "demenar lo segle" is attested in Peire d'Alvernha's "Be m'es plazen" (Peire d'Alvernha, *Liriche,* ed. Alberto del Monte [Turin: Loescher-Chiantore, 1955], p. 78): "D'aut chai em bas / Qui per compas / No sap lo segle demenar; / E ben hi falh / Qui tan tressalh / Que non hi puesc' a temps tornar." The trans. reads: "Cade d'alto in basso chi non sa vivere con misura; e ben vi fallisce chi salta tanto in là da non poter all' uopo tornare indietro."

Zenker (*Die Lieder Peires von Auvergna* [Erlangen 1900], quoted by Levy, PSW, VIII trans.: "wer in massvoller Weise die Welt nicht zu nehmen versteht." Neither trans. is fully convincing.

It has also been suggested that vs. 657 "en .II." is a misinterpretation of "endos," where "endos" is a Cat. form of "amdos," with the meaning "here [in you] have come both senses" (i.e., the sense of gaiety and of benevolence or good will which the jongleur had seen in Dauphin (cf. vss. 655 and 656). Vs. 658 could then be interpreted: "qu'*en lo* segle volgr' amenar," with MS. abrev. to "qu'e·l" or "qu'e·l segle volgra *remenar.*" The trans. is: "which I would like to reintroduce into the world."

All the interpretations proposed make sense. The first is preferred because the stylistic parallel is probable, and the errors of the MS. can be accounted for mechanically.

661-62. I.e., "a light-minded person would never induce me to ponder deeply on his problem."

666. "cor": flex -s omitted?

673. "le": this form, instead of the normal "lo," is inexplicable here except as a Toulousan dialectalism. The same form occurs in *So fo,* vs. 297 of MS. b (Barcelona fragment).

674. Jeanroy suggests emending "de pretz" to "bos pretz, thus making it the third member of a compound subject. The conjunction "e" ("de pretz") renders impossible the association of "de" with "camjatz" (changed from"). The construction "e, de pretz, c'avia poder," in which "de pretz" is associated with "e camjatz" parenthetically, would be most unusual and would leave "e ... c'avia poder" also an unusual construction. Jeanroy's emendation is therefore adopted.

675. Inverted construction: "voles saber p.q̄. amors. ..."

677. "sol": perhaps "sol*c*," with scribal haplography of *c* and the following e; "soler" is defective, however, with no ex. of a perfect (Appel, *Provenzalische Chrestomathie,* p. xxxix). Cf. vs. 544.

678. "pro e bo": flex. -s unnecessary. Or possibly -s is missing from "mant home" (obj. pl.). The inconsistency indicates a probably scribal error.

679. "sazos": flex. -s unnecessary. "sazos" cannot be the subject, and indicates a scribal correction for the sake of the rhyme after "pros e bos." Since Raimon Vidal probably did not write "sazos," "pros e bos" may have occurred in the exemplar of R, with correction of "sazos" in R.

681. "que": the following subordinate clause is parallel with that of vs. 675 (E. Herzog) which in turn is parallel with vs. 672.

682. i.e., "there are not three barons [that maintain standards] as thus they used to." Tobler (Cornicelius, *So fo,* p. 69) suggested "C'aissi·s teni' entre·ls baros." However, variations in the flex. of "bar—baro" are frequent in Raimon Vidal and attested by metre.

685. "Mas per dintat": Levy (PSW, II, 91) quotes the passage (accepting Tobler's emendation to vs. 682) and comments: "Deute ich *per dintat* richtig 'in seltenen Fällen'? Vgl. *viltat,* das ja im ersten Beleg (Kolsen,

G. de Born. No. 2, p. 23) als Gegensatz zu *dehntat* hingestellt wird, in der Bedeutung 'Fülle, Menge.' "

Appel: " *'Per dintat'* kann wohl sinnlicher als mit 'in seltenen Fällen' etwa mit 'als Leckerbissen' übersetzt werden."

"dintat" can be explained as a reflex of DIGNITATEM with homorganic assimilation of the nasal consonant to the following voiceless stop. "per" is possibly a misreading of ₽ for ₽ (cf. vs. 1044 where the same scribal error may be assumed). "pro" can then be considered as meaning "enough" and functioning as an adverb. In the first case the translation would read: "and you have never sufficiently found worth. ...." With a following plural noun, however, "pro" can mean "many" (e.g., "pro jorns," Levy, PSW, VI, 564, 2). On this analogy it may be considered to modify a singular abstract noun, with trans. "enough worth." The trans. adopted, "worth enough," does not favor either function.

691. "dalfi": cf. vs. 654, n.

700. "mesclat": Bartsch, Bohs, and Jeanroy read "selat." (Bartsch and Bohs omit the preceding "me" which Jeanroy re-established and then explained the extra syllable by postulating "ac'setz" for "aguessetz.")

In R the differences between the letters e and c are very slight; in most cases the environment leaves no room for doubt as to which was intended. In the present case the graph could be an e, but more closely resembles a c. Interpretation of the graph as c solves the problem of the extra syllable and provides a satisfactory meaning: Levy, *Pet. Dict.*, "soulever (une querelle)."

717. "Mais": the emendation is necessitated by vs. 721, contrasting the manner in which "saber" is acquired.

723. "poder donar": here perhaps the equivalent of the simple infin. (Levy, PSW, VI, 408, 3), but more likely a Catalanism with attenuating force, cf. modern popular Barcelona speech, where "poder" = "potser" 'perhaps' (with [ę] for [ẹ]. *DCVB*, VIII, 808 quotes the saying *"Poder,* no es pot posar en carta ni en paper" ([ę] in "poder," "paper") and interprets: "significa que quan es diu *potser* (o *poder*) hi ha poca seguretat en el que s'afirme o nega." The form was used in O. Cat., as can be seen from the MS. of Eiximenis, *Dones* A45Rb (:I, podř B), checked by F. Naccarato on the photocopy, Francis Naccarato, "Eiximenis' *Libre de les dones*" (unpublished dissertation, University of Chicago, 1965). The passage refers to the husband who killed his adulterous wife: "pensa ab quina cara ne ab quina esperança pot demanar a Deu misericòrdia l'om qui la muyller ha morta—e *poder* en cors e en anima—per vergonya dels hòmens." Also in 47Ra (:I): "e poder no serà axí" where a syntactic origin can be seen: "POTERE NON ESSERE HA(BE)T SIC" instead of the modern form "POTERE HA(BE)T NON ESSERE SIC."

729. "de se*n*": the MS. "dese" is a scribal error; "desen" ("immediately") has weak -n.

738. Another interpretation would be to punctuate: "del paire, nostre rey cortes" in apposition to "paire," which in turn is in apposition to "del rey n'Anfos," though one would have expected the simpler form "la cort del rey n'Anfos, lo paire, nostre rey cortes" if Alfonso the Chaste is meant, as opposed to his son Alfonso of Provence.

739. The sentence could end at "mes" (according to the MS.). "mes" is then to be understood as "spent" (cf. Levy, PSW, V, 268, 3, "meten,":

"freigebig"), and the following then is trans." "and I saw so much honour given to everyone, and so many deeds and actions..."

It is necessary to make a distinction here between "metre" with an object and without, in cases where "giving" or "spending" are concerned. In instances where a direct object is stated the meaning of the word is apparent from the context; in instances where an object is absent this specialized meaning of "metre" is indicated by a synonym or paraphrase, in all ex. found in Levy, Appel (*Provenzalische Chrestomathie*, pp. 68, 7; 97, 45—the latter by contrast: "Mais ha de pretz, Monges, al mieu veiaire, / Sel que fai pretz de petitz e de grans / e *met* ab ioi, don ho puesca traire, / no·n a us ricx avols mal acoindans"), and in Crescini (*Manuale*, pp. 51, 7; 49, 37, 47, 29. Such a synonym or paraphrase does not occur in the present instance. Further, the verb "donar" has to be assumed. The emendation to "Aitan" with a new sentence beginning vs. 741, seems the preferable solution.

740. "Aitan": emendation by Bohs. The error ("E tan") may be explained by the fact that the sentence marker separates vs. 739 from vs. 740. Thus a scribe would read: "ai tan d'onor ... lay vi faitz ..." and correct to "E" with the conjunction usually used between sentences. The sentence must end at verse 740, however, for there is no second half introduced by "que" of the comparison begun by "(E) tan. ..."

747. "era": the apodosis does not always require a past conditional, especially in popular language.

749. See vs. 181 n.

752. "l'autr'an": Herzog suggests "ehemals."

764. "autri": a rare form, found however in Appel, *Provenzalische Chrestomathie*, No. 107, vs. 128 ("nos autri"). If rare in O. Occ. it is even rarer in O. Cat., occurring in Rossillonese (J. Corominas, "Vidas de santos roselloneses del manuscrito 44 de París," *Anales del Instituto de Lingüística de la Universidad de Cuyo*, III (1945), 126-211, 34.

772. "E p*u*is": present in a distorted exemplar, the emended form could give rise to "apilhs" of the MS. Less likely is the Catalanism "ab ells," since AB > *ap and ILLOS > ilhs are phonetically unacceptable.

778. "homs (non) avars": the verse has an extra syllable. The "non" does not agree with vss. 780-81 (see note and trans.).

779-81. Vs. 779 is short one syllable. No solution to the problem here can be considered wholly satisfying. The form "anclot" occurs at the end of vss. 779 and 780; vs. 780 is not necessarily a dittography. The passage calls for emendation though the sense is not clear and admits several interpretations. Bohs emends vs. 779 to "anc *ar*lot" and vs. 780 to "an *d*ot" and trans." "Sie fanden in der Provence nie einen Geizhals noch einen gemeindenken unter den Grafen, die vielmehr stets der ihnen zugefallenen Morgengabe der Trefflichkeit sich durch Freigebigkeit würdig erwiesen." While the word "arlot" might be used even with reference to the counts of Provence by as ribald and irresponsible a poet as the monk of Montaudon, it is highly unlikely coming from Raimon Vidal.

It has been suggested that the passage be emended and trans. as follows: "non trobavon, ni ancanoit, / Als contes que tostemps an doit / E mantengut pretz ab donar": —"they didn't find any miserly men nor, till just now, the counts, who have always taught and maintained excellence by giving." "Ancoi," properly "even today," is often found used in the sense of "even now"; "ancanoit" (literally "even last night") could consequently be used in the sense of "even recently"; the word may contain a veiled malicious allusion to the counts of Anjou who replaced the Catalan dynasty of the Raimon Berenguers, the Anjous having in fact the reputation of being stingy people. (The past tense of "non trobavon homs avars" is then important by contrast.) "doit" is a past part. of "dozer," "to teach," being an archaic though usual form. A scribe who misunderstood either "doit" or "ancanoit" might in vs. 781 change e to de (because of the neighboring "doit" and "donar"), and the following copyist would then have to move "mantengut" after "pretz."

A further possibility, adopted here for want of a better, is to assume an original "dot" in vs. 780 (with subsequent misreading of d for cl, which in turn produces the dittography in vs. 779, further assisted by a combination in vs. 799 of an -l). The missing syllable is supplied by er-, which may have been represented by the graph ꝛ which, although usually occurring in word medial or final position, may have been found initially, although omitted by the scribe. The "lot" of vs. 779 then refers to the subject of "trobavon" (the troubadours, vs. 756). "Lot" is attested in Raynouard, *Lexique*, IV, 102 ("lent, lourd") and is current in Mod. Prov., for which Mistral (II, 226) gives as meaning "lent, pesant, lourd, tardif, paresseux." Vs. 781 "mantengut" refers to "pretz." The problem of the vowel does not exist, since both "dot" and "lot" have [ǫ].

783. "en Guilhem lo blon": objective case for subject.

784. MS. "Dunun" (in rhyme with "blon") should perhaps read "Guion." There is no record of a "Dunon" as count of Auvergne, and the dates of Guion coincide with the period referred to, as Anglade has noted (*Onomastique des troubadours* [Montepellier: Publications spéciales de la Société des Langues romanes, 1915], p. 209).

785. "comte": objective case for subject. "dalfi": see vs. 654, n.

791. The subject is treated as sg. with flex. -s but considered as pl. with respect to the verg "dizian."

792. Verse omitted in R, with no rhyme for "mons."

793. Since Pons de Vernet is attested, the MS. "Alvernhet" is the interpretation of a scribe unfamiliar with the Catalan nobility, who preserved the -et as a diminutive for reasons of scansion. Vernet is in the county of Perpignan, diocese of Elna.

796. "totz": the -z is unnecessary and unusual in the context.

789-99. MS.: "En .R. Gaucelm ad estanh / e de tot mal fait a Pinos." Bohs, p. 302, identifies ".R. Gaucelm" as Raimon Galceran de Pinós, and in so doing is confronted with a meaningless "ad estanh" and an extra syllable. He solves the problem by emending to "*s*'estranh / de tot mal fai*re* a Pinós" and trans. "Herr Raimon Gauseran enthielt sich in Pinós jeder schlimmen Tat." In so emending a further problem is created, unsolved, that of the hiatus between "faire" and "a."

Postulating Catalan toponymical references misunderstood by a non-Catalan scribe, Corominas suggests "E·n Raimon Gaucelm a *L*'Estanh / de tot Malfet *tro* a Pinós and notes that Gaucelm is a common name, and L'Estany is a well-known small town, with an old and beautiful monastery, between Vic and Manresa; Mafet, also called Malfet (the most popular form today and attested in the mediaeval period), is about 10 or 15 miles west of Pinós, itself about 6 or 8 miles west of Cardona.

The emendation to "Galseran" is perhaps not as drastic as would first appear; a defective copy of "E·n Gauseran d'Estanh" might easily be read "E·n Gauselm ad estanh" where the examplar had Gau ꝑ ādestāh, with omitted or unclear graphies for -er and -n; the "Gaus" would then be interpreted as an abbreviation for "Gauselm."

Unfortunately it has not been possible to discover a trace of either a "Raimon Gaucelm de L'Estanh" or a "Raimon Gauseran d'Estanh."

The "L'Estany" mentioned by Corominas, situated between Manresa and Vic is listed as "Estany" in the *Diccionario geográfico de España* (17 vols.; Madrid: Prensa Gráfica, 1956-62), Vol. IX, which tends to support the assumption based on an analysis of scribal error that "Raimon Gauseran d'Estanh" should be read. It would also appear likely that "Raimon Gauseran d'Estanh" and "Raimon Galseran de Pinós" are one and the same person (see Index of Names).

The barony of Pinós lies to the east of the Llobregat, with its north-south boundaries running from the Coll de Jou to Malanyeu (Juan Serra Vilaró, *Baronies de Pinós i Mataplana* [2 vols.; Barcelona: Balmes, 1930], II, 15-16). Thus, Estanh and Malfet lie considerably to the south of the barony of Pinós. Furthermore, within the barony there is no town or castle called Pinós. The apparent anomaly is resolved when one considers that the name of the barony was that of the family that ruled it, and derived from another of their possessions. Serra Vilaró mentions two possibilities (I, 92) Pinós de Biure and Pinós in the Segarra, both amply attested as belonging to the family. Pinós in the Segarra is not far from Malfet, but it is possible that Raimon Vidal meant Pinós de Biure, to the east of the Llobregat, implying a large stretch of territory in which there was no lack of worthy barons. Pinós de Biure, or Sant Pau de Pinós, near Berga, is mentioned by A. Stimming (*Bertran von Born*, p. 177, n. 49) and Thomas (*Bertran de Born*, p. 59, n. 8) with respect to Raimon Galseran, though neither gives any reason for the identification. The juxtaposition of Malfet in the text would however indicate Pinós in the Segarra. By a reverse association it would seem that Malfet and Estanh belonged to Raimon Galseran de Pinós even though they are not mentioned as part of the property of the barons of Pinós. Many of the early records were destroyed, so that lack of documentation cannot be considered evidence to the contrary, and while neither Malfet nor Estanh are mentioned in the will of Galseran III (Serra Vilaró, I, 98-105), who was the son of Raimon Galseran de Pinós, the properties could have passed out of the possession of the Pinós family before January 11, 1277, the date of the will. It was Galseran III who built up the town of Bagá, capital of the barony (Serra Vilaró, I, 94); this fact explains why Bagá is not mentioned by Raimon Vidal with reference to the father of Galseran III, Raimon Galseran de Pinós.

802. "*U*rgelh," MS. "erguelh": although there are at least three towns or villages called Montergull in North Central Catalonia, the mention in the preceding verse of Guillem de Cardona, who was influential in the affairs of the county of Urgell, indicates that it is the latter which is intended and not Montergull.

MS. "erguelh" is then the result of two scribal misinterpretations of the text. The first consisted of a Catalan scribe writing o- (or perhaps e-, on the analogy of, though not confused with, O. Cat. "ergull") for unstressed *u*-. The second consisted of a scribe writing e- for pretonic o-' and reading the written -ge- as [ge] instead of [dže]. The conditioning factor in the first instance was, according to Ronjat (I, 306), the presence of a following palatal, while Carl Appel, *Provenzalische Lautlehre* sec. 37, lists r, l, m, n, s and j as causative (described as "Sonanten": better, "continuants").

The second scribe was probably Toulousan since Levy, PSW, V, 519, gives "ergolh" in G. de Montanhagol, VIII, 39 (also in *Flamenca* 12; Nov. pappagallo). Ronjat notes the change in Toulousan, Sarladais, Bergeracois, and Ambertois, while Mistral (II, 445) notes "ergoil" as a Limousin form.

While the same change can be seen in O. Cat. "ergull" an O. Occ. scribe must be postulated to account for the confusion between -guelh and -gelh, since the etymon *URGOLI cannot give -elh in O. Cat.

The confusion can be explained semantically. "En Guillem lo ric (e) en erguelh" makes sense of a sort.

806-08. If in 806 an impersonal verb is assumed (y ac) the flex. -s on "d'autres baros" is correct, and similarly in 807 "francx et arditz." In which case the rhyme with "auzit" is faulty. If on the other hand "foron" is assumed in vs. 806, then the flex. -s in all the preceding cases is incorrect, with "coratjes—baro" as a faulty rhyme. The former explanation is preferred.

809-10. The rhyme "Montcada—matinade" admits two interpretations. "Montcade" is an archaic form (< Monte Càteno < MONTEM CATANI), and its rhyme is then "matinad'e. ...." Ending a verse with a conjunction is a liberty not found elsewhere in Raimon Vidal. More likely is a Catalanism by a later scribe with post-tonic [-a] > [-e].

810. The verse is a syllable short. "*ai*tal" would provide a natural solution.

819. Entença lies between Tremp and Benavarri.

820. "mantenc": emendation by Bohs.

822. "tornar": after mentioning Aragonese nobles Raimon Vidal reverts to the Catalans. Hence, "*a*l comte" (vs. 823) which is more comprehensible than "I shall return the count to you."

823. The counts of Castelló d'Empuries were traditionally called Pons or Huc.

839-40. The ending [-*t͡s*] of "Monelhs" indicates that in vs. 839 the flex. -s on "ysnels" and probably also "valens" is not a scribal error of morphology but must be attributed to Raimon Vidal. So also the palatalization of final [-*t*] in "ysnels," which is a Catalanism.

842. The verse has an extra syllable, an error by homeoteleuton. After having written the final -ro of "baro" the scribe then returned to "foro" as his starting-point and repeated "mā."

843. The verse has an extra syllable due to a scribal error.

849. The missing verse may be supplied with "*ieu non vuelh alongar los plaitz*," suggested by Corominas.

850. The marginal punctuation marker indicates that the sentence ends at the end of the verse. It has been suggested that the verse might be improved by a slight emendation: "ad obrar, vi'! e ad als faitz"; or "vi' ad el faitz!" (VIAM AD ILLUM FACITIS); or, "viatz! e·l faitz!" ("quickly, and do it [already]!").

855. "auz*i*": MS. "auz si": possibly "auzi" in the exemplar of R, which would explain the omission of -i- as an error by homeoteleuton.

860. "*en* englelterra": "*en*" omitted by homeoteleuton. e for a corresponds to E. Cat. pronunciation of unstressed -a, though not necessarily so here; cf. It. Inghilterra."

863. "Jofres": -o- for Occ. -au- is a Catalanism, or a French form.

866. "enamoratz": "excited by." Perhaps "partial, impassionate, prejudiced against," a meaning still found in seventeenth-century Spanish (cf. vs. 906).

872. Bohs trans. the passage: "Dieser machte das Wissen zu seinen Schutzwällen und schuf sie voller Kenntnisse in seinem Sinne" on the basis of Raynouard, *Lexique*, V, 377, "rempart, mur de circonvallation." " 'Lo torn de Rossilho no t'es salutz' "; *Gir. de Ross.* f. 12." Cf. Levy, PSW, VIII, 289, 8, "Umkreis," 9, "Stadtmauern," 10, "Umgang." Levy (PSW, VIII, 293) quotes vss. 869-875 and comments:

> Aber *acquestz* bezieht sich doch gewiss, ebenso wie das folgende *Aquist,* auf die beiden vorhergenannten fürsten. Ist nicht "velors" Subjekt? Der Sinn des Ganzen scheint mir zu sein: "da die beiden selbst so trefflich waren, konnten sie auch darüber urteilen, wer von den anderen Menschen gut, wer schlecht war," aber die Einzelheiten sind mir nicht klar. Ist E [vs. 872] = *et* oder *en*? Oder ist etwa *Ad* zu ändern? Ist [vs. 873] in Gedanken ein *fetz los* zu ergenzen und *son lor*?

The sense then would be "saber e conoissensa feiron sos torns en aquest, en son coratje." A singular "fetz" can pass with a compound subject. The meaning of "torns" remains a problem in this context.

But in vs. 872 "aquestz" (as opposed to "aquist," vs. 874), "fetz" and "sos" (as opposed to "lors") are all singular and must refer to vs. 870, N'Anfos: whereas "aquist" (vs. 874) may refer to either the last two men mentioned or to all of the great men of the preceding passage. If "conoissens en" = "conoissens(a) en," and if "torns" = "inheritance" (Levy, PSW, VIII, 292) "Erbanspruch [?]," 26; "erfolge," 27; "Erbschaft"), the sense becomes clearer without the need of emendation. It does not seem far-fetched to understand from the passage that the son inherited his father's good qualities, with "fetz" denoting active participation.

811. "Marsa*n*": the omission of -n may be a mechanical error (a for ā) or may indicate the dialect of a scribe.

884. "baros": objective plural for nom. sg. (Cornicelius, *So fo*, p. 69).

885. "adreg": a final affricate with flex. -s > t(z) usually (i.e. [ʃ] assimilated to [s]. Does the reverse take place here, or is flex. -s omitted? The former is possible, cf. Mod. Cat. where the two admitted pronunciations of "boigs, roigs" are "boč, roč" or "boits, roits." In O. Cat. examples of alternation between "matex" and "mateys" are found in many texts such as Eiximenis' *Dones*. If flex. -s is omitted, the error is probably due to a scribe since "membratz" has -s. In any case the form is exceptional in this MS., where "adreit" is normal.

890-93. An alternative trans., with a comma after "joglar" would read: "they defeated (and plundered) their knightly enemies and protected jongleurs but defended knights who were in the right."

891. "aquest": flex. -s omitted.

897. "majors": rhymed with "guizardos": Bohs emends to "baros"; however, the form indicates the typical Catalan loss of final -r before -s.

904. "troberatz": Jeanroy reads "troberatz"; the MS. however has -a-.

905. "aura": the reading is difficult. "pessat": (cf. 906, "enamorat") the flex. -s is probably an error of the copyist.

907. "bastion": the reading is difficult.

910. "entezas": No examples have been attested of "*entes, -za" in O. Occ., where instead the regularized form "entendut" is used (Levy, PSW, III, 61; Raynouard, *Lexique,* "tendre"; Mistral "tendre"—tenut, tendut), with the sense of "attentive, zealous, intelligent, well-versed" (Levy, *Pet. Dict.,* s. v.). "entes" is however the past part. of "entendre" in Cat., used adjectivally as "que enten; intel·ligent (en una ram de coneixements determinat)" DCVB, V (I), 56, and which has produced the derivative "entesar." Similarly adjectival is "tes, -a," "rigid." The word may therefore be a Catalanism, attested by the rhyme and corresponding to the O. Occ. "entendut" (cf. vs. 149).

911. "pares": Catalanism.

913. The sense of "ab bel'onha" is obscure, and may indicate a scribal error. "Onha" does not occur elsewhere, the usual form being "onh" ($<$ UNCTUM), not a post-verbal subst.

920. Verse omitted, rhyming with "gens." Perhaps "*gai' e cortez' et avinens*" (Corominas).

921. "creire": MS. "creaire" is an error since "preveire" has no -a-. The verse is then one syllable short, which is supplied by emending "onrat" to "onrar" and adding a conjunctive "e" (Bohs).

930. "perdos": a derivation from PERDERE would simplify interpretation, but the reflex is "perdoa." "en perdos" cf. vs. 28: "in vain" does not explain the conjunction "e" of vs. 931.

931. MS. "de lieys" needs emendation. Derivation from LEGEM does not explain the diphthong "-ié-"; more likely from the Cat. "deler, dele," "ardour," or the less common related from "delerar," "to go astray, to babble." ("deler DĒLĒRARE, with Osc. or Umbr. Ē for Lat. Ī.) (J. Corominas, "Notes etimològiques," *Butlleti de Dialectologia Catalana,* XIX [1931], 26.)

921-39. The content of these verses is puzzling. One can infer that the nobility, while preserving the semblance of religious conformity to the extent of endowing religious institutions (922) did not care for the established church or resented its influence (924) though they loved God (921). It seems too that they were quite content to let such a situation remain as it was (925-29). Some or most were weak and without cohesion (932-33, 936-37). Against these came a "pardon" and "knowledge," to which they could offer little resistance and which they were forced to accept (934-35, 940); and as a result of which they became hypocrites.

It seems that "perdos" and "sabers" are used as abstracts to veil an allusion to some coercive force that could demand a change of opinion so fundamental that those who accepted it were not the same men they had been, losing their moral substance.

If one attempts to reconcile these obscure allusions with historical events, the only coercive force at the time was the Church. "Sabers" may then be understood as religious orthodoxy unwillingly accepted, with "perdos" as armed invasion, i.e., the Albigensian crusade (Levy, PSW, VI, 235). Levy based his definition on P. Meyer's note, p. 216, vol. II of the *Chanson de la croisade contre les Albigeois* where, for vs. 4002, as for vss. 686 and 763, he noted that: "Par *perdo,...* on entend une oeuvre à laquelle est attachée une indulgence." While Martin Chabot does not go so far (*Chanson de la croisade albigeoise,* I, pp. 21 and 77, n), preferring to read a specific reference into the word, the present text confirms P. Meyer's interpretation.

That the nobility south of the border was not entirely orthodox, in spite of the efforts of Pere II, may be seen in the letter of Pons d'Arsac,

Archbishop of Narbonne, in which he orders the excommunication of "hereticos et eorem fautores et deffensores, Bravantiones, *Aragonenses,* Cotarellos, Basculos..." (Vic and Vaissete, Vol. VIII, col. 341, Doc. XXXI). Heresy among those who were not nobles is described in a letter dated 1250 and published by Pere Pujol (No. XV in *Documents en Vulgar dels segles XI, XII, & XIII procedents del bisbat de la seu d'Urgell* [Barcelona: Palau de la Diputació, 1913], pp. 22-25). See also Peire Vidal, *Liriche,* II, 301, No. XXXV, vss. 85-89:

>Al rey Peire, de cui es Vics
>e Barsalon' e Monjuzics,
>man que meta totz sos afics
>en destruire·ls pagans de lai,
>qu'ieu destruirai tots sels de sai.

There is one further observation. If the passage does in fact refer to the change in personality of an entire society due to the pressure of orthodoxy, the event can only have taken place after the major defeat of the Albigensian cause at the battle of Muret. Up to that time the efforts of Innocent III were without effect. While it is true that on several occasions Count Raymond of Toulouse affirmed his support of the Church, on as many subsequent occasions he denied it by word or deed; at the time of the death of Peter of Castelnau he remained as obdurate as he had ever been. There is no evidence that the measures taken by the Archbishop of Narbonne produced any lasting or general effect.

936. "sels": object for nom. pl. "silh" (Levy, "Anh.").

941. Alternatively, read "azaut sabeir[e] conoissen "and trans.: "graceful and wise connoisseurs."

955. "Aitals homes": flex. -s unnecessary.

956. "non": both Bartsch and Bohs read "non." It is not in the MS., though it clearly should be.

958. "*Az* adzaut ho*me*": Bohs emends "Ad *azaut* hom(e)." "si tot si malhs": Bohs notes "Wohl von *malha* = maille, Masche, Panzerring, ist "si malhar" abgeleitet mit der Bedeutung "sich panzern, sich verschliessen gegen."

"malhar" is found in O. Occ. only with the meaning "to make chain mail" or "to hammer" (Levy, PSW, V, 65) and is not reflexive. Bohs's interpretation is a post-substantival formation from "malha," "hauberk, mail shirt."

O. Occ. "malhar" may be seen as a reflex of MALLEARE and MACULARE.

MALLEARE preserves its meaning "to hammer"; "malha maleo percutit" in *The* Donatz Proensals *of Uc Faidit,* ed. J. H. Marshall (Oxford: Oxford U. P., 1969). So in Mod. Gasc. "malhà" - "macquer, battre la paille, le lin, le linge."

MACULARE, according to Du Cange, is "vulnerare, vel vulnerando deformare."

Possible semantic crossing can be seen in Du Cange, V, 198: "Malleare: malleo seu gladio dimicare; malleo contundere: ...ad terram prosternitur, et caput eius clavis hostium undique Malleatur, donec animam suam cum sanguine suo pedibus equinis exaleret." cf. Eng. "maul," (derived from O. Fr.): (1) a large mallet, (2) "vulnerare, vel vulnerando deformare," where the def. from MACULARE is correct.

"Malha" must be understood as "to strike, to beat," here in the sense "to struggle along with." The meaning in context is therefore "although you have to struggle along with fools."

The semantic variations of MACULA, however, permit acceptance of Bohs's hypothesis. MACULA "malha" means (a) "mesh"; (b) "mail shirt, hauberk" (Levy, PSW, V, 65), with a post-substantival verb "malhar." The sense of (a) to "enmesh" is not found in O. Occ. unless the present case is an example: "... there is no knowledge or behavior that it is of so much value to a clever man as the art of the jongleur, although he has to enmesh himself with fools," i.e., have to do with. One would expect "ab" instead of "vas," however. The sense of "enmesh, to cover with meshes" is found in O. Occ. "enmalhotar" (cf. O. Fr. and Mod. Fr. "enmailloter"), applied to infants and hawks (Raynouard, *Lexique*, IV, 131); MACULARE is found in this sense only in O. Fr. (Godefroy, Maillier" 2), although Mod. Prov. "maia" - "ménager, épargner, choyer" (Mistral) and Mod. Dauph. malé - "choyer, dorloter" (*FEW*, VI, 13), indicate an extension of meaning based on O. Occ. "malhar" with unattested meaning "to swaddle."

The sense of (b) "mail shirt, hauberk") can be seen in a post-substantival derivative found in the *Donatz proensals*: "malha facit hamos in lorica." A metaphorical extension of meaning is found in O. Occ. "de frevol malha" = "lâche" (*FEW*, VI, 13). A further extension of the word could well be a reflexive form "se malhar" = to put on a hauberk" which, with the concept of protection already seen in (a) could be "to protect oneself with a hauberk," or simply "to protect oneself." With such a meaning "vas" is quite compatible.

959. "*fay*": supplies missing verb and rhyme with vs. 960 "gay". Emendation by Bohs.

965. "U(s) malvat(z) fol(s)": since "desconoissen" has no flex. -s it may be assumed that the error is not due to R. V.

969. "melhor trezaur": flex. -s omitted.

970. "*m*estiers," MS. "estiers": emendation by Bohs.

976. Neither Bartsch nor Bohs read "E," yet the MS. is clear.

982. Bohs emends to "Mas *co*se*z*ens es aurs, so·m par," adopting Levy's suggestion (Levy, PSW, I, 387); Jeanroy rejects the emendation as meaningless and suggests "sos sezers." "Le véritable siège de l'émeraude, c'est l'or (où l'on doit l'enchâsser)." Herzog prefers Levy's emendation to that of Jeanroy. The reading accepted is based on the fact that "sols" with adverbial -s is attested in O. Cat., where "sos" for "sols" is a known phonological evolution. A non-Cat. scribe would not have understood, and omitted the "-e."

Jeanroy notes the similarity of the passage to one by Guilhem del Olivier (Bartsch, *Denkmäler*, p. 49; Appel, *Provenzalische Chrestomathie*, p. 109, vs. 6[f]), where two "coblas" use the image of the gem. The similarity is so striking that the poems are worth quoting in full. Since R. V. usually acknowledges his quotations it is possible that it was G. del Olivier who borrowed from R. V. rather than vice versa. The figures denote corresponding passages in *Abril issia*.

No. 75:
>Tot enaisi com peira preziosa
>qu'es de gran pres, tanh que mielhs (se)
>si cast

980-
82 en anel d'aur qu'en anel de lato,
    joves dona plazens e gracioza
    deu mielhs estar ab sels que sabon pus,
    cant a tort, que ab los necx gamus;
    c'ab los cortes pren homs cortezias

983-85,
991 et ab los pecx fadencx e gamuzias.
    Per que dona jove qu'en pretz enten,
    s'apenre vol, meta s'ap l'enten.

No. 76:
982 Qui en anel d'aur fai veir' encastonar
980,
981 o en lato maracde que ricx sia,
973 ges sel c'o fai non sec la drecha via
982 aquel maracdes se deu ab l'aur mielhs far
     per dreg dever el veir' ab lo lato:
978 e pros dona per la senblan razo
     deu ben gardar ab cal li tanh qu'estia,
     s'aver vol laus ni pretz ni cortezia.
     E pus devers requer a cauza muda
     se quel cove, ben deu don' eleguda
     requerer sel per que er mais valens
     o non esquieu lurs apariamens.

"aur": flex. -s omitted.

986. The syntactical link between vs. 985-86 is weak, causing a problem of interpretation. The solution adopted here is to emend "se" to "so," a procedure that may be justified because "se que" is found for "so que" in Mod. Gasc. Then "so" is the antecedent for the "c' " of vs. 987, and "tot atretal" is adverbial. The trans. is thus "exactly in the same way, he thinks he can do what God would never permit."

An alternative is to consider the "no" of vs. 987 as "n'o," with "o" referring to vs. 986. The "n' " must then be considered a French negative particle. Although an example may be seen in *So fo* Ms. b, vs. 267, there it may well be a scribal error ('n'en' for "non") and, although some examples can be found in Levy, PSW, V, 413-14, the use of the northern form is rare in O. Occ. The trans. in this case would then be: "And he that wants to, and believes that he can, find wisdom among the ignorant, thinks that he is becoming just like them, which God would never permit for a single day."

987. "dieu": flex. -s omitted.

988. "saber": flex. -s omitted. "homs ferms": flex. -s unnecessary. Probably a scribal error, corrected because no flex. is used or is possible in vs. 989 because of the rhyme.

991. "mals apres": functions with a double meaning: (1) "those who are ill learned: and (2) derived from "mal m'en pren" — "I am unhappy" > "unfortunate" > "wretched" > "a wretch, rogue"; "malaprès, -eso" often has this meaning in O. Cat. and O. Sp. (Juan Ruiz).

992. "forfaitz": flex. -s unnecessary (Jeanroy).

993-94. "conoissetz" with [e] and "pretz" with [ę] is perhaps a Cat. error.

NOTES 113

996. "fatz": Both Bartsch and Bohs read "seratz" (Bohs emends to "serratz"). The character (ſ for f) is difficult to read, but the bar seems to run horizontally (f), not oblique (ſ: "ser"). There is no problem of scansion if the diaeresis of "ya" is admitted. Since a syllabic boundary usually occurs between [i.a.] (cf. vs. 1014) the scansion becomes an additional argument in favor of "fatz." (Jeanroy notes: "les ms. a la leçon excellente 'fatz.' ")

999. "e·ls bos e·ls mals": ("homes"). The dir. obj. of the sentence has been changed from sg. to pl., cf. "aitals," vs. 1001.

1000. "cabals": presumably ironic (so also Herzog).

1003. "sabrer" is the Cat. form of "sabrier" (< SAPORARIUM, -ERIUM). "sabrier" in the figurative sense occurs in Peire Vidal, *Liriche*, ed. Avalle, II, 228. No. XXIX, vs. 37 and note, also Levy, PSW, VII, 410, where "sabrer" is found with other undiphthongized forms in a quotation from Blacatz, p. 5 (Otto Soltau, "Die Werke der Troubadour Blacatz." *Z. r. Ph.*, XXIII [1899], 23).

1004. "penson": Levy, *Pet. Dict.*: "s'occuper de, prendre soin": trans.: "see to it that...."

1003-05. Perhaps amend to "que puesc' on lo.s lunh*ar* de lor," with "que" as a colloquial repetition of "c'" in 1004. The present text could then be explained as follows: a corrector would have placed an interlineated "hom" a little to the right of "puescon" (indicating that "puescon" should be changed to "puesc' (h)om") and a copyist would have misunderstood that "lunhar" should be changed into "luenh'hom."

Any reconstruction must take as its starting point the parallel in meaning between vss. 1003-05 and 1006-09, indicated by "atressi (1008). The two sentences are parallel in syntax though not identical. The subject of both is vs. 1003, "silh que conoisson sab*r*er," unstated in the second sentence. The main verb of the first sentence is "penson" (1004), balancing "volon" (1008). "volon" is followed by an infinitive "lunhar." But while "volon" is followed by a simple infinitive, "penson" is followed by a subordinate clause "que puesc'on" — "that one can," i.e., "may legitimately" (balanced by 1009 "aisi co.s tanh") — which in turn should be followed by an infinitive. Accordingly the MS. reading "luenh hom" is emended to "luenh*ar*." The dir. obj. of the infinitive is "lo" in the first case (1005), "los" in the second (1008). The antecedents of both dir. obj. pronouns are stated. In the case of the second sentence it is "los marritz" (etc., vss. 1006-07), while in the first it is "om ab mens de saber." The "-s" of ms. "los" is then seen to be the indirect obj. anticipating "de lor."

1007. "blasme": subject of "a," with flex. -s omitted.

1010-11. "no·y gardon": trans. "do not consider slander." The two verses are a restatement of vs. 1007. The "y" refers to "maldir," which is also qualified by "negu."

1013. "dels entendedors": i.e., "entendedors de saber."

1019. The verse is a syllable short. Bohs emends to "malv*a*t," but a repetition of "de" would be better. "malvat(z)" is "bad, wicked, pitiful, miserable," while "mal" can mean "impolite, rude," which suits the context "escuelh" much better. The two are contrasted in Levy, PSW, V, 40. "Als pros serai bendisenz et aclis / Et als malvaz serai, q'aisi·s partis, / Braus et esquius e mals et orgoillos."

1022. Massó Torrents, *Misc. Prat. de la Riba*, p. 368: "De les noves rimades que commencen 'Rasons es e mesura.' " The text corresponds to vss. 155-158 of Eusebi's ed. (*Romania* XC, 14-30). In vs. 1023 Raimon Vidal's version agrees with IKR against GQNc, but diverges from R in vs. 1025 by omitting -s from "terra" and "hom," and in vs. 1026 showing "a" for "e."

1027. "saber": flex. -s omitted.

1030. "...car son nec de saber": "nec," here, "bereft of," with added meaning of "dumb, secret" (Raymond T. Hill and Thomas G. Bergin, *Anthology of Provençal Troubadours* [New Haven: Yale University Press, 1941], glossary), in contrast to "sonaran."

1036. "dira*n*," MS. "dirai": emendation by Bohs, of an evident scribal error.

1040. "an sazo": Bohs emends to "a sazo," thereby eliminating the verb. However, "dig" is plural. The form "aver sazo" (Levy, PSW, VII, 496) is supported by other ex. and by Raynouard, *Lexique*, V, 164.

1041. "empeguir": The word is found also in *Abr. Iss.*, vss. 1311, 1355, 1476, and 1721. It is used today in Majorca and Minorca, with the meaning "to get shy, keep silent," cf. Fr. "rester interdit" (Corominas). Defined as "avergonyir" in DCVB, IV, 783, with an example from Auzias March. Probably a Catalanism, although it appears in the *Donatz proensals* and Terramagnino da Pisa, vs. 20 (*Romania*, VIII [1879], 185), and is listed by Mistral as "engourdir."

1042. ".ls": indir. obj. plur. A Catalanism.

1043. "passatz": flex. -s unnecessary.

1044. MS. "prezonatz": flex. -s unnecessary (Bohs). The MS. form is due to mistaking ꝑ for p and emending a to e: "p[ro]razonat." "pro" is ironical.

1052. ".ls": indir. obj. plur. noted as a Catalanism by Bohs.

1012-53. This section, treating of uninformed and tasteless critics of the jongleur and his art, is reminiscent of the *Razos de trobar* (Stengel, p. 68):

> Li auzidor qe ren non intendon, qant auzon un bon chanter, faran semblant qe for ben lentendon e ges no lentendran, qe cuieriant se qelz en tengues hom per pecs, si dizon qe no lentendesson. Enaisi enganan lor mezeis, qe uns dels maior sens del mont es qi domanda ni uol apenre so qe non sap.

1055-63. The left-hand side of the column is difficult, and in some cases impossible, to read.

1055. "trist": "-ri-" illegible to Bartsch and Bohs; it can however just be discerned.

1056. "ses": Bartsch and Bohs read "son," but "-es," though faint, is clear. Since "son" is rejected, which was the main verb in previous eds., that position is filled by "vol*r*an" and "cujaran" (vss. 1059, 1061).

1057. "ni ren": "-i r-" is very faint; the "-e-" seems to have a stroke over it ("-en"). Bartsch and Bohs read "re."

1058. "C*ades*": The "*-ade-*" is quite illegible. The emendation was proposed by Bartsch and adopted by Bohs. Perhaps emend "amat" to "a*n*at" and trans.: "as soon as some time has elapsed [of their years of apprenticeship]."

1059. "vol*r*an": two letters are illegible, though read by Bartsch and Bohs.

1063. "a*ver* cora*r*jes": legible in full for Bartsch and Bohs.

1071. "mals fatz o bas": the m. pl. objective here refers to a compound object: "noves d'amors, chansos e autres chantars." Within 160-odd lines occurs the confusion "fatz"-"faitz" three times, and the reverse once (vss.

1071, 1208, 1233; and vs. 1187). In the latter case the emendation is justified since FATUUS cannot possibly give *faitz. In the former cases the few examples and the fact that they are found close together may indicate the editing of a scribe. Against this, and leading to the assumption of homophony on the author's part, is the rhyme "palaitz" "ensenhatz" of vss. 115-6; such a liberty appears exceptional. The MS. reading has been preserved except in the case of vs. 1187, even where, as in vs. 1233, "faitz" is attested by another MS.

1077. "cascus" flex. -s unnecessary.

1078. In addition to being in part illegible the text may also be corrupted. Repetitions of words and phrases such as "azaut" (1078, 1080), "us" (1078, 1090), "captenemens" (1079, 1088). "d'omes conoissens" (1080, 1088) indicate possible homeoteleuton.

1086. "sos faitz es mostratz": (MS. "son fat e mostratz"). The emendation is adopted from Bohs. The inconsistency in the use of flex. -s is obvious. If "son" is accepted as the verb, then "fait" (nom. pl.) is correct and "mostratz" is an error, all the more glaring for being the rhyme-word. In addition, the meaning of "mostrat" in such a context is not at all clear. It is unlikely that R. V. would commit such an error. If therefore "mostratz" is accepted as correct, a corresponding -s must be added to "fait," but in that case "son" cannot be the verb. The lack of an article before "faitz" and "mostratz" is an indication that in this case they would be obj. pl. The problem is solved by emending "son" to "sos" and "e" to es." Thus "faitz" becomes nom. sg. and "mostratz" is the past part. of a compound verb form. The antecedent of "sos" still remains vague and is assumed to be impersonal. For confusion of the letter s with a nasal, see vs. 390 n. For confusion between "fatz" and "faitz" see vs. 1071 n. The fact that such confusion is possible only with flex. -s is an argument in favor of an original "faitz" written "fatz" and edited by a scribe to "fat."

An alternative reading is to place the period after vs. 1086 without emending the verse. The sentence would then end: "... so that, when you tell stories to people, a meagre payment may not be given to you because they [your words and expressions] are trite and foolish." The "a" of vs. 1087 then becomes a verb. In that case the "vos dic" of vs. 1090 must be subordinated, perhaps by a slight re-arrangement: "per so vos dic, e car es us." In any event "lors" (vs. 1088) would be better emended to "sieus" — "e·ls sieus," if the first explanation be accepted, "los sieus" if the second. "sieu" with the meaning "their" and its hypercorrection is not uncommon in the thirteenth century. If the first explanation is accepted however, "sos" and "lors" do not have the same antecedent, and "cascun mestier" can be considered collectively.

The first explanation is adopted for this reason, and because the relationship of the ideas is both more complex and more symmetrical. The second alternative makes equally good sense, however, and does not tamper with the text. Sentence-markers in the MS. occur after vss. 1088 and 1090 and can be disregarded.

1088. "lors": the antecedent is here assumed to refer to "cascun mestier," here considered collectively.

1092. "sabatos": final syll. is illegible, supplied by rhyme.

1094. "cotel": the form without -l- is attested (Appel, *Provenzalische Chrestomathie*, p. 118). Possibly however a diminutive of "cota" ("tunic") though not attested in masc.

1095-96. The ending of "plaz-" was "-er" because of the rhyme "tener." However, "son plazer" is a construction that is unusual; more likely would be "plazen," in which case 1095 "e·l cap gen tener" would be emended to "e·l captener gen." The flex. -s on "aitals" is unnecessary.

1097. "may*strat*": "affected": Levy, *Pet. Dict.* "fait, arrangé, inventé avec art." Pejorative in Levy, PSW, V, 5. The passage is quoted in Raynouard, *Lexique*, IV, 118 and trans.: "Que convenablement et non trop façonnés vos vêtements soient taillés." However, "vestir" is not syntactically related to "maystrat." Cf. O. Cat. "m(a)estrejar," "make up," Fr. "maquiller" —"arrange artistically," a common meaning.

1099. Rhyme missing, though the sense is not affected.

1102. "com si venion per orat": presumably because a jongleur's clothes would consist of presents to him cf. v. 632.

1103. "adzautimens": flex. -s unnecessary (subject of "venon"). "tan," MS. "cas": emendation by Bohs.

1106. "pec": MS. "pecx," evidently a scribal emendation to the cliché "pecx captenemens" without realizing that here "pec" functions as a verb.

1108. "vostre": flex. -s omitted.

1116. "homs": flex. -s unnecessary. Perhaps trans. the verse: "how such a man may live an active life."

1121. "s'i a*dutz*": the reflexive form in this context would be unusual. The only ex. in Raynouard, *Lexique*, III, 82, refers to a river (trans. "s'écouler"). The emendation is acceptable if the "s'" is considered an intensifying conjunction "e...si." The syntactic position is not unusual after the noun, cf. Levy, PSW, VIII, 650: "E tuit aquist si l'abandoneron...." An alternative is to emend: "... e conoissensa, sia*tz sau*putz; / et ab lo saber, atretal / vos dic, e car ..." and trans." "virtues, and knowledge as well, be wise, and about skill I tell you. ..." Here "siatz" must scan as one syllable, which is possible in atonic position, cf. vs. 1391 and *So fo*, MS. b, vs. 169.

1123. "ta mal": omission of -n is due to proclisis before a labial, cf. Gasc. where "ta" occurs before any initial, vowel, or cons.

1125. An alternative trans. is: "although he thereby does not improve his heart, —and to frank and learned people too, of course, —worthy and well brought up men are not pleasant to him; so in any case, among fools and mean people [1130]."

1127. "faire gaug": "to be pleasant" is good idiomatic Catalan. Although not found in O. Occ. (not listed in Raynouard, *Lexique*; Levy, PSW: or Mistral), "hè gòi" with the same meaning is found in the Gasc. of Val d'Aran (however, Ronjat notes in sec. 117 that "goi" may be due to Cat. influence), and occurs in O. F. (Tobler-Lommatsch, IV, 1719: "faire joie a aucun," *FEW* IV, 81). The form may therefore be O. Occ. as well.

1119-34. The construction of the sentence parallels that of vss. 1086-97, in which causal clauses are followed by the main verb, followed by one or more additional clauses, followed by the predicate of the main verb, in both cases a subordinate clause.

1137. "hon": the verse is a syllable short. Possibly original "home," which would also explain vss. 1293 and 1459.

1140. "faducx azauts": perhaps "fat velh azaut" (MS. "saduey a...").

1141. emendation based on 1147. The verse is a syllable short.

1147-48. Massó Torrents, *Misc. Prat de la Riba*, p. 368: "De la primera cobla de la cançó 'Dels quatre mestiers valens'" (L. T. Topsfield, *Les*

Poésies du troubadour Raimon de Miraval [Paris: Nizet, due 1972], No. IX. vss. 8-9)." The first stanza is as follows:

> Dels quatre mestiers valens
> per que cavalliers a pretz
> es bel solatz avinens
> us dels melhors,
> e sel que mielhs acuelh Amors;
> per qu'ieu m'esfors ab els et ab chantars
> com pels cortes fos grazitz mos afars;
> c'om malazautz, sitot s'es pros,
> non es gair' ad ops d'amar bos.

1149. "adzautimen": flex. -s omitted.
1153. "us": ethical dative.
1160. "l'us ... l'autres"; flex. -s unnecessary. The errors are due to Peire Rogier since they cannot be emended without destroying the metre.
1155-61. Massó Torrents, *Misc. Prat de la Riba*, pp. 368-69: "Cinquena cobla de 'Seigner En Raimbaut, per vezer' (Bertoni, *B. Amorós*, p. 303, No. 223, verses 29-35; Carl Appel, *Peire Rogiers, das Leben und die Lieder des Troubadours* [Berlin: G. Reimer, 1882], p. 63)." The text differs from Appel's edition, but resembles other MSS. as follows: 1155 s.v. el, CGR: caber CEU, parer R. 1156 en locs sias R. 1158 mantener R. 1159 c'aisi·s E. 1160 l'us ACDGJKRU, autres ACDJK. The variants in Bertoni's edition of the text are listed by Appel as *ß*. The version used by R. V. corresponds most closely to R; as Appel mentions (*ibid.*, p. 61): "*ß* schliesst sich in der sechsten Strophe eng an ER," though the resemblances to C are obvious too.
The passage is glossed by Juan Ruiz, *Libro de Buen Amor*. 728c and 729ab:

> Con los locos fázes' loco, los cuerdos dél bien dixieron
> ....
> El sabio vençer al loco, con consejo no es tan poco:
> Con los cuerdos estar cuerdo, con los locos ferse loco.

1165. The phrase seems to be a proverb. See also 1163 and 1170.
1168. "a percas": "a" for "ab"? though "a" may be part of an adverbial locution.
1170. "esper": flex. -s omitted. Error of R. V. because of rhyme.
1171. "aver *per* sen": the verse is a syllable short. Emendation by Bohs, on the analogy of vss. 1173 and 1174.
1173. "acabatz": flex. -s unnecessary (Bohs).
1175. "esgart": flex. -s omitted, although it is parallel with "sens" and "sabers." "ome": flex. -s omitted though "conoissens" at the rhyme clearly agrees with it.
1176. "ric": flex. -s omitted. The verse has one syllable too many.
1177. The verse appears to be a proverb becaues of its ellipsis. Both Bartsch and Bohs read "falh," though "folhs" is clear in the MS. An additional ellipsis whereby the verb "falh" is read as an adj. "folhs" is still not unlikely in a proverb (cf. "A bon chat bon rat"). The palatalization of the l may indicate a Catalanism, but the change also occurred in S. Languedoc (Dept. Aude) and was tolerated in O. Occ. poetry. One must suspect either an original "folh"—possibly a Catalanism on the part of the author,

understandable if the proverb were Catalan—or an original "falh" emended to "folhs." The reason for such an emendation is far from clear; even if an original "falh" were hard to read, "falh" would still remain the most obvious choice for a correction. Consequently, an original "folh" appears the best alternative and is preserved.

The MS. reads "folhs marrimens," but the flex. -s may be an error since the following rhyme should not take -s.

1178. "mor *en* estranhamen," MS. "moron estranhamens": Bohs preserves "estranhamens" and emends to "movon" and trans." "die Torichten leben fremd [?] (bleiben unbekannt?)," which he clearly considered unsatisfactory.

If "mor *en*" is accepted for MS. "moron" then the subject "pec" must be singular, "pecx," and, preferably though not essentially, "malpercassan" of the following verse should also take a flex. -s. Furthermore, "estranhamen" ("banishment," "éloignement") cannot take a flex. -s in the context since there is no reason to assume a plural of an abstract noun; the same consideration applies if the word is emended to "estre*n*hemens" ("poverty"). As a result, it becomes necessary to remove the flex. -s from "marrimens" of the preceding verse, since a rhyme "ens — en" is highly unlikely, and consistency demands that the -s of the qualifying adjective "folhs" also be removed.

In removing the flex. -s from "estranhamens" and "marrimens," however, an improvement is effected in the text with respect to the rhyme-scheme. Instead of four rhymes ending in "-ens" which would be highly unusual, vss. 1175-76 are seen to end in "-ens" while vss. 1177-78 end in "-en." Moreover, the scribal error of homeoteleuton which required the scribe to edit elsewhere in an attempt to make sense can easily be seen. Reasons of sense, rhyme-scheme and the mechanics of copying, all independent of each other, induce the acceptance of the emendation proposed.

1179. "mal" is a prefix here, as in 1189, cf. 1208.

1180. "c'a": emendation by Bartsch, adopted by Bohs.

1182. "a enac": it has been generally assumed that "Aenac" was the name of a troubadour to whom this is the sole reference. Corominas suggests that the form does not refer to a troubadour, but is derived from Cat. "enagar," "to orient, convince." The abstract noun "enac" is also known. This interpretation is strengthened when one considers that "us trobaires" is a meaningless statement of the obvious if "Aenac" were a person, but is necessary if "a enac" means "for the persuasion of many".

1184-89. Massó Torrents, *Misc. Prat de la Riba*, p. 369: "(Unica menció coneguda d'aquest trobador)." He punctuates the four verses as follows:

> En Amor a tal plazer sens
> que *qui*·l sabia traire,
> cascus seria milhs amaire
> que·l fatz que en cocha pren.

Verses 1185 and 1187 are of seven syllables. While the "*a*" of 1188 is necessary for the sense, there is no indication that seven syllables in the other verses are not correct. (Vs. 1185 could be emended: "que qui *be*·ls ..." and vs. 1187: "... los pren".)

1184. "Tals plazer": The omission of a flex. -s on "plazer" is more easily explained as a scribal error because of the following s- than the

NOTES

presence of -s on "tal," cf. "plazer" (non. pl. vs. 1189). "sen": flex. -s omitted.

1185. ".lh": the MS. ".lhs" is phonetically inexplicable and can best be explained as a scribal error. The infrequent form "traire [a]" (Levy, PSW, VIII, 363, "zu einem Ziele hinführen"), of an original "que qui·lh en sabia traire" would be confused with the more usual "traire de" because of the pron. "en." Thus, "lh," instead of being the indir. obj. sg. referring to "amar" would be taken as a dir. obj. form referring to "plazers" and an -s added. Such an error appears the more likely since palatalization of -!- in third pers. pronouns, though present in both O. Occ. and O. Cat., differs according to the pronoun in the two languages.

Stylistically, "traire [a]" is preferable to "traire (de)." The sense of the passage, taken with the preceding verses, is that sustained effort is needed in order to succeed; that the effort (or pleasures) that one *brings to* a task far exceed any pleasure a lazy person can *get out* of a situation.

Bohs's solution ("Que qui·l sen") is simple and attractive, but does not explain ".lh," nor did he consider it satisfactory in meaning: "In der Liebe hat verständiger Sinn so viel Reiz, dass jeder, der Verstand zu betätigen wusste [?], ein besserer Liebhaber wäre.... "que·ls": flex. -s an error by analogy with "fatz."

1187. "fa(i)tz": scribal error due to similar environment in vs. 1190, "Per que·l fait[z]." Emendation by Bohs.

1188. "a desplazen": the verse is one syllable short and is structurally parallel to the following the verb of both being "venon." Consequently the missing syllable is supplied by "a." Emendation by Bohs, adopted by Massó Torrents.

1190. "fait[(z)]": scribal error due to similar environment in vs. 1187.

1194. "lo*n*c": emendation by Bohs to "tan," cf. the following verse "tan ver." However, better to assume a missing bar of nasalization.

1195. "dieu": flex. -s omitted (Bohs).

1197. "no·n" MS. n̄ = nen: A negative is necessary for the sense. R. V. says that God did not make this age so consistently bad that an ambitious (etc.) man could *not* get gifts from it in order to rise ... i.e., it is possible to rise. A negative in vs. 1197 would parallel those in vss. 1194, 1195. A scribal error may be assumed in which "nō" in the exemplar would be misread for "nē" and written "n̄."

A similar case occurs in *So fo*, MS. b, vs. 267, where a negative is demanded by the context, and the solution of assuming a scribal error is preferred. Examples of "n" = "not" found in Levy, PSW, V, 414, must be treated with caution since many are taken from manuscripts of northern provenance.

1208. "fatz": see vs. 1071 n.

1208-09. Superscribed over the initial letter of vs. 1209 is an "a," an indication that the order of verses should be changed in the opinion of the writer. Though the letter resembles the handwriting of the scribe, it may not have been he who wrote it.

If the scribal indication is accepted and the order of verses changed, the trans. then would read: "and for the ambitious, good prospects; but he who is not adjusted to the times [1210] can hardly get along even with effort." It then becomes necessary, however to emend "que" to "qui" ("mays qu*i* non es al segles fa*i*tz"), which does not seem warranted. A further consideration is that in vss. 145-146, where the order of verses must be reversed without question, there is no indication furnished by the scribe. The occasion where an indication is furnished must therefore be treated with caution.

In view of vs. 1189, vs. 1209 might be emended to "e·l *mal*-percassans bos atraitz greu y pot per forssa caber," and trans." "A very attractive thing will hardly be allotted to the unambitious man even with the use of force."

1211. "vostri": Such plurals are common today in Aude, Ariège, Lauragais, Haute Garonne (Ronjat, pp. 516-17).

1215. Verse missing to supply a rhyme for "donat."

1226. Flex. -s omitted: "mas gaugz e bo*s* saber*s* adzaut*z*."

1227. "Arnaut": flex. -s omitted.

1228. "que": the relative pronoun is repeated needlessly, causing an incomplete relative clause, cf. vs. 1005.

1233. "fatz": see vs. 1071 n.

1231-41. Masso Torrents, Misc. Prat de la Riba, p. 369: "de la mateixa obra 'Rasons és e mesura.'" The passage corresponds to vss. 64-76 of Eusebi's ed. (*Romania* XC, 14-30), the text and variants of which are as follows:

> (De totas encontradas.)
> estranhas e privadas,
> aprenda de las gens
> fatz e captenemens,
> e deman et enqueira
> l'esser e la maneira
> dels avols e dels bos,
> dels malvatz e dels pros.
> Lo mal el be aprenga
> el mielhs gart e retenga;
> tot cant es deu saber
> e deu ben retener,
> pueys poiras mielhs defendre
> quil volra sobreprendre.

69 e dels pros *GIKNc* del malvais et dels pros *Q* — e del bons *GIKNQc* — 71 los mas els bes aprenda *R* lo ben el mal apregna *GQ* — 72 e mels *G* lo m. *N* — Order of vss. in *R*: 75, 76, 73, 74 — 73 es laid saber *GNQc* — 74 el ben sol retener *GNQc* el ben deu r. *IK* — 75-76 omitted *IKN* — 75 e pot s'en *c* — 76 si nuls lo vol *GQc* mesprendre *G* reprendre *Qc*.

MSS. of Arnaut de Mareuil's poem are: *GIKNQRc* (*d* is a copy of *K*). As in previous cases (vss. 603-606, 1022-1025), R.V.'s version agrees with *R* agains the others, e.g. vs. 1236. In vs. 1238 *R* and R.V. have "aprenda" while *GQ* show "apregna" and all other MSS. "aprenga." In vs. 1239 however, *R* has "retenga," thus admitting an improper rhyme which was emended by R.V. or his source to "entenda." A further similarity is the fact that *R* inverts the order of two couplets, writing 75, 76, 73, 74. R.V. omits 73, 74 and ends the quotation at the point where they would be found. In spite of general agreement between the two texts against the others, and the fact that the *R* version of Arnaut de Mareuil's *Ensenhamen* occurs only a few pages before *Abrils issia* (ff. 134-135) written by the same scribe, R.V.'s text is not a direct copy of *R* since, if we assume correlation by the scribe, the texts would be identical, which they are not (see vs. 1022, n.). Eusebi's stemma recognizes two traditions, α and η, the latter represented by *R* only (and now by R.V.'s version), the former by all other MSS. In editing vs. 76 (vs. 1241) Eusebi followed *R*, rejecting the reading of *GQc* (*IKN* omit). Yet in this case R.V. agrees with *GQc* (with the exception of "hom" for "nuls" and the "mesprendre" of *G* against the "reprendre" of the others), i.e. representatives of α and η agree, to the exclusion of *R*. In this case the original must have read "si nuls lo vol reprendre." Syntactically the relationship between the quotation and the context is closer than usual. Although vss. 1228-29 are structurally similar to vs. 1230 ("per" with infin.), the first is a final clause and applies to Arnaut de Marueil while the second is a consecutive clause and applies to "those who want to improve themselves."

The end of the quotation is related syntactically to the following verse since the latter contains the subject "selh" of the last sentence. There is no reason to assume that a verse is missing.

1243. One syllable short.
1249. "vostre fag": flex. -s missing.
1250. "vostre": flex. -s omitted.
1251. "vostras": here has an ethic function.
1253. "sel": flex. -s omitted. The verse is a syllable short.
1254. "pres-valen": (cf. vs. 593). In this example it can be seen that the form must be hyphenated or even considered as one word, since the normal "pretz" (in this MS.) has been reduced to "pres" to simplify the consonant cluster [-tsv-] > [-sv-], which occurs at the juncture of prefix and root, e.g., "esvelhar."
1263. "hom": needless here, being repeated in vs. 1264. The error is probably due to the resemblance of "hō" and "bē."
1264. "suau": flex. -s omitted.
1265. "fait": flex. -s omitted. "bon": flex. is omitted.
1266. "noble": flex. -s omitted.
1276. It is possible to interpret the beginning of the sentence ironically: "those men want to act with boldness, feeling. etc., but are just as much out of their element acting in this way as a fish is on dry land." However, if "aquilh" (vs. 1273) refers to the same people as "aquels" (1277) then they later become kings, prelates, etc., who maintain law and order. In that case it must be assumed that future kings seek knightly virtue with as much ardor as a fish on dry land desires water, though this is not stated. It is in any case difficult to see just what fish have in common with the moral virtues, and a corrupted text may be suspected.
1281. "sel ... noble cor": flex. -s omitted.
1282. "proans": No active participle is attested for "proans," nor is the meaning clear. Possibly the word should be divided "pro ans" ("enough years") and the phrase rendered "nor have many years of youth," i.e., "who have only a few years of youth left."
1284. "et (vās) vilans": homoeoteleuton from the verse above.
1289. "ab us semblans": possibly "abus semblans," in which case there should be no comma after "semblans."
1291. "valens": must be understood here in a relative sense, i.e., worthy from the point of view of those who are vain and false (vs. 1283).
1293. One syllable short. See vs. 1137 n.
1296. "vencutz": flex. -s unnecessary.
1297. "menutz": flex. -s unnecessary.
1304. "qui·l solassava," MS. "qui la solassava": the vs. in the MS. has an extra syllable and the "la" is without antecedent. If the exemplar of R

read "quil assolassava," a form due to the dialect of the scribe, a subsequent copyist to whom the form was unfamiliar would emend to the present MS. version.

1307. "us es us": Bartsch and Bohs both have "non es us" though the MS. is clear. Bartsch reads "razos." Bohs emends to "*ben* sazos," following Levy (PSW, II, 384).

1309. Verse missing to rhyme with "conoissens."

1310. "que fan lurs caps d'esquerns a dir": Mistral ("fa soun cap") trans. "en faire à sa tête." Levy (PSW, III, 383, and II, 384) trans. as "nach seinem Kopf handeln."

1311. "fassa*n*": emendation by Cornicelius (*So fo*, p. 73), adopted by Bohs.

1317. "sens lur adutz .I. tan lait fait": Two syntactic interpretations are possible. The first, adopted here, is to consider "sens" as the subject and ".I. tan lait fait" as the object, in which case the trans. is: "Wisdom brings such an ugly deed to them that they have valiant and good hearts." Alternatively, ".I. tan lait fait" may be the subject, and "sens" the object, in which case the -s of "sens" may be considered correct if it represents Latin SENSUS rather than Germanic SINN, or it may be an error attributable to a scribe. If "sens" is considered the object, the trans. then is: "such a shameful deed that it brings them to wisdom and to having a valorous heart." In either case R. V. appears to be referring to a heedless conscience suddenly made aware of moral values by considering a particularly shameful deed. It cannot be inferred from the text if the deed is performed by the person whose conscience is thus aroused against it, which would describe a state of repentance, or if the deed is performed by another, which induces moral indignation. In any case, it is the change itself, rather than the cause, which interests him.

1319. "Aquels": object for subject ("aquilh") Levy.

1321. Possibly vs. 1320 had a Cat. "fer" for "far," with "vezer" as the rhyme and prefixed by adverbial "car" (cartener, carpregar).

1334. "lurs vas": flex. -s unnecessary.

1339. "vils": flex. -s unnecessary. The hypercorrection is due to a scribe because of "acostumat" in the following verse, at the rhyme.

1345. The verse is a syllable short. The emendation proposed by Corominas is based on the "-ver" of "aver" being interpreted by a scribe as a repetition of "vergonha."

1346. MS. "lar ... los": Bartsch and Bohs read "larc ... bos."

1351. The verse si a syllable short. "*a*trobatz" is a possibility.

1355-66. Vs. 1357 is repeated intact in the MS. after vs. 1358, and expunctuated. The rhyme "dan - contenso" is faulty. Even if a Catalanism "don" (< "daun") is assumed, "dan" has weak -n but "contenson" has stable -n, a rhyme that is found nowhere else in R.V. and is highly unlikely in other troubadours. It is safe to assume that the passage is corrupt, and that two verses are missing that would supply the necessary rhymes. Corominas suggests emending 1357 "per contenso" to "en baralhan" to rhyme with "dan", and restoring the expunctuated verse, assumed to be textually correct, to a position after vs. 1359 (vss. 1358-1359 must rhyme). The corruption can easily be explained as a mechanical error with attempted correction. A tentative restoration of vs. 1361 would read: "*que lor mostra com ilh son pro.*"

There are several other possible interpretations of the meaning. Bohs emends vs. 1358 ("an en pessamen") to "amon pessamen" and trans.

> Was wieder an anderen unrühmlich ist, das ist die eitle Vielrederei, welche unter den Wackeren und den Übrigen oftmals zum grössten Schaden entsteht, bei Gelegenheit eines Streites, bei den einen, weil sie Nachdenklichkeit lieben, bei den anderen, weil sie wacker und ausserdem edel gebildet sind.

Herzog rejects Bohs's emendation and trans.

> Was wieder an andern unrühmlich ist, ist die Eitelkeit, die zwischen den Wackern und den andern (d. h. nicht Wackern) zum höchsten Schaden durch Wettstreit entsteht, bei den einem denn sie haben darüber Ärger (*an en pessamen*) nämlich, dass die andern wackrer sind, und bei den andern, weil sie (wirklich) trefflich sind...."

1356. "a son dan": Levy, (PSW, II, 6,) lists one ex. of "eser al dan de alcun" (*Flamenca*, p. 6315; "que tot lo mon a son dan sia," trans.: "d'avoir tout le monde contre elle"). Here the antecedent, in a construction identical with that of *Flamenca*, is "vaneza."

1375. "torns": Levy (PSW, VIII, 293) quotes the present ex. with meaning "manieren"? "Benehmen"? "Wesen"? which can be inferred from the context with justification, but also adduces vs. 872, where the meaning is different (see n.).

1376. The verse is a syllable short.

1377. "silh": Bartsch and Bohs read "ilh," though the "s" is clear.

1380. "A": Bartsch and Bohs read "Ja," though the marginal cap. A is clear.

1381. "Homen": flex. -s omitted. "valor": flex. -s omitted.

1391. "aital home": flex. -s omitted.

1392. "Ni·l": flex. -s omitted.

1395. MS. "donas": Bartsch and Bohs read "donan," though the -s is clear.

1401. "mespre*tz*": emendation by Bohs.

1417. "pro": flex. -s omitted because of preceding "als."

1421. "us": nom. pl. "u*n*."

1424. "e d'aver flac": apparently a repetition from the preceding verse, edited by a later scribe to fit sense and syntax.

1431. The verse is a syllable short with the necessary elision of -e on "metre" with the following "e" of the MS. Raynouard's "dessoven" (*Lexique*, V, 497) should be eliminated since the unique ex. is taken from the present text. The problem of scansion is avoided by assuming that the scribe of the exemplar has written "adesoven" for "ades soven."

1435. "Home": flex. -s omitted.

1438. "*de*": emendation by Bartsch, adopted by Bohs.

1443. "*sen*": emendation by Bartsch, adopted by Bohs.

1458-59. "poiretz" with [ẹ] and "etz" with [ę] indicates a Catalan rhyme.

1459. "hom": the verse is short one syllable. cf. vs. 1137 n.

1460. "cascu": flex. -s omitted.

1464. "Als": Bohs emends to "els," which is needless.

1474. Levy (PSW, VI, 561) trans.: "vertraulicher Umgang."

1488. "l'endenh": Jeanroy suggests "ledenh."

1489 "parlar": flex. -s omitted.

1487-94. The oblique plur. "Homes" is qualified by a relative clause that ends with "val," vs. 1490. The main verb, according to the MS., is "ajatz" with an adverbial "car," trans.: "you should cherish these men." Apart from the fact that "homes" is qualified by pejorative adjectives and phrases ("flac captenh," "vils parlars," etc.) the reading "ajatz car" is suspect because vs. 1494 states "he who follows them in that ("paratje escarnir") acts very badly." It is almost impossible to believe that R.V. would recommend association with men whom he has unreservedly condemned in the strongest terms. The thought of the sentence is paralleled by the following: "Mendicx de cor ... vos sian lonh...." Accordingly, "ajatz" is emended to "*fu*jatz."

The problem then is how to interpret the following "car." If it is QUARE then the "car" introducing vs. 1493 is redundant. But while R.V. repeats his ideas he does not use redundant conjunctions (although he repeats a relative pronoun, vs. 1228). One of the two forms "car" must then be interpreted adverbially, "immediately" ("car" of 1491 begins a subordinate clause parallel to "can non poiran al" and is on a different syntactic level). According to syntactic position both could function as either adverb or conjunction. The adverbial clause of time, "can non poiran al" can also refer to either "fujatz" or "fan paratje escarnir"; it is probable that this clause and the temporal adverb "car" refer to the same verb. If applied to "*fu*jatz" the sense is: "Shun [these men] immediately, when they can do nothing else." The underlying idea is not clear. If the adverbial locutions are applied to vs. 1493 the trans. then is: "shun [these men], for when they can do nothing else they immediately slander [make fun of] nobility," which is understandable.

The remaining problem is vs. 1492. It can be read either as "o car non l'auzar es falhir," or as "o car non l'auzarés falhir." The first ("not to dare it is to fail") bears no perceptible relation to the context. The second ("or because you will not dare to fail it") is better. In both cases "it" refers to "paratje." The third possibility (accepted here) is to remain closer to the MS. word division and read "falhir" as a noun. The underlying idea is that their sense of values is inverted and they willingly do what is wrong. In which case, "non lauzar" should probably be hyphenated on the analogy of "presvalens" (vss. 593 and 1254). The parallel between a secular and theological morality can be seen; "non-lauzar" is a sin of omission.

1495. "mendicx": the erroneous flex. -s of the MS. is due to the scribe since the rhyme-word "valen" is correct.

1497. "sies": perhaps a Catalan spelling for "sia.s" with ethical dative as in "no sai que *s*'es" (Raimbaut d'Aurenga, No. XXIV).

1508. "no·l": flex. -s omitted. "calcat": Levy, PSW, I, 187.

1511. "aver cors": trans.: "have a body" (?)

1519. "tals": flex. -s unnecessary. "que·l": flex. -s omitted.

1521. "feitz": Levy quotes the word in the present passage in PSW, III, 442 ("träge, lassig") as an alternative past part. of "fenher". "fenh" used adjectivally is quoted by Levy from the *Breviari d'Amor*, vss. 18401 and 19654, and Amadieu de Sescas (Bartsch, *Denkmäler*, p. 112). The word is ə hapax, but could have existed as the regular reflex of FICTUS beside the more frequent "fenh" (< *FINCTUS). While "estrenher — estreit" and "cenher — ceing (sen)" represent STRINGERE — STRICTUM and CINGERE — CINCTUM, which is the normal phonetic development of the past participle, PINGO, with a past part. PICTUM produces an analogous past part. "(de)penh" < *PINCTUM (C. Appel, *Bernart de Ventadorn*, No. XXXIX, vs. 23). In verbs of both classes the absence of a nasal consonant in the Perfect may have helped to preserve the semantic identity of past participles "estreit," "frait," and "feit." For Crescini "feitz" in the present passage was just as admissible as "fenh." ("Per il testo d'una delle canzoni di Bernart de Ventadorn," *Homenaje a Menéndez Pidal* [3 vols.; Madrid: Hernando 1925], II, 117-18.)

1528. Alternative trans.: "give them merit enough to create a position of authority [which they can fill adequately]."

1532. "sol"; see vs. 544, n. MS. "no sabon que sens nos": While "ses" and "senes" are the usual forms in O. Occ., "sens" is Catalan, so that a Catalan scribe could have changed a "quesesuos" to "que sens nos," though the original may have had "ets" for "es."

1538. "lor": "castiar" usually takes a direct object. The form "lor," in contrast to the more normal "lur" in this MS. (but see vss. 1558-59) may indicate a scribal error of r for s (𝟚 for 𝒮). Alternatively, a Catalan hypercorrection for Cat. "los" as indir. obj.

1543-46. These verses appear as the motto to G. Kolsen's edition of Guiraut de Bornelh.

1543-44. The meaning apparently is, that it is sensible to want to talk to people of good will (vs. 1527) and that a graceful compliment will be the only (and perhaps sufficient) reward that can be expected, since the barons are less generous, or more cautious (vs. 1538) than they used to be because they have been snubbed.

1545. "esgardamen": cf. vs. 1529.

1549. Massó Torrents, *Misc. Prat de la Riba*, p. 370: "De la cançó 'Gen m'aten' (Kolsen, *G. de Bornelh*, p. 118, No. XXIII, vss. 67-72)." Kolsen's trans. is as follows: "...und (ich) halte es nicht für schädlich wenn die Minne mich bedrängt und demütigt; denn dereinst werde ich doch noch guten Erfolg darin haben." 1547 "non" is the only variant from the text adopted by Kolsen. Other variants listed by him are due to misreadings in previous editions.

1553. "afortit": flex. -s omitted.

1553-54. The text is corrupt. After "tanh que" a subjunctive is expected. "tenh" is first sg., while "om afortit" is third sg. Vs. 1554 is short one syllable, and can be best remedied by emeding to "A *far* sos faitz..." Possibly however emend to "A*ja* sos faitz ..." and construe: "aisi tenh [que] tanh c'om afortit a*ja* sos faitz pus cabalos."

1555. "vilan": flex. -s omitted (cf. vs. 1559, "avol gen").

1556. "*a*pres," MS. "ho pres": the emendation, by Bohs, supplies both missing syllable and sense.

1557. "sab*e*r," MS. "sabor": emendation by Bohs.

1565. "e·ls lors": flex. -s unnecessary ("mestier" of the preceding vs. is sg.).

1571. "lurs prezic": the MS. is marred by an ink-blot; since the words are not italicized by Bartsch or Bohs the damage must have occurred later. The -z is omitted from "prezic," and from "ric" in the following verse. As related forms correctly show -s the omission is probably a scribal error.

1573. "ven s'esbefar," MS. "vēses be far": emendation by Bohs. "esbefar" is not found in Raynouard, *Lexique*, or Levy, PSW. Mistral (I, 971) has "esboufa, eboufa" — v.n. et refl. 'Pouffer, pouffer de rire.'" O. Occ. "bufar" with the Mod. Occ. and Cat. "bufa" indicate an original -u-, cf. O. Fr. "esbuffer," "se jouer de, tromper" (Godefroy, III, 397; Tobl. Lomm., III, 809; *FEW*, I, 597 b). The related form "befar" is however found in the Breviari d'Amor, vs. 27780, quoted by Karl Stichel, *Beiträge zur Lexikographie des altprovenzalische Verbums* (Marburg: Elwert, 1890):

> Quar temps y a de prezicar
> temps de rire, temps de befar.

The form is probably a Catalanism, found also in Jaume I *Cronica*, ed. and trans. J. M. Casacuberta (5 vols.; Barcelona: Editorial Barcino, 1926-60), pp. 102, 126, 268 and defined in *DCVB* as "perdre el coratge; cedir en l'energia que es tenia" (s. v. "esbafar," with the usual E. Cat. "e" = [ə] for unstressed "a").

1577. "sembla qui," MS. "semblan": final -n due to confusion with the following "semblan"; "repren," MS. "reprenden": due to confusion with "defenden" of the following verse.

1588. "estranh": flex. -s omitted. (Bohs).

1589. "tenon," MS. "ten hom": the scribal error is probably due to the impersonal "om" of the preceding verse.

1612. Alternatively, "de sazo" can be set off by commas, to mean "[you should tell] at a suitable time."

1614. "si·ls": -s added because of sense and by analogy with vs. 1618.

1616. "novas": probably not "news" which had just been told by the jongleur.

1620. "linhatje": flex. -s omitted.

1625. "cors": flex. -s unnecessary.

1627-28. "estretz ... dretz": flex. -s unnecessary. "estretz de": cf. Raynouard, III, 226, "privé de." The verses may have been reversed because of the repetition of "e·l cor(s)," vss. 1623, 1626. In any case the two ideas are treated concurrently in the same sentence (vss. 1625-29): (1) bodily posture should be graceful, (2) speech should be free from vulgarisms. Because of the rhyme-scheme it is impossible to separate the two elements completely.

1673. "establimen sieu": flex. -s omitted (Levy).

1678. "semblan"; the indicative after "cays que" may be a hypercorrection by a Catalan.

1689. The verse is short one syllable, due to the misreading of an exemplar, with "los" edited to ".ls".

1694. "filh": flex, -s omitted. The verse may be an allusion to Peire Vidal, cf. Boutière-Schutz, pp. 351-52:

> E·ill fo dat a entendre qu'ela [sc. sa muiller]
> era neza del emperador de Costantinopoli, e
> qu'el per lei devia aver l'emperi per rason....
> E·n portava armas emperials e fasia se clamar
> emperaire e la muillier empararitz.

1695. "joglar": flex. -s omitted.

1696. "sapcha bo": see Levy, PSW, VII, 400, "gefallen." "l'anar": flex. -s omitted (Bohs).

1697. "venir": flex. -s omitted. "bos": repeats the "bo" connected with "sapcha" of the preceding verse. The flex. -s may be due to a false analogy with "saboros."

1701. "vilas": because of "locx" the etymon might be Villas, in which case shift of stress must be assumed in order to rhyme, which would be exceptional in O. Occ. although found in O. Cat. (J. Corominas, "The Old Catalan rhymed legends of the Old Seville Bible," *Hispanic Review* XXVII [1959], 361-383). It is more probable, however, that "vilas" represents O.Occ. "vilars" with Cat. reduction of -rs to -s. Levy (PSW, VIII, 774) notes that the word is rare; Mistral, "vilar, vialar"; "village, hameau (vieux)": Du Cange "villare": "villula, vel viculus decem aut 12 domorum seu familiarum" provides the etymon. The word is found in Cat. *DCVB*, X, 809, defines it as "(1) Vila petita, Llogaret. (2) Propietat rústica plantada d'oliveres," with specialization of the meaning found also in Levy, "small property, country house." The word was probably part of R. V.'s vocabulary since Du Cange quotes Charta Caroli C. ex Archivo Gerundensis Ecclesiae: "Et in pago *Bisuldunensi* villam, quae nominatur Baschara cum suis Villaribus ... (ca. 869)." It is in the sense of "country house," "small estate," that the word could be used here. R.V. may be saying that manners today are discourteous, but that some isolated people ("per locx ni vilas") still will recognize learning. The best explanation is that it is an adjective agreeing with "lo segles," with "per locx" interposed.

1709. "joglar": flex. -s omitted. The passage is corrupt, with "nes" because of "neys" (1710) or "nes" (1711). In context the train of thought is that a jongleur's reputation is acquired by being good in his profession (vss. 1702-05); even if he is not known in high places he should go there, because his professional competence will be recognized (at once). Though immediate recognition will also be given to men with readiness of tongue, all they can do is talk (vs. 1716) (as opposed to the other skills of a jongleur).

1710. "al..car": flex. -s omitted (Bohs).

1712. "Amarviment," MS. "amarvit men": If "men" is understood as a noun ("mind, wit") the adj. "amarvit" should be fem., adding an extra syllable to the verse. Better perhaps to read a misplaced -t in the exemplar, with the word-break as a scribal emendation. "Amarviment" is a hapax but of regular formation.

1721. "blasmatz": flex. -s unnecessary (Bohs).

1722. "fatz": flex. -s unnecessary.

1724. "mens": Bartsch and Bohs read "mas." The MS., however, has "m̄s" ("mens"), not "m̃s" ("mas").

1725. "com trop blasmars": An alternative interpretation is "c'om trop blasmars," where "trop" is considered a verb. If "trop" is considered an adverb, however, (the explanation adopted here), it is for reasons of style, where it forms a parallel to vs. 1722 "trop lauzar" where the adverbial function of "trop" is clear; it also forms a contrast to vs. 1721 "assatz blasmatz," although in neither case are the grammatical constructions parallel. "trop lauzar" of vs. 1722 is dependent on "vulhatz." The following clause is then to be considered elliptical, with an unexpressed subject, i.e., "no vulhatz trop lauzar ... car [trop lauzars] es atressi com trop blasmars."

1730-42. Massó Torrents, *Misc. Prat de la Riba*, p. 370: "Setena cobla de 'A enas sai d'on m'aprenh' (Raynouard, *Choix*, III, 361)." Variants with the present text are as follows: 1728 Mas qui; 1730 qu'esquerns es e non re al.

1733. "capdelh," MS. "capduelh": The MS. form probably due to a scribal error, from the verse following.

1734. "esvelh," MS. esvuelh": even if -u- is regarded as a dittography, "esvelh" as an adj. is difficult. It is not attested elsewhere and its formation is that of a noun. In any case, flex. -s is omitted.

1735. "trist": flex. -s omitted (Bohs).

1736. "recrezen ... vist": flex. -s omitted (Bohs).

1746. "dis": "dic" is preferable. Perhaps a scribal error, since in vs. 1752 "dis" is better.

1760. "fresc": flex. -s omitted (Bohs).

1765. "aperceubut": flex. -s omitted, to rhyme with the following verse.

1766. "reconogut": flex. -s omitted. Probably a scribal error, since in the next verse of parallel construction the -s is present.

1768. "astruc": flex. -s omitted.

1770. "cor": instead of "car," a Catalanism.

1771. "partir": flex. -s omitted (Levy). The verse is two syllables short. Possibly an original "lo *de*partir, nos *en* venguem."

INDEX OF NAMES

Albert de Castelvielh (vs. 795)

The history of the family is complicated by the practice, common among the Catalan nobility, of transmitting first names from father to son. "Albert de Castelvielh" is documented from 1149 to 1206; while such a span is not inconsistent with the lifetime of a single individual, documentary evidence shows that there were in fact two men of the same name, uncle and nephew.

Albert de Castelvielh is first found in 1149 in the *"Llibre Blanch" de Santas Creus*; his signature usually appears after that of Guillem de Castelvielh which, with the fact that Albert is referred to as "frater eius," indicates that of the two brothers, Guillem was the elder.[1] According to Coll i Alentorn, Guillem was the third of that name in the family dynasty, and married Belasqueta de Vilademuls, sister of Ramon de Vilademuls.[2]

The influence of Albert at the court of the Count of Barcelona considerably exceeded that of his brother, for Albert is named executor of the will of Raimon Berenguer IV, while his brother's name is found as a simple witness only, considerably further down on the list; after another four signatures is found that of "Guillelmi

---

[1] *LIBSC* Docs. No. 42, 56, 80, 89, 90, dated January 31, 1149; July 13, 1153; May, 1158; June 15, 1160; and June 16, 1160 respectively. *LFM* I, Nos. 247 and 244, dated August, 1151, and October 4, 1154, respectively, given also by Bofarull, *Colección*, IV, 192, No. 69 and 224, No. 82; further sources given by Bofarull are: VIII, 31, No. 5, February, 1154; IV, 240, No. 97, April 1157; VIII, 34, No. 8, February, 1162.

[2] Miquel Coll i Alentorn, *La llegenda de Guillem Ramon de Montcada* (Barcelona: Alpha, 1957), pp. 95-96.

de Castrovetulo, iunioris," indicating that Guillem had a son grown to manhood by this time.[3] Albert de Castelvielh was one of the party including Guillem de Montcada who accompanied Raimon Berenguer IV in 1162 on his way to Milan to meet Frederick Barbarossa when the count died.[4] His influence at court continued, for we find him in February 1163 in the train of Alfons I, in August 1167 at Arles in Provence, and in July, 1168 at Tarragona and in August at Poblet.[5] He is called adviser to Alfons I and Baron of the royal court in 1169,[6] and "vices regis."[7] He was with Alfons at Saragossa in January 1170, in March, 1171, at Tarragona in July, 1171, a year later at Barcelona,[8] and in the same month at Poblet.[9] In 1173 he followed the court regularly, being found as a witness to royal documents in May at Perpignan, in June at Barcelona, July at Fons d'Aldara and in October at Lleida.[10]

He died between April and December, 1174,[11] for at Perpignan at that time Guillem de Castelvielh received from Alfons the castles of Tiviça, Mora, Garcia, and Marsà; Albert de Castelvielh is named as "quondam avunculum tuum." Further in the same document is found:

> Et ego Guillermo de Castro Veteri proper hec supradicta beneficia diffinio vobis, domino meo Ildefonso, regi, atque penitus remitto illos quinque milia morabetinos, quos Arbertus, *avunculus meus, mihi in suo testamento dimisit* et omnia alia debita et perdedas ac missiones ac expensas quas pro vobis vel propter vestrum servicium fecerim in Mon-

---

[3] *LFM*, I, 534, at Huesca, October 11, 1162. Guillem the Younger is first found in August, 1153: "Guillelmi de Castroveteri *el macip* (Bofarull, *Colección*, IV, 210, No. 77).

[4] Coll i Alentorn, *Guillem Ramon de Moncada*.

[5] J. Caruana "Itinerario de Alfonso II de Aragón," *Estudios de edad media de la corona de Aragón*, Vol. VIII, pp. 8-24 (page numbers refer to pages of the "Itinerario.")

[6] *LFM*, II, 191, No. 681.

[7] *Ibid.*, I, 266, n. 1.

[8] Caruana, "Itinerario," pp. 40, 53, 56, 60.

[9] *Cartulari de Poblet,* ed. Eduard Toda and others (Barcelona: Institut d'Estudis Catalans, 1938). He also witnessed documents there in January, 1156, May, 1157, August, 1168, and June, 1172.

[10] Caruana, "Itinerario," pp. 68, 69, 70, 72.

[11] Last mentioned at Huesca (Caruana, "Itinerario," p. 76).

tepessulano sive in aliis quibuscumque locis usque in hodiernum diem.[12]

Since Guillem used his legacy from Albert to pay off obligations incurred to Alfons in Montpellier, it is probable that Albert was still alive when the court was in Montpellier in 1172. From the documents quoted earlier, it is apparent that the Guillem de Castelvielh who is one of the principals in this deed can be none other than the Guillem de Castelvielh "iunioris," son of the Guillem de Castelvielh who was the brother of Albert. Since, also, Guillem no longer uses "iunior," it follows that Guillem who was the brother of Albert had already died. The word "avunculus" must therefore be understood as "uncle," not "grandfather,"[13] which is the relationship given by Miquel i Rossell.

Since, according to the same document, Albert is clearly dead, M. Coll i Alentorn is in error when he assumes that the Albert de Castelvielh who accompanied Raimon Berenguer to Milan in 1162 and the one who witnessed Alfons' will in 1194 are one and the same.[14]

The Albert de Castelvielh who was mentioned by Raimon Vidal is presumably the second of that name, who was the son of Guillem III of Castelvielh and of Belasqueta de Vilademuls, sister of Raimon de Vilademuls. His sister Guilleuma[15] married Guillem Raimon de Montcada, and thus he was related to both parties in the dispute culminating in the assassination of Berenguer de Vilademuls, Archbishop of Tarragona, by Guillem de Montcada in 1196. In the lengthy feud between the families of Cabrera and Urgell, Albert de Castelvielh sided with the latter; he captured and imprisoned Pons de Cabrera until Alfons ordered Albert to release him.[16]

---

[12] *LFM*, I, 253-54.
[13] *Ibid.*, II, 441 (Index. art. "Arbertus de Castro Vetulo"; "abuelo de Guillelmus de Castro Vetulo"). Confirmation is found in the deed authorizing the sale of a third of Tortosa by the Genoese to Raimon Berenguer (Bofarull, *Colección*, IV, 216, No. 78, November 1152): "Tercius erit Guillemus de Castelvel aut frater eius Arbertus aut filius ejus Guillielmus."
[14] Coll i Alentorn.
[15] Another sister, Alemanda, is mentioned in *LlBSC*, No. 390, August 9, 1197.
[16] Miret i Sans, "Notes per la biografia del trovador Guerau de Cabrera," *Estudis universitaris catalans*, IV, 310.

His reputation was sufficiently widespread (politically or as a patron of troubadours) for him to be included in the list of nobles that accompanied Alfons on his visit to Peire Vidal to persuade the troubadour to begin writing poetry again.[17]

The personal property of Albert de Castelvielh was extensive, for he inherited from Berenguer de la Guardia in 1192 the castles of La Guardia, Piera, Castelltort, Granera, Castellnou de Bagas, and the parish of Bruc,[18] with the castle of Falset somewhat later.[19] His importance is further attested by the fact that he witnessed the alliance between Portugal, Leon and Aragon in 1191, and Alfons' will in 1194.[20] As of 1206 his name is no longer found as a witness to documents, nor is that of his son Berenguer, whose signature immediately followed Albert's in the *"Llibre Blanch" de Santas Creus*. It is probable therefore that Berenguer had died and that the Guillem whose name appears subsequently was a younger son who inherited the title.

Alberu (vs. 635)

In rhyme with "negu"; one could therefore expect the [y] to be preserved in a modern place-name, though such is not to be found. The nearest forms are: Alberon, near Arles, dept. Bouches-du-Rhône,[21] Albières, dept. Aude, and Aubière, Puy de Dôme.[22] Serious objections can be made against all three for phonological reasons.

---

[17] Boutière and Schutz, pp. 246-47.

[18] *LFM*, I, 371-73, No. 347, October, 1187; San Cugat de Vallés, I, 313.

[19] "... post longas contenciones et placita que fuerunt inter domnum Ildefonsum ... et Arbert de Castro Veteri" according to the *LFM*, I, 256-57, No. 243, September, 1192. Other holdings of the family included originally Pontons, Odena, Castellvell, Benviure, Far, San Vicente, and Vilarrodona; later were added Flix, Falset, Marsà, Garcia, Mora, and Tiviça (*ibid.*, I, xxii-xxiii).

[20] Caruana, "Itinerario," pp. 194, 219.

[21] Mentioned in the *Gesta Comitum Barcinonensium*, ed. Lluis Barrau Dihigo and Jaume Massó Torrents (Barcelona: Institut d'Estudis catalans, 1925), pp. 13, 46, 136, and in the *Histoire de Languedoc*, VIII, col. 382 (gift by Anfos to the abbey of Franquevaux).

[22] Proposed by Bohs; see Mistral, I, 171. Here too Anfos was besieged by the Count of Toulouse in 1166 but rescued by Bertrand de Baux (Charles de Catel, *Histoire des comtes de Toulouse* [Toulouse: P. Bosc, 1623], p. 210; *Histoire de Languedoc*, VI, pp. 23-4. See also pp. 33 and 68 of the same vol.

Alfons (vs. 737)

Alfons II of Aragon, I of Catalunya, 1152-1196. For his relations with the troubadours see Martín de Riquer, "Los problemas del *roman* provenzal de Jaufré," *Recueil de travaux offert à Clovis Brunel* (2 vols.; Geneva: Droz, 1955), II, 444-46.

Alfonso VIII of Castile (vs. 766)

Reigned from 1158-1214, and married Eleanor of England.

Arnau de Castellnou (vs. 795)

The family of Castellnou of Vallespir [23] is not well documented. An "Artalli de Castro-novo" is found in 1156 and 1159. [24] Arnau de Castellnou was Provincial Master of the Templars, documented from 1267-1274. [25]

Arnaut Guillem de Marsan (vs. 881)

Author of an *ensenhamen* "Qui comte vol apendre," perhaps the first of the genre. [26] In it he recommends knightly prowess among other things, as a sure way to a lady's heart, and boasts of his own successes. Among his conquests he includes N'Escarronha (q.v.)

> En apres conquis mais
> per qu'en dei esser gais

A Peire d'Alberon is mentioned on p. 137; he also witnessed the will of Raimbaut d'Aurenga (Walter T. Pattison, *Life and Works of the Troubadour Raimbaut d'Orange* [Minneapolis: University of Minnesota Press, 1952], p. 218).

[23] Bernat Desclot, *Crònica*, I, 136-38.

[24] Bofarull, *Colección*, IV, 232, 279, Nos. 87, 111.

[25] Joaquin Miret i Sans, *Itinerari de Jaume I, "el Conqueridor"* (Barcelona: Institut d'Estudis catalans, 1918), pp. 400, 497.

[26] Rita Lejeune, "Le date de l' 'Ensenhamen' d'Arnaut-Guillem de Marsan," *Studi Medievali*, N. S., XII (1939), 171: "Le poète est un pionnier." The poem is published in full by Bartsch, *Provenzalisches Lesebuch*, pp. 132-39. Partial publication by Raynouard, *Choix*, II, 301, and V, 41; Mahn, *Werke der Troubadours*, III, 366; Appel, *Provenzalische Chrestomathie*, p. 163. Translation with notes and analysis, A. Parducci. *Costumi ornati: Studi sugli insegnamenti di cortigiani medievali* (Bologna: Zanichelli, 1927), pp. 24-26, 251-58, 259-72.

>   ma dona n'Escarronha
>   la gensor de Gascuenha.

Assigned to the end of the thirteenth century by Jeanroy, Stimming, and Parducci,[27] Arnaut-Guillem de Marsan's poem was dated with greater probability by Rita Lejeune who placed it at 1170-80, "où Arnaut Guillem atteignit sa maturité": in September of 1170 he was old and influential enough to accompany Eleanor of England to Tarrazona in Castile, where he witnessed the act of donation given by Alfonso VIII of Castile to his bride.[28] Arnaut Guillem belonged to the cadet branch of the family of Marsan. His father was Guillem II. The family held the property of Marsan, in the Landes, with their capital at Mont-de-Marsan.

A later Arnaut-Guillem de Marsan, viscount of Louvigny (documented 1242-1255) was probably the grandson of the poet. There is no reason to associate him with the man mentioned by Raimon Vidal.

Astarac ("Pro baro vas Astarac") (vs. 879)

It is difficult to identify such a vague mention. Perhaps Centule d'Astarac.[29] A later "worthy baron" was Bernart IV d'Astarac (1249-1291),[30] to whom Amanieu de Sescas devoted the closing verses (434-472) of his "Ensenhamen," speaking of him in terms of the highest praise.[31]

"Coms de Barcelona" (vs. 869)

Raimon Berenguer IV, who governed from 1131-1162.

---

[27] Jeanroy, "Notice" in the *Grande Enciclopédie* of Lamirault "contemporary of Raimon Vidal"); Stimming, *Grundriss*, II, 51; Parducci, *Costumi ornati*, p. 24; all quoted by Lejeune, pp. 161-62.
[28] The deed is printed by J. González, *El Reino de Castilla en la época de Alfonso VIII*, 3 vols. (Madrid: Escuela de Estudios medievales, 1960), Vol. I facing pp. 192-93.
[29] P. Meyer, *La Chanson de la croisade contre les albigeois*, vol. II, p. 443, n. 3. See also Martin-Chabot, vol. III, p. 255, n. 8.
[30] Identified by Milá y Fontanals, *De Los trovadores*, p. 423, n. 6.
[31] Parducci, *Costumi ornati*, translation p. 278, p. 282 n.

Berenguer d'Entença (vs. 819)

One of the "ricos hombres" of Aragon and lord of Saragossa, according to a document of 1187,[32] Alfons II gaves him Teruel to colonize. He kept it for two years, being replaced by Bertran de Santas Creus.[33] Nothing is heard of him until he became governor of Calatayud in February 1180, taking over from Pere de Castell Azol.[34] In May, 1182, he appears as "in Calataiub et in Ferica." From February 1187 to January of the following year Saragossa is not given as a synchronism, while Berenguer is mentioned as "dominus in Borga." He continued in Saragossa, witnessing the alliance between Portugal, Leon and Aragon against Castile in 1191. In the same year at Monzon he is mentioned as being "senior ipsius civitatis per manum domini regis."[35] The earliest record of him is a document of December 27, 1170;[36] he is last found in April, 1196, "(senior) in Fontibus et in Aljaferino."[37] His daughter Jussiana d'Entença[38] married Hug III d'Empuries. "Berenguer" was the usual first name in the family, repeated from father to son. The most famous was the leader of the Catalan company, Megaduke of Byzantium. Entença is on the border of Catalunya and Aragon, between Tremp and Benavarri.[39]

---

[32] Caruana, "Itinerario," p. 160.

[33] Milá y Fontanals, *De los trovadores*, p. 340, n. 9. February 1, 1172 at Saragossa, "Berengario de Intenza seniore in Turol," Caruana, "Itinerario," p. 59. The town traditionally was occupied by Alfons on October 1, 1171.

[34] Caruana, "Itinerario," p. 122. Assignment of the document to 1180 rather than 1181 appears justified since, although a document of June 1180 lists Pere de Castell Azol in Calatayud (drawn up by the queen's notary), later documents starting from July show Berenguer.

[35] *Ibid.*, pp. 138, 167, 188, 194, 199.

[36] *Ibid.*, p. 52.

[37] *Ibid.*, p. 226.

[38] She was his daughter, according to Luis Salazar y Castro (*Historia genealógica de la casa de Lara* [4 vols.; Madrid: Imprenta Real, 1694-97], vol. I, p. 43), though Miret i Sans (*Itinerari de Jaume I*, p. 575) hesitates between "sister" and "daughter." The fact that Berenguer's signature appears as late as 1196 and Jussiana's as early as 1174 can be interpreted either way.

[39] F. Soldevila, *Historia de Catalunya* (3 vols.; Barcelona: Alpha, 1962), vol. I, pp. 319-322.

Berenguer de Robian (vs. 882)

No evidence is available concerning a Berenguer de Robian. He must have been Occitanian rather than Catalan, for he is mentioned in conjunction with Bernart d'Armagnac, Arnaut Guillem de Marsan, and Bernart de Cumenge. The village of Roubià, dept. Aude, arr. Narbonne, is mentioned in the *Histoire de Languedoc,* VIII, cols. 318 and 1737 ("de Robiano"), while the names "Arnaldus de Robiano" and "Adalaicis de Robiano" are found in Vol. VII, cols. 248 and 231. Adalaicis was the wife of P. de Torozella; her name is found in a document of March, 1262.

Bernart d'Armalhac (Armagnac) (vs. 880)

Bernart IV, Count of Armagnac and Fezensac, is mentioned by Bertran de Born as "en Bernardos" in the "sirventes" "Puois Ventadorns e Comborns ab Segur," identified by the accompanying "razo." [40] The context in which he appears is political, since Bertran de Born was trying to stir up opposition to Richard the Lion-Heart.

Bernart had four sons, Geraud IV, Arnaut-Bernart (or Bernart-Arnaut), Peire-Geraud, and Rogier. [41] Bernart-Arnaut was a troubadour who exchanged "coblas" with Na Lombarda. [42] The story is related in her "Vida" and clarified by Dejeanne, [43] who assumed that Bernart-Arnaut is the Bernart d'Armalhac mentioned by Raimon Vidal. Bernart-Arnaut inherited the title from his brother in 1219 and died in 1226. [44] While the larger context of "Abrils issia" indicates a period during the lifetimes of Alfons II, Henry, Richard, and Geoffrey (sons of Henry II of England), i.e. before the beginning of the thirteenth century, the narrower context varies in time, e.g., Arnaut Guillem de Marsan lived ca. 1170-80, Berenguer de Robian

---

[40] Stimming, *Bertran de Born,* No. V, 19 and p. 68; Thomas, *Bertran de Born,* No. III, 19 and n. 10, which gives his dates as 1160-1190.

[41] *Histoire de Languedoc,* VI, 778.

[42] Boutière and Schutz, *Biographies,* pp. 416-417.

[43] Jean-Marie L. Dejeanne, "Les 'coblas' de Barnart-Arnaut d'Armagnac et de Dame Lombarda," *Annales du Midi,* XVIII (1906), 63-68; A. Jeanroy, *Jongleurs et troubadours gascons des XIIe et XIIIe siècles* (Paris: Champion, 1923), pp. 16-18.

[44] Fritz Bergert, *Die von den Trobadors genannten oder gefeierten Damen* (Halle: Z.r.Ph., XLVI, 1913), p. 51.

lived ca. 1190, Bernart de Cumenge governed from 1181-1225. It is not inconsistent with this context therefore to regard the troubadour as the one to whom Raimon Vidal refers.

Bernart de Cumenge (Comminges) (vs. 883)

Bernart IV governed from 1177 to 1225 as count of Comminges and Couserans. His father was count Dodon, called Bernart, and his mother was the daughter of Alphonse-Jourdain, count of Toulouse, according to Ch. Higounet,[45] who corrects the relationships given by the authors of the *Histoire de Languedoc* (nephew of Raimon V of Toulouse).[46]

He and his son Bernart took an active part in the war against the Albigensian crusaders, as vassals of the count of Toulouse and Pere I and allies of the count of Foix.

He was the husband of Marie de Montpellier, daughter of Guilhem VIII of Montpellier. She later married Pere I. Bernart was induced to repudiate her for both political and personal reasons.

While previous commentators [47] are unanimous in identifying the "Bernardos de Cumenge" with the Bernart de Comminges mentioned above, the question must be raised whether his son may not be the one to whom Raimon Vidal refers. In the *Chanson de la Croisade albigeoise*[48] the poet always distinguishes between the "comte de Cumenge" and "Bernart de Cumenge," the latter reserved exclusively for the son. Raimon Vidal usually distinguishes between higher and lesser nobility, using titles for the former, e.g., the "pros marques" (de Lombardia), the "comte Ferran," the "comte Dalfi," or the simple names of a high dignitary so well known as to need little or no explanation from him—"Guillem, sel de Montcada," "en Miquel ... en Arago." For the lesser nobility he gives the full name, but rarely the title, e.g., Arnaut Guillem de Marsan. Although not completely consistent, the practice is constant enough to suggest

---

[45] Charles Higounet, *Le Comté de Comminges de ses origines à son annexion à la couronne* (2 vols.; Toulouse-Paris: E. Privat, 1949), I, 152, n. 2.

[46] *Histoire de Languedoc,* VI, 125; VII, 7, n. 7. In Vol. VIII, col. 408, he is described as "filius sororis comitis Tolosae," and in VIII, col. 575, the will of Raimon VI, as "Ber. convenarum comitis, consanguinei mei." He was cousin to Raimon VI.

[47] Cornicelius, p. 98; Bohs, p. 303.

[48] Martin-Chabot, II, 266, n. 4.

that it is the son, Bernart de Cumenge, mentioned in the *Chanson de la croisade albigeoise.*

The use of the diminutive "Bernardo" indicates the son rather than the father.

The Count of Cumenge is mentioned by several troubadours. Aimeric de Peguilhan directed the poem "En greu pantays" to him, with the highly equivocal dedication:

> Coms Cumenges, grat e merces vos ren
> quar ses donar m'avetz donat aitan
> qu'endreg d'onor val un don aut e gran. [49]

He is mentioned also by A. de Sescas in his "Ensenhamen de las Domnas," [50] by Bernat de Tot lo Mon, "Los plazers," [51] by Folquet de Lunel in his "tenso" with Guiraut Riquier, [52] and by Guilhem de Montanhagol in "on mais a om de valensa." [53] All four troubadours belong to the thirteenth century and, with the possible exception of Aimeric de Peguilhan, [54] could not have referred to the father.

Bertran de Saissac (vs. 889)

Son of Uc de Saissac, [55] Bertran de Saissac was for a long time the friend and adviser of Roger II, Viscount of Béziers and Carcassonne. His influence was considerable, since he was present at the treaty between Roger and Alfons II, [56] and he was wealthy, since

---

[49] W. P. Shepard and F. M. Chambers, *The Poems of Aimeric de Peguilhan* (Evanston: Northwestern University Press, 1950), No. XXVII, p. 36.

[50] Bartsch, *Lesebuch*, p. 146.

[51] Appel, *Provenzalische Inedita*, p. 46.

[52] Mentioned by Anglade, *Onomastique des troubadours*, p. 202.

[53] Coulet, p. 149. The "coms Cumenges" mentioned is Roger, in Coulet's opinion. Jeanroy (*Poésie lyrique*, I, 284) rejects Roger, while Ricketts proposes Bernard VII (*Les Poésies de Guilhem de Montanhagol* [Toronto: Pontifical Institute of Mediaeval Studies, 1964] p. 72).

[54] Higounet assigns the mention to Bernart IV; beyond question is Bertran de Born's reference (Stimming, *Bertran de Born*, p. 7).

[55] *Histoire de Languedoc*, VI, 64.

[56] Signed in Carcassonne, November 1179 (*LFM*, II, 332 and 340, Nos. 856, 863). He was probably instrumental in reconciling the two, or securing less harsh terms for Roger II. This, at any rate, seems to be the meaning of vss. 23-24 of Guilhem de Berguedan's "sirventes" "Reis, s'anc nuls temps," ed. Martin de Riquer, *El Trovador Guilhem de Berguedan y las luchas feudales de su tiempo* (Castellón: 1953); see also p. 26.

in 1189 he lent his overlord 25,000 melgorian sols, receiving as security Roger II's rights to property at the abbey of Caunes which included the town and two castles. [57] He enjoyed the trust of Roger II to a high degree, being called in 1191 to arbitrate a dispute between Roger and Peire Olivier de Termes concerning the mines of Termenès. [58] On the death of Roger in 1194, Bertran became the guardian of the Viscount's son, Raimon-Rogier. According to the codicil of the will of Roger, [59] Bertran de Saissac was confirmed in his position as guardian for another five years, to 1199, supplanting even Raimon-Rogier's own mother. [60] In this capacity he had control over the domains of the dioceses of Béziers and Agde, and the family fiefs in the Rouergue, Albigeois, and Toulousain, with partial control over the domains in the Carcasès, Razès, Lauraguès, and Termenès. Bertran de Saissac was also named executor of the will.

In August of the same year he bound himself and his ward to consult Gaufred, Bishop of Béziers, and Étienne de Servian in all matters concerning the dioceses of Béziers and Agde; to protect them against attack; not to establish any provost ("veguer") in the dioceses without their consent; and to expel all heretics and to refrain from introducing any more. [61] It has been suggested [62] that in so doing he placed the control almost entirely in the hands of the Bishop and thus weakened the temporal authority to the point where the viscounty was easily overrun by the crusaders some years later. This may be doubted, as his handling of the Abbey of Alet shows.

The Abbot of Alet, Pons Amelii, died in 1197. The monks duly elected Bernard de Saint Ferréol. The choice displeased Bertran, who imprisoned the new abbot and drove away his supporters. To ensure that his own nominee was legally elected he restored the former abbot, digging up his body and placing it at the head of

---

[57] *Histoire de Languedoc*, VI, 135; VIII, cols. 396-97, No. 46.
[58] *Ibid.*, VI, 143; VIII, cols. 412-14, No. 53.
[59] *Ibid.*, VI, 153-55.
[60] Adelaide, Countess of Burlats. She was celebrated by Arnaut de Mareuil (Boutière and Schutz, pp. 32-35). Bernart's influence was such that Milá y Fontanals (*De los trovadores*, p. 295, n. 17) calls him "caudillo del partido anti-aragonés."
[61] *Histoire de Languedoc*, VI, 157-58.
[62] *Ibid.*, VI, 158, n. 2.

the council table. Thus gently reminded of their own mortality, the monks saw the wisdom of electing Bertran's choice, Bozo. On his release Bernard de Saint-Ferréol appealed to the Bishop of Carcassonne who, being as afraid of Bertran as the monks, refused to give an opinion and sent the case to his metropolitan, the Archbishop of Narbonne. Far from supporting Bernard de Saint-Ferréol, the Archbishop pronounced in favor of Bozo, perhaps because he had just received a large sum of money from him. Bozo, in fact, sold off the property of the abbey "pro mercatus abbatice" until it was nearly ruined, and showed himself lenient, if not favorable toward the heretics. It thus appears that Bertran de Saissac was not particularly influenced in his actions by the clergy, and probably did not feel his written agreement as being unduly constraining,[63] even though he seems to have been of a legalistic turn of mind.

Moreover, Bertran de Saissac was himself a heretic, according to Pierre de Vaux-Cernay;[64] the agreement between Bertran and the bishop of Béziers in which he undertook not to import any more heretics into the town indicates that he had previously done so.

Bertran de Saissac was the patron and friend of troubadours[65] and was mentioned in a "sirventes" by Guillem de Berguedan:

> De tot en tot era de perdre l'or
> tro.l de Saissac i mes autre demor.

However, his closest relationship was with Raimon de Miraval. He is mentioned in the "Vida" as his patron and one of the great barons of the region,[66] but more revealing still, he has an entire strophe dedicated to him in the "sirventes" "A Dieu me coman, Bayona":

> A'n Bertran de Saissac chanta
> Sirventes e mais chansos,

---

[63] *Ibid.*, VI, 158-59.

[64] Quoted *ibid.*, VI, 220.

[65] He was not, as Comas y Pujols claims, a patron of Peire d'Alvernha, who in his "Cantarai d'aquestz trobadors" mentions a *Bernard* de Saissac. Bernard de Saissac was a member of a collateral branch of the family, perhaps slightly before the time of Bertran. He is mentioned in 1174, when Roger II granted to him and Isarn Jourdain a hill on which to build the castle of Mont-Revel (*Histoire de Languedoc*, VI, 64). Bertran de Saissac may have been a patron of Peire Vidal, who wrote: "Et anc mais colps tan no·m plac, / Qu'ieu sojorne a Saissac / Ab fraires et ab cozis." (Peire Vidal, *Poesie*, I, 146, No. XVII, vs. 20).

[66] Boutière and Schutz, p. 375.

E di-l que no-s tenh' az anta,
Car premier non l'ai somos;
E ja de luy no-t partras blos,
C'un caval c'a col de ganta
No-t don per amor de nos
Si dars non l'atalanta. [67]

The translation is as follows:

Au seigneur Bertran de Saissac chante des sirventés et, de préférence, des chansons, et dis-lui de ne pas se tenir pour offensé que je ne me sois pas adressé à lui tout d'abord: tu ne le quitteras les mains vides sans qu'il te donne pour l'amour de moi un cheval qui aura un cou de cicogne — bien qu'il ne se plaise point à fraire des dons.

Andraud sees in the attitude of the troubadour an inferior in rank but on good terms of long standing. [68]

According to Andraud the residence of the Saissac family was in the valley of the Orbiel, between Miraval and Carcassonne and Béziers, explaining in part the poet's familiarity. Andraud assigns the date of death of Bertran de Saissac at 1199 to 1202, the first because there is no mention of another guardian to Raimon-Rogier, the second because in this year the deed whereby he ceded all his possessions to the Count of Foix contains the mark of Olivier de Saissac but not that of Bertran. He noted also that Ave, the widow of a lord of Saissac, in 1209, may have been the wife of Bertran.

Blacatz (vs. 782)

The life and works of Blacatz have been described by O. Soltau. [69] Blacatz died in 1236.

---

[67] Ed. L. T. Topsfield, *Les Poésies du troubadour Raimon de Miraval* (Paris: Nizet, due 1972).

[68] Paul Andraud, *La Vie et l'œuvre du troubadour Raimon de Miraval: Étude sur la littérature et la société à la veille de la guerre des Albigeois* (Paris: E. Bouillon, 1902), p. 53.

[69] Otto Soltau, *Blacatz, ein Dichter und Dichterfreund der Provence* (Berlin: E. Ebering, 1898); "Die Werke des Troubadours Blacatz," *Z. r. Ph.* XXIII (1899), 201-48.

Boniface I of Montferrat (vs. 773)

The best account is given by J. Linskill (*The Poems of the Troubadour Raimbaut de Vaqueiras*, pp. 8-37); se also the three epic letters by Raimbaut, and accounts by Villehardouin and Robert de Clari. Leopoldo Usseglio's history of the court of Montferrat and the Gaya Scienza is based on old and faulty editions, e.g., he repeats Raynouard's attribution of *Abril issia* to Peire Vidal (pp. 437-48). [70]

Castilho (vs. 636)

Probably Castillon-en-Couserans, a village in the department of Ariège, on the Lez, a tributary of the Salat which in turn flows into the Garonne. The village is ten kilometers southwest of Saint-Girons and forty-eight kilometers west of Foix as the crow flies.

Castellvi (vs. 804)

The most famous Castellví (O. Cat. Castell-vill < castell-vell) is Castellví de Rosanes, four miles west of Martorell and ten miles east of Vilafranca del Penedès.

Dalfi d'Auvergne (vss. 139, 517, 654, 691, 785, 851, 861, 945

A protector of troubadours and a troubadour himself, Dalfi d'Auvergne ruled from 1169 to his death in 1234. His poetic activity has been investigated by Stroński ("Quelques protecteurs des troubadours," *Annales du Midi*, XVIII [1906], 474-93. For Dalfi see pp. 476-83).

Diego López de Haro (vs. 767)

Usually accepted as the "Diego" of Raimon Vidal. [71] The most complete account of him and his relations with the troubadours is

---

[70] Leopoldo Usseglio, *I Marchesi di Monferrato in Italia ed in Oriente durante i secoli XII e XIII*, Vols. C-CI of the *Biblioteca della società storica subalpina* (2 vols.; Casale Monferrato: Miglietta, 1926). For the history see II, 169-278; for the relationships with the troubadours, see II, Part IV, "La Gaya Scienza in Monferrato," 321-417.

[71] Bohs, p. 225; Cornicelius, pp. 92-94; Milá y Fontanals, *De los trovadores*, p. 126, n. 3; Menéndez Pidal, p. 127.

that of J. Anglade, "Les Troubadours provençaux en Biscaye," *Revista de filología española*, XV (1928), 343-353. The simple reference "Diego" corresponds to that of the "Vida" of Rigaut de Berbezilh, where the reference is accepted by G. Favati and A. Varvaro, [72] and is found in Aimeric de Peguilhan. [73]

N'Escaronha (vs. 914)

Escaronha was married to Bernart II de l'Isle-Jourdain. [74] Their son Jourdain was married to Esclarmond, by whom he had a daughter also called Escaronha. [75]

Raimon Vidal probably refers to the former Escaronha, born ca. 1125, [76] and who was a celebrated beauty. Arnaut Guillem de Marsan boasted that she was his mistress, [77] and Guiraut de Bornelh mentions her in a pastoral: [78]

> Toza, n'Escaronh'es guitz
> de pretz, que.m dat, companhera
> cortez'e fin' amairitz,
> per que.l mals me fug de tera. [79]

though he was apparently less successful than Arnaut-Guillem, for in vss. 26-30 he says:

---

[72] Favati; Varvaro, p. 75. Varvaro considers the passage an interpolation given by two MSS. out of five. This view does not of course invalidate the identification. I. Frank was evidently mistaken in his reading of the text when he asserted that Diego de Gamberes was mentioned with an uncle, Guidrefe de Gamberes (I. Frank, "Les Troubadours et le Portugal," *Mélanges d'études portugaises offerts à M. Georges Le Gentil* (Lisbon: 1949), pp. 199-226.

[73] William P. Shepard and Frank M. Chambers, *The Poems of Aimeric de Peguilhan*, No. XXVI, vs. 4, p. 146.

[74] *Histoire de Languedoc*, VI, 143; VII, Note xlii, 118-9; Bernart died in 1189 according to O. Schultz-Gora ("Besprechungen," *Z. r. Ph.* [1888], 544), who quoted from *Coutumes de la ville de l'Isle-Jourdain*.

[75] *Histoire de Languedoc*, Vol. VIII, col. 461 (Jourdain's will, dated September, 1200).

[76] Bergert, p. 40; A. Kolsen (*Guiraut von Bornelh, der Meister der Trobadors* [Berlin: C. Vogt, 1894], p. 24) calculated the date from the fact that her son was old enough to endow a monastery in 1161 (*Histoire de Languedoc*, VI, 10).

[77] See "Arnaut Guillem de Marsan."

[78] Kolsen, *Sämtliche Lieder des Trobadors Guiraut de Bornelh*, Vol. I, No. 56, vss. 71-74; II, 101-102.

[79] Punctuation according to K. Lewent, *Zum Text der Lieder des Guiraut de Bornelh* (Florence: L. S. Olschki, 1938), p. 80.

> Qu'era me sui departitz
> de una fals' abetairitz
> que.m fa chamjar ma charrera
> e fora.m chabdals e guitz,
> si no fos tan volatera.

Kolsen has suggested that "Escaronha" was celebrated by the poet on other occasions under the "senhals" of "Senher," "Bels senher," "Segurs," "Flors de lis," and "Jois," and that the "Alamanda (d'Estanc)" of the "Vida"[80] is not his lady but his lady's maid.[81]

Count Ferran and his brothers (vss. 769-70)

The most satisfactory identification is that provided by Cornicelius,[82] who saw in them the Infantes de Lara, Don Fernando, Don Gonzalo, and Don Alvaro. The three Infantes de Lara for long opposed Doña Berenguela and Fernando III at the beginning of his reign (to 1219).

---

[80] Kolsen, *Guiraut von Bornelh, der Meister der Trobadors*, pp. 23-33.

[81] The "tenso" between Giraut de Bornelh and Alamanda (*ibid.*, No. LVII) was well known since Bertran de Born used the melody (Stimming, *Bertran de Born*, VI, 25 and 162). In the "Vida" of Na Lombarda (Boutière and Schutz, p. 209), Bernart-Arnaut d'Armagnac wrote a poem to Na Lombarda in which he says:

> Lombards volgr'eu eser par na Lombarda,
> qu'Alamanda no·m plaz tan ni Giscarda

and puns in the second verse on ladies' names indicating a country. Since Bernart-Arnaut and Alamanda both lived in Gascony it is possible that the Alamanda of Guiraut de Bornelh and of Bernart-Arnaut were one and the same; the possibility becomes a probability when it is recalled that Bernart-Arnaut addresses the second stanza to "Seigner Jordan," who can perhaps be identified with Bernart de l'Isle-Jourdain, although, as Alamanda and Jourdain, son of Escaronha and Bernart II, may have been contemporaries, it may be the latter rather than Bernart II who is addressed in the second stanza of Bernart-Arnaut's poem. Without any convincing reason Jeanroy claimed that "Alamanda" was fictitious ("Les femmes poètes dans la littérature provençale aux XIIe et XIIIe siècles," *Mélanges de philologie offerts à Salverda de Grave* [Batavia: J. B. Wolters, 1933], p. 186, n. 6.

[82] Cornicelius, pp. 94-95. Cornicelius pointed out that the "comte Ferran e sos fraires" may be presumed to be Castillian because of the mention of Alfonso VIII and Don Diego and López de Haro. The identification was accepted by Bohs, Anglade ("Les troubadours provençaux en Biscaye," *Revista de Filología española*, XV, 350). Milá y Fontanals identified the "comte Ferran" with the son of Alfons, mentioned frequently in the chronicle of Jaume I (*De los trovadores*, p. 339, n. 7).

The Count of Foix (vs. 635)

Raimon-Roger (1188-1223); see Charles Baudon de Mony, *Relations politiques des comtes de Foix avec la Catalogne*, (2 vols.; Paris: A. Picard, 1896).

Emperaire Fredericx (vs. 859)

The Emperor Frederick I, Barbarossa, who ruled from 1152- 1190.

Garcia Romieu of Calatayud (vss. 817-18)

One of the Aragonese knights who accompanied Alfons on his mission to cheer up Peire Vidal,[83] he is documented in 1208, 1209,[84] 1211, and four times in 1212.[85] In June of that year, he was at Toledo and took part in the battle of Las Navas de Tolosa. He was a man of extraordinary bravery, for on that day when courage was commonplace he was singled out for mention by Rodrigo de Toledo:

> Nemo potuerit omnia particulariter intueri, scilicet qualiter agilitate facili praevenerit fugientes; quam viriliter Eximenus Cornelli cum turba suorum advenerit agentibus primos ictus; qualiter Garcias Romerii et Aznarius Pardi cum aliis magnatibus Aragoniae et Cataloniae belli dubia magnifice peregerunt.[86]

In November he was present at the betrothal of Guillem Ramon de Montcada and Constanza, daughter of Pere II at Tauste. In April,

---

[83] Boutière and Schutz, p. 368; Favati, p. 276. A "Blascol Romieu" precedes Garcia's name in the "Vida" and is mentioned by Peire Vidal (ed. Avalle, No. V, vs. 7). "Garcia Rumei" and "Blaschus Rumei" are found in that order in Bofarull, *Colección*, VIII, 94, No. 34. The reversal of the order of names in the two cases indicates that they were probably brothers. Garcia Romieu is described as "senior in Calatajub" in the same document while Blaschus is "senior in Tirasona" (October 1, 1203). However, "Ximenus Romeu, alferiz domini regis" in November, 1169 (*ibid.*, VIII, 47, No. 13) also is found with Blasco in December 1180 (*ibid.*, VIII, 67, No. 21).

[84] *Ibid.*, VIII, 105, No. 38 and VIII, 108, No. 39.

[85] Miret i Sans, "Itinerari de Pere I," *Butlletí de la Reial Academia de Bones Lletres de Barcelona*, Vol. I (1904).

[86] Rodrigo de Toledo, *De Rebus Hispaniae*, ed. Lorenzana (Madrid, 1793), p 136, quoted by Coll i Alentorn (Desclot, *Crónica*, I, 29).

1213, he was at Saragossa and three days later at Huesca.[87] He took part in the battle of Muret, where he was one of the king's troop[88] and where he may have died, for the name is not found on any documents until 1228, where there begins a long series that does not end until October 1271.[89] This Garcia Romieu, one of the "ricoshombres de Aragon" (April, 1254), was probably the son of the one referred to by Raimon Vidal.

Gaston de Bearn (vs. 786)

Gaston V of Bearn died childless in 1170; as a result the estate passed to his sister Maria, who in the same year put herself under the protection of Alfons II at Jaca, paying hommage to him for the fiefs of Bearn.[90] She married Guillem Ramon de Montcada, by whom she had two boys in 1173, possibly twins, Gaston and Guillem Ramon, and a daugther Saurina.[91]

The fiefs of the viscount of Bearn went to Gaston, while Guillem Ramon received the patrimony of Montcada. During the minority of Gaston, Bearn was governed by his guardian Pelegrin de Castell Azol.[92]

On the death of his mother Maria in 1187, Gaston did hommage to Alfons II for Bearn and all his lands (including Saragossa, Fraga, and Jaca) except those which he held in fief from the Count of Poitiers (Richard the Lion-heart).[93]

In 1192 Gaston married Petronilla, daughter of Bernart de Cumenge at Muret. As a dowry she brought him the county of Bigorre.[94] In 1193 he captured the town of Ortès which had been taken previously by the Viscount of Tartas.[95]

On the marriage of his sister Eleanor to Alfonso VIII of Castile, Richard the Lion-heart had given her Gascony as her dowry. In

---

[87] Miret i Sans "Itinerari de Pere I."
[88] Gerónimo Zurita y Castro, *Anales de la Corona de Aragón* (6 vols.; Saragossa: Portonarijs, 1610), Lib. II, p. 100.
[89] Miret i Sans, *Itinerari de Jaume I*.
[90] Pierre de Marca, *Histoire de Béarn* (Paris: Camusat, 1640), pp. 466-68.
[91] *Ibid.*, pp. 472-83.
[92] *Ibid.*, p. 489.
[93] *LFM*, I, 28, No. XX.
[94] *Ibid.*, I, 29, No. XXI.
[95] Marca, p. 503.

1204 Alfonso entered Gascony to enforce his wife's claim, which was recognized by Gaston, who met the king at San Sebastian, greeting him as duke of Gascony.[96]

From the beginning of the Albigensian crusade Gaston appears to have thrown in his lot with the Count of Toulouse, his father-in-law Bernart de Cumenge, the Count of Foix, and Savaric de Mauléon.[97] Gaston joined the offensive against Simon de Montfort in 1211, and with the Count of Toulouse and his other allies besieged Simon de Monfort in Castelnaudary.[98] In the following year the army of the crusaders entered Gascony,[99] and devastated the region of Brulhois which belonged to Gaston. Simon de Montfort and Gaston arranged to meet to discuss terms for a truce in Agen, but Gaston did not appear for the meeting.[100]

Pere el Catòlic, moved to action by the successes of Simon de Montfort against his vassals, petitioned the Pope that the lands which had been conquered from Gaston and others should be restored.[101] In his reply Innocent III censured Simon and the Archbishop of Narbonne for converting a crusade into a war of conquest, and instructed them to meet with Pere to discuss terms for a settlement. In his memoire to the council of Lavaur dated January 13, 1213, Pere pressed for the restitution of the lands of Gaston, who was not, he declared, a heretic. The bishops, however, were not disposed to pardon someone who had done such harm to the church; from among an "infinite" number of possible charges they accused him of aiding and harboring heretics; of being a persecutor of the church; of participating in the siege of Castelnaudary; of harboring the murderer of Pierre de Castelnau; of maintaining "routiers." In the past year, they said, his "routiers" had entered the cathedral of Oloron and cut the cord holding the pyx containing the sacrament, which spilt on the ground. A soldier had dressed in a priest's vestments and had held a mock mass, for which they held Gaston

---

[96] *Ibid.*, p. 506.
[97] *Histoire de Languedoc*, VI, 349.
[98] Pierre de Vaux Cernay, *Hystoria Albigensis*, ed. Pascal Guébin and Ernest Lyon (3 vols.; Paris: H. Champion [Société de l'Histoire de France] 1926-39), I, 253.
[99] Martin-Chabot, I, 280: "Trastot o an conquist e la terra Gaston."
[100] P. de Vaux Cernay, II, 37.
[101] *Ibid.*, II, 67.

responsible. For these reasons Gaston was held excommunicate and anathema but, the council added, he could be received back into the church after confession and restitution.[102] In their letter to the Pope justifying their accusations, the bishops made specific mention of Gaston of Bearn. Gaston meanwhile paid hommage to Pere for his estates so that Pere could vouch for the fact that he was not a heretic and at the same time hold as security the castles of Lourdes, Oloron, Montaner, Cadillon, and Miramont.[103]

The attempt at pacification seems to have been of no use. Later the same year Gaston, the Count of Foix and Bernart de Cumenge sacked the monastery of Grandselve.[104] Gaston was probably not at the battle of Muret in person, although he sent troops. In 1214, the long-drawn-out struggle with the church ended for Gaston; he was confessed by the Bishop of Oloron, and gave to the diocese the town of Sainte Marie to indemnify it for the damage he had caused.

In 1215 he died, without children, like his uncle before him, and after his death was known as Gaston the Good. His brother Guillem Ramon de Montcada succeeded to the viscounty, but was recognized by the Bearnais only after several years.[105]

During his short life Gaston was mentioned by several troubadours. Bertran de Born devoted a stanza to him in "Quan vei pels vergiers desplejar" and mentioned him again in "S'ieu fos aissi senher ni poderos."[106] Aimeric de Peguilhan dedicated "S'ieu tan ben non ames":

> Lo pro.n Guaston sal Dieus
> de Biarn, qu'ieu sui sieus
> per totz temps, so.us afi,
> ez elh mieus atressi,
> a guiza de senhor,
> quar fa de gran major

---

[102] *Ibid.*, II, 78-80.
[103] Marca, p. 524, n. II.
[104] P. de Vaux Cernay, II, 92.
[105] Guillaume le Breton, *Philippiade*: "Et quos misere Navarri et quos nutrierat Carcasso, Comesque Bicorrus, Conveniunt omnes numero bis milia centum," (a figure which seems exaggerated). Quoted by Marca, pp. 527-35.
[106] Stimming, *Bertran de Born*, No. XIII, vs. 27, p. 88; No. XXV, vs. 38, p. 113. The "razo" accompanying the first poem notes: "... el vescoms de Bearn e de Gavarda, so era en Gastos de Bearn, qu'era chaps de tota Guasconha."

son pretz, e no.us recre,
que.l mielhs met sobre.l be.

Aimeric also dedicated to him the poem "Puois descobrir," the "tornada" of which is as follows:

Seign'En Gaston, vostr' onranssa
onra Gascoigna d'aitan;
c'aissi cum carn salva sals,
la salvatz dels peiors mals.

The poems may have been written when Aimeric was staying at Gaston's court.[107]

Na Gensana (vs. 918)

Bartsch and Bohs both read "Gensana," confirmed by the present reading of the MS. Milá y Fontanals however says: "R. Vidal cita una Jensiana [sic.] *de sai* como que brillaba en la época de D. Alfonso ..." (*De los trovadores*, p. 287). The "sic" indicates that Milá had made an independent and inaccurate reading. Milá quoted the name with respect to Jussiana, perhaps because he considered her the wife of Pons de Mataplana, whom he identified with Uc de Mataplana. It would therefore appear natural for Raimon Vidal to mention the wife of his patron. There is however documentary evidence that Pons and Uc were brothers ("Hugo de Mataplana et uxor mea Beatricis et ego Pontius de Mataplana, frater predicti Hugonis"),[108] and nowhere does it appear that Pons was ever married.[109] Martín de Riquer identifies three ladies named Jussiana,[110] one the wife of Bernat de Villardida, with documentary evidence of 1194; the second, the wife of Pere de Cervera son of Pons de

---

[107] Shepard and Chambers, No. XLIX; No. XLII. It is the opinion of the editors that Aimeric may have spent some time with Gaston. References to a Gaston de Bearn by Peire Cardenal (*Poésies complètes du troubadour Peire Cardenal*, ed. René Lavaud [Toulouse: Privat, 1957], No. XXIII, vs. 26) and by Cerveri de Girona in the "Testament" and in "Can era paucs" (F. A. Ugolini, "Il Canzoniere inedito di Cerveri di Girona," *Atti della R. Academia nazionale dei Lincei*, Ser. VI, V [1936], 644) are to Gaston VII.

[108] *LIBSC*, No. 162, quoted by Martín de Riquer, "Las poesías de Guilhem de Berguedan contra Pons de Mataplana," *Z. r. Ph.* LXXI (1955), 3.

[109] Riquer, *Z. r. Ph.* LXXI (1955), 13.

[110] *Ibid.*, pp. 13-14.

Cervera, documented from 1193-1242;[111] the third, Jussiana d'Entença, who married Hug III d'Empuries, was the sister of Orea, countess of Pallars, mother of Pons Hug II and grand-mother of Hug IV.[112] She is documented from 1174-1178, and Riquer identifies her with the "Juziana" of the third stanza of "Ben ai auzit" by Guilhem de Berguedan.[113] Comas y Pujols identifies this last Jussiana with the "Gensana" of *Abrils issia*;[114] since she is mentioned by Guilhem de Berguedan she must have welcomed troubadours[115] and since she is qualified as being "de sai," whereas the Countess of Urgell is "de lay,"[116] presumably following the indication of Milá y Fontanals. (So also Bergert: "... vermutlich *Jussiana*, die Gattin des 1197 verstorbenen Pons von Mataplana"[117] and Anglade.[118]

There seems no justification for the assumption that "Gensana" and "Jussiana" are identical,[119] especially as "Jussiana" in G. de Berguedan's "Ben ai auzit" scans as four syllables while in *Abril issia* "Gensana" scans as three. Documentary evidence is however lacking, though "de say" indicates that she was a Catalan. (The difference between the qualifications "de sai" and "de lai" may indicate a distinction between Catalunya and Urgell.)

---

[111] See also Miret i Sans, *Los viscondes de Bas en la illa de Sardenya* (Barcelona, 1901), p. 36 quoted by Riquer.

[112] Miret i Sans, *Itinerari de Jaume I*, p. 575; F. Monsalvatje y Fossas, *Los Condes de Ampurias vindicados* (Olot: Bonet, 1917), p. 94. According to Salazar y Castro (*Historia genealógica de la casa de Lara*, vol. I, p. 43) she was the daughter of Berenguer d'Entença. A lawsuit in 1189 resulted between Pons Hug and the canon of Saragossa concerning an agreement *facta inter Domnam Jussianam Comitissam matrem eius* (i.e. Pons Hug), by which time she was probably dead.

[113] There is still another Jussiana; Hug III d'Empuries and Jussiana had two sons, Hug and Pons Hug; the latter was the father of the fourth Jussiana, who married Bernart Guilhem de Montpellier, son of Guilhem VIII of Montpellier and uncle of Jaume I (Miret i Sans, *Itinerari de Jaume I*, p. 575, correcting Blancas, *Linajes de Aragón*, and the chronicle of Jaume I. See also Salazar y Castro, II, 43.

[114] Comas i Pujols, p. 87.

[115] It does not follow, since Guilhem de Berguedan was a knight with lands held in fief to Uc de Mataplana (Riquer, *Z. r. Ph.* LXXI [1955], pp. 1 and 18) and did not depend, like a jongleur, on the generosity of patrons.

[116] See "Count and Countess of Urgell."

[117] Bergert, p. 40.

[118] Anglade, *Onomastique des troubadours*, p. 252.

[119] Riquer rejects the possibility.

"Guidrefe de Gamberes" (vs. 768)

There is no record of a "Guidrefe de Gamberes." Milá y Fontanals suggested [120] that Pedro Ruiz de los Cameros may have been intended. The form "Gambiros" for "Cameros" is found in the "Vida" of Guillem Magret; [121] "... Pois si rendet en un hospital en Espaigna, en la terra d'En Roiz Peire dels Gambiros." [122] The allusion in the "Vida" is to Pedro Ruiz, about whom not much is known. He was a relation, probably the son, of Ruy Diaz de los Cameros, who commanded an army corps at the battle of Las Navas de Tolosa. [123] Ruy Diaz had a brother Alvar Diaz. At the beginning of the reign of Ferdinand III of Castile (ca. 1219), Ruy Diaz revolted against the king, shortly after the final revolt of the Infantes de Lara. Summoned to the court to answer charges of disorder, he fled without giving up the castles he had been ordered to. Ferdinand enforced his justice by buying him off, giving him 14,000 maravedis in gold in exchange for the castles. [124]

If the form "Guidrefe" is assumed to arise as a result of scribal error it is possible to trace the form back to either Pedro Ruiz or Ruy Diaz. The mention of Pedro Ruiz in the "Vida is however more consistent with the reputation as a patron of troubadours given to him by Raimon Vidal.

Guillem de Cardona (vs. 801)

Guillem de Cardona was the only son of Ramon Folc IV, Viscount of Cardona, and cousin and vassal of Ermengol VIII of Urgell. [125] He inherited his estates in 1174 or 1175. [126] His name is

---

[120] Milá y Fontanals, *De los trovadores*, p. 339, n. 6; p. 126, n. 3.

[121] Boutière and Schutz, p. 493; Favati, pp. 300 and 506.

[122] Cameros, a sierra divided into two parts, Camero Viejo and Camero Nuevo, in Logroño province. The only date that can be assigned with any probability to Guillem Magret is 1204, according to Fritz Naudieth, "Der Trobador Guillem Magret," Z. r. Ph., Beiheft LII (1914), 79-144; 94-101.

[123] Alfonso X, *Primera crónica general de España*, ed. Ramón Menéndez Pidal (2 vols.; Madrid: Bailly-Ballière, 1955), Vol. II, chap. 1012.

[124] *Ibid.*, II, 719.

[125] Diego Monfar y Sors, *Historia de los condes de Urgel*, ed. P. Bofarull y Mascaró (2 vols.; Barcelona: Montfort, 1853), I, 426. Ermengol mentions Guillem de Cardona as "consanguineum meum" in his will, *ibid.*, I, 434;

found at rare intervals in documents of little significance for the next twenty years.[127] In 1197, however, war broke out between Ermengol of Urgell and Raimon Roger, Count of Foix. Guillem de Cardona distinguished himself in the struggle, which lasted until 1203.[128] In the treaty between Ermengol and Raimon Roger, Guillem de Cardona is specifically exempted from reprisals.[129] As a further guarantee, the allies and vassals of the two counts bound themselves by marriage alliances. Elicsenda, Guillem de Cardona's daughter, was given in marriage to Arnau de Castelbon who had just been released from the prisons of the Count of Urgell.[130] Guillem's signature is missing from the agreement; he may have disapproved of the marriage.

Relations between Ermengol and his countess Elvira had never been good. In the same year they concluded a pact in which they forgave each other past offenses and resolved to love each other in the future. Ermengol prudently stipulated, however, that in case they separated Elvira should stay at Cardona, and on her behalf Guillem de Cardona guaranteed the concessions made by Ermengol. He also witnessed the deed.[131]

Guillem de Cardona was an executor of Ermengol's will, drawn up in 1208, in which provision was made for him to possess in his own right the fiefs he held from Urgell should Ermengol or his daughter Aurembaix die without issue.[132] He was also named inheritor of the entire estate if all other members of the family were to die with no children.[133]

His responsibilities to the family of Urgell did not end with the death of Ermengol, for when Pere I engaged his son Jaume to

---

and in the will of Ermengol's father, Ermengol VII, Guillem de Cardona appears as "nepotem meum" (*ibid.*, p. 420). The will is dated 1177.

[126] Joaquin Lorenzo Villanueva, *Viaje literario a las iglesias de España* (Madrid: Imprenta real, 1806), V, 248.

[127] *LIBSC*, p. 255, No. 258 (1183); p. 366, No. 366 (1193); *Cartulari de Poblet*, p. 359, No. 16 (1190); p. 251, No. 13 (1196).

[128] Monfar y Sors, I, 426.

[129] Baudon de Mony, I, 129; II, 60.

[130] *Ibid.*, I, 55-57 (Pièces justificatives No. 29). Elicsenda is described as "filiam Guillelmi de Cardona, neptam vestram" (i.e., of Ermengol). Elicsenda's mother was Geralda, daughter of Elicsendis and her first husband Guillem de Alcarraz (Riquer, *Z. R. Ph.* LXXI [1955], 7).

[131] Monfar y Sors, p. 432.

[132] This subsequently occurred.

[133] *Ibid.*, pp. 433-37.

Aurembaix in 1210, Guillem signed the contract and probably assisted in drawing it up. [134]

The engagement of Aurembaix to Jaume was clearly a political move, by which the county of Urgell would eventually accrue to the Count of Barcelona. The advantage to Elvira lay in the fact that the alliance would afford protection against the incursions of Guerau de Cabrera, who shortly beforehand had refused to recognize the right of the Countess Elvira to inherit the county of Urgell from her husband; as the nephew of Ermengol and the nearest surviving male relative he claimed it for himself. His armies invaded the county, capturing towns and castles, while Guerau adopted the title of Count of Urgell. Guillem de Cardona was as ineffective as the countess in resisting Guerau de Cabrera, which explains why she contracted the engagement of their children. Although Pere I had every interest in seeing to it that Guerau de Cabrera did not usurp property that would later come to the Count of Barcelona, he refused to respond to Elvira's appeals or to adjudicate the case until Elvira deeded the county to him during her lifetime. Pere accepted the offer, but turned over the task of getting rid of Guerau de Cabrera to Guillem de Cardona, who with his son Raimon Folc was to administer the county for a period of five years (1210-1215). It is not surprising that the Cardonas, who had failed before, were not successful in getting rid of Guerau de Cabrera; after all, their sole reward for five years' administration and fighting was to be several castles. Elvira, considering perhaps that her interests could be protected only by someone who stood to profit directly, married Guillem de Cervera, while Guillem de Cardona turned his attention to politics on a larger scale. [135]

He became one of the closest advisers of Pere I, following the king on his travels. [136] In 1212, he was at Toledo and took part in the battle of Las Navas de Tolosa. [137] The following year he fought

---

[134] Miret i Sans, *Boletín de la Real Academia de Buenas Letras*, IV, 19. The engagement did not last a year. In 1211 Jaume was engaged to the daughter of Simon de Monfort.

[135] Monfar y Sors, pp. 438-44.

[136] Miret i Sans, *Boletín de la Real Academia de Buenas Letras*, IV, 21-23: Barcelona, March 6, 1211; Lleida, March 21, 1211; Vich, March 29, 1211.

[137] Bernat Boades, *Libre dels feyts d'armes de Catalunya* (Barcelona: Biblioteca catalana, 1878), p. 313; Alfonso X, II, 690.

at Muret but apparently managed to escape and continue fighting, for in the year after that he, with Nunyo Sanç and Guillem de Montcada, made war on Simon de Montfort in an attempt to recover Jaume I, now a hostage at Carcassonne in the hands of the crusaders.[138] As a result of a bull from Innocent III, Simon de Montfort handed over custody of Jaume I to a number of Catalan barons at Narbonne, among whom was Guillem de Cardona.[139]

No more is heard of Guillem de Cardona until 1222, when Jaume I gave the lands of Urgell to Guerau de Cabrera, except for those parts held by Guillem de Cardona. This arrangement was in accordance with the will of Ermengol VIII, at least as far as Guillem was concerned.

The following year Guillem de Montcada revolted against the authority of the crown. Jaume I was able to impose his authority thanks to the assistance of Guillem de Cardona, Guillem de Cervera, and Nunyo Sanç,[140] but the effort took three years and was only ended with the treaty between Guillem de Montcada and the Cardonas, which Count Ramon Folc and his brother Guillem signed in 1226.[141] These however were the sons of Guillem; he had died before the treaty and his place had been taken by his children. The younger son Guillem[142] became Provincial Master of the Temple and exercised a position of great power in Catalunya under Jaume I.

Guilhem dels Baus ("lo Blon") (vs. 783)

Guilhem dels Baus was the son of Bertrand des Baux and Tiburge d'Aurenga, sister of Raimbaut d'Aurenga. Guilhem inherited the title of Prince of Orange from his mother, together with half the town.[143]

---

[138] Jaume I, I, 28.
[139] Miret i Sans, *Itinerari de Jaume I*, p. 18.
[140] Desclot, II, 78, n. 1; II, 80. n. 1.
[141] Miret i Sans, *Itinerari de Jaume I*, pp. 62-63.
[142] Mentioned in a document of 1229: "Guillelmus de Cardona, quondam, filius Guillelmi de Cardona" (*LlBSC* p. 391, No. 391).
[143] Raimbaut d'Aurenga's will has been published by Walter T. Pattison, *The Life and Works of the Troubadour Raimbaut d'Orange*, pp. 25-27. The will is quite ambiguous, as is the "Vida" of the poet, where the family relationships are recognized by Pattison and Boutière-Schutz p. 444 as erroneous.

During the Albigensian crusade the policy of Guilhem was very simple: he tried to be on the winning side. At the beginning he did not commit himself, though as a vassal of the Count of Toulouse he must have taken up arms later. When the Count of Toulouse was forced to undergo the humiliating public penance prescribed by the papal legate Milon, Guilhem took part in the event and had to give up the castles of Vitrole, Montmirat, and Clarensans.[144] Shortly thereafter Guilhem tried to free himself from an overlord who had lost much of his power, but without success, for in 1210, threatened by the arrival of additional crusaders under Simon de Montfort, he made a truce with Raimon of Toulouse.[145]

A later attempt to achieve independence was more successful. In 1215 he approached the Emperor Frederick II and, on the basis of a long-standing but nebulous claim to Provence, was granted a charter making him King of Arles and Vienne.[146] He enforced his claim by invading the lands held by the Count of Toulouse in Provence. On being ordered by the Pope to restore the lands to the papal legate cardinal Sainte-Maire de Aquiro, he refused, and instead went to Rome to reinforce his claim. In this he was unsuccessful, as the council decided in favor of the young Count of Toulouse.[147] The Count managed to obtain the neutrality, if not the alliance, of Guilhem in the following year, though the treaty was soon broken by Guilhem.[148]

His kingdom did not last long. He was caught by the people of Avignon, who were faithful to the Count of Toulouse. They flayed him alive and cut him in pieces.[149]

Guilhem dels Baus was a patron of troubadours and a poet himself. Raimbaut de Vaqueiras was for a long time at the court of

---

[144] *Histoire de Languedoc*, VI, 281.
[145] *Ibid.*, VI, 333; VIII, 590-91.
[146] Jean-Louis-Alphonse Huillard-Bréholles, *Historia diplomatica Friderici Secundi* (Paris: Plon, 1852), I, Part II, 353.
[147] Paul Fournier, *Le Royaume d'Arles et de Vienne* (Paris: Picard, 1891), p. 103.
[148] Martin-Chabot, II, 98, Ser. 154, vss. 55-58.
[149] Nicolas de Bray, *Gesta Ludovici Octavi*, ed. André Luchesne, *Historiae Francorum Scriptores* (5 vols.; Paris: Cramoisy, 1649), V, 317.

Orange.[150] As a poet, Guilhem exchanged "coblas" with a "Raimbaut" and with Gui de Cavaillon, and with Uc de St. Circ.[151]

Guillem de Montcada (vs. 809)

Either Guillem Raimon Dapifer, the Great Seneschal (1120-1174)[152] or his son Guillem Raimon, who killed the Bishop of Tarragona.[153] A third Guillem died at Majorca in 1229.[154]

Guilhem de Montpellier (vs. 884)

The well-known figure of Guilhem VIII de Montpellier requires no special treatment here. The events of his life are amply described in the pages of the *Histoire de Languedoc,* Vol. VI. Guiraut de Calanson dedicated to him his long and pretentious "Celeis cui am de cor e de saber,"[155] and Raimbaut de Vaqueiras his "Leu sonet."[156] He was the patron of Peire Ramon de Tolosa[157] and the friend of Arnaut de Mareuil,[158] but for so influential a figure he is comparatively seldom mentioned, and not always favorably. Folquet de Marseille's love for the "emperatriz" (Eudoxia, daughter of Manuel Comnenus) is alleged by the "razo" as the reason for her divorce.[159]

---

[150] J. Linskill, *Raimbaut de Vaqueiras,* pp. 10-13; pp. 27-8 rejecting the "senhal" *Engles* as applying to Guilhem, and pp. 38-9 for discussion of the "coblas."

[151] H. P. de Rochegude, *Le Parnasse occitanien* (Toulouse: Bénichet cadet, 1819); A. Jeanroy and Salverda de Grave, *Poésies de Uc de Saint-Circ* (Toulouse; Privat, 1913) No. XXXIX.

[152] A. Rubio i Lluch, *Don Guillermo Ramón de Moncada, gran senescal de Cataluña* (Barcelona, 1886), quoted by Coll i Alentorn, p. 155; J. Miret i Sans, "La Casa de Moncada en el vizcondado de Bearn," *Butlletí de la Reial Academia de Bones Lletres,* Vol. I (1901).

[153] Coll I Alentorn.

[154] Jaume I, II, 44.

[155] Willy Ernst, "Die Lieder des provenzalischen Trobadors Guiraut von Calanso," *Romanische Forschungen,* XLIV (1930), 322: "A Monpeslier a·N Guillem lo marques T'en vai, chanso; fai l'auzir de bon grat Qu'en lui a pretz e valor e richat."

[156] J. Linskill, *Raimbaut de Vaqueiras,* No. II.

[157] Boutière and Schutz, p. 347.

[158] *Ibid.,* p. 36.

[159] *Ibid.,* pp. 475, 478.

Guion d'Auvergne (vs. 784)

The county was divided between him and his cousin Dalfi, both using the title of Count of Auvergne. He exercised singularly little influence on political affairs of the period, and cannot be said for certain to have been a noted patron of troubadours. While references to "en Gui" are not uncommon, positive identification is difficult.

In 1208 he inherited the possessions of Guilhem de Rodez, [160] who died without issue.

He joined the crusaders in the Albigensian crusade in the late spring of 1209, for on April 26 he assigned the dowry of his wife Petronilla de Chambon. He was on the point of leaving for the crusade. [161] He was one of the commanders of the first army corps, [162] though not whole-hearted in the undertaking, since he prevented the crusaders from taking the town of Casseneuil for reasons of personal profit, [163] which led to a quarrel with the Archbishop of Bordeaux. The crusaders at this time were not united under a single command, but consisted of two main army corps, each under several leaders. In order to achieve unity as far as possible, the Pope ordered the crusaders to forget their private differences and specifically absolved Guion d'Auvergne from the crime of having imprisoned his own brother, who was Bishop of Clermont.

He is referred to indirectly by Richard the Lion-heart in a French "sirventes" addressed to Dalfi:

> Vai sirventes, je t'envoi
> en Auvergne, e di moi
> as deus comtes de ma part
> s'ui mès font pès, Dieu les gart. [164]

He is mentioned directly in Dalfi's reply to Richard:

---

[160] *Histoire de Languedoc,* VI, 269.

[161] *Ibid.,* VI, 287.

[162] Martin-Chabot, I, 41: "Aqui es lo coms Guis, us Alvernhes cortes."

[163] *Ibid.,* I, 43: "Ab tot so lo prezeran, no fos le desturbier Quer lor fe lo coms Guis, car el n'ac gran aver E si c'ab l'arsevesque s'en pres a tensoner."

[164] Rochegude, p. 14.

E taus esterlins pesatz
donetz mon cosin Guion
so dison siei compagnon
tostemps segron vostr'estrieus
sol tan larc vos tenga Dieus. [165]

Venality emerges as his main characteristic.

Jofre de Rocabertí (vs. 827)

A Gaufred de Rocabertí witnessed a document at Gerona in 1190; [166] at Perpignan in June 1192, [167] and in September of the same year. [168] In December, 1194, he was a witness to the will of Alfons. [169] He was in Gerona again in 1196 when he witnessed another document. [170] In 1200 he witnessed the "Cortes" of Barcelona. [171]

There is a gap of eleven years until a Jofre de Rocabertí is encountered again, as witness to two documents of March 6 and 11, 1211, and on March 21 of the same year he signed three documents. [172] According to Milá y Fontanals he fought at Las Navas de Tolosa, [173] and the following year was at the disaster of Muret.

Another gap of sixteen years intervenes, until in 1229, Jofre de Rocabertí promised twenty knights with 100 infantry, armed and maintained until Majorca should be taken. That he in fact went to Majorca is stated by Desclot, [174] who says that he was a member of Nunyo Sanç's company. He must have died shortly thereafter, for in the same year "Dalmacio de Rupebertini" is mentioned as the Viscount. [175]

---

[165] *Ibid.*, p. 85.
[166] Caruana, "Itinerario," p. 183.
[167] *LFM*, II, 140.
[168] *Ibid.*, I, 31.
[169] Caruana, "Itinerario," p. 219.
[170] *LFM*, II, 284.
[171] Cortes de Aragón, Valencia y Cataluña, I, Part I (Madrid: 1896), 85.
[172] Miret i Sans, *Butlletí de la Reial Acdaemia de Bones Lletres de Barcelona*, Vol. I (1904), 21.
[173] Milá y Fontanals, *De los trovadores*, p. 126 (based on Beuter).
[174] Desclot, II, 92.
[175] Monsalvatje y Fossas, *Colección diplomática*, II, 114. Desclot may have been mistaken in this instance, for in January, 1228, Dalmau de Rocabertí signed the "Cortes" of Barcelona, using the title of Viscount (*Cortes de Aragón, Valencia y Cataluña*, I, 119).

Raimon Vidal mentions that Jofre de Rocabertí was the nephew of Raimon de Vilademuls (1176-1199). The only attested sister of Raimon was Belasqueta, who married Guillem III de Castellvell; Jofre may have been a child by a previous marriage to a Rocabertí, or Raimon de Vilademuls may have had another sister. The latter explanation seems the most probable. The only child of Raimon de Vilademuls was Maria, who married Hug IV d'Empuries. On the death of her father the property passed to her, but in 1226 (the date of her death?) it went to Jofre de Rocabertí. [176] One must assume that the Vilademuls estates devolved on each of the children in turn, the system of the "droit de viage." [177] Apparently the estates of Las Rocas that Maria inherited from her mother were not affected by the system, for they remained in the possession of the counts of Empuries.

Given the dates of Raimon de Vilademuls and his relationship with Jofre, it seems probable that the Jofre of the period 1188-1198 is the same as he of Las Navas and Muret. It is possible too that he went to Majorca. Assuming a minimum age of twenty-one in 1188 he would have been sixty-one or older at the time of the expedition to Majorca; like Pons de Vernet, certainly not too old to have led his own men.

L'Estanh (vs. 798)

Situated between Manresa and Vich.

Lo Puey (vs. 623)

Le Puy, dept. Haute-Loire.

---

[176] Monsalvatje y Fossas, *Los Condes de Ampurias vindicados*, p. 102.

[177] The "droit de viage" or "droit de retour" obtained in Poitou, in particular with the Viscounts of Thouars and the family of Mauléon (H. J. Chaytor, *Savaric de Mauléon* [Cambridge: Cambridge University Press, 1939], p. 3).

The system is to be found in Catalunya combined, in the case of the Counts of Pallars in the tenth and eleventh centuries, with joint tenure of the title of count. Thus, in the tenth century, Count Ramon had two brothers, Borrell and Sunyer. On the death of Ramon without issue, the inheritance passed to Borrell. Borrell's son Ermengol inherited the title on the death of his father, but governed jointly with his uncle Sunyer (Ramón d'Abadal i de Vinyals, *Catalunya carolingia*: Vol. III. *Els Comtats de Pallars i Ribagorça* [Barcelona: Institut d'Estudis catalans, 1955], p. 142 et. seq.).

En Lobat (vs. 574)

Anglade [178] sees in Peire Cardenal's "D'un Sirventes far," vs. 28, a reference to "en Lobat." The text is as follows:

> ... car, si liges entr'els libres antix
> vos trobares de lops aitan adreitz
> que n'an passat manz fals baros enix.
>
> D'els non vai segurs laics ni clercs
> ni monges niers ni blancs ni gris
> que bels manjars ni bels jazers
> l'oste ni l'ostal non garis,
> si lai a draps ni astz ni pals ni pix;
> que al levar s'en van ab los espleitz,
> so que non fes en lobatz ni'n urtix. [179]

Translated by Lavaud: "ce que ne fit jamais seigneur loup ni seigneur tigre." In view of the fact that in the previous stanza (quoted) P. Cardenal judges wolves to be more cunning than the "fals baros enix," Lavaud's translation appears justified, and the passage refers primarily to wolves. However, a pun on the name "Lobat" is also intended, as can be seen in a partimen between the Monge de Montaudon and Albert de Sisteron. [180] The Monge says:

> ... s'ill valon mais don vos estes confraire,
> donc valc lo mais Lobatz, non fes Rotlans,
> que per un do que fan, tolon tres tans;
> e nos sabem gen do e condugz faire
> e vos raubar gleizas e vi'andans.

In this passage the reference to a person rather than an animal is clear because of the association with Roland. Secondly, the friends of Albert de Sisteron are represented as robbing churches, of whom Lobat is the best, paralleling the robbing of the black, white, and gray monks in Peire Cardenal's "sirventes." It appears then that the moral ascendancy of Lobat, according to Peire Cardenal, consists in refraining from plundering his host; he, at any rate, was not

---

[178] Anglade, *Onomastique des troubadours*, p. 178.
[179] Peire Cardenal, *Poésies complètes*, pp. 314-15, No. LII, vs. 28.
[180] Appel, *Provenzalische Chrestomathie*, No. 97, vs. 53.

"fals." The distinction is important, since in the Albigensian crusade it would characterise an anti-crusader from a mere soldier of fortune or routier, in theory at least.

Lobat is mentioned by Raimbaut de Vaqueiras in "El so que pus m'agensa," vs. 66:

> Barral, sel de Marcelha
> vi gent armat
> sul destrier c'a la selha
> negr' e.l pel plat,
> e val be mil tans celha
> sel d'en Lobat. [181]

One feature common to the three excerpts quoted above and the mention by Raimon Vidal is the fact that no title or place of origin is given for Lobat. This omission leads to the supposition that Lobat was very well known, or was a bastard. Both may apply in the case of Lop de Foix, brother of Roger-Bernard, Count of Foix. [182] Lop de Foix took part in the Albigensian crusade, fighting with his father. He was wounded in a skirmish near Toulouse, took part in a raid on the Lauragais and was at the battle of Baziège, 1219. [183] His illegitimacy was inferred by Martin-Chabot [184] from the fact that he was not mentioned in Roger-Bernard's will. He did possess some property, however, having rights on Fanjeaux and part of the domain of Mirepoix. [185]

It seems likely that Lobat was the illegitimate son of Raimon-Roger and Loba de Pennautier, [186] whose liaison caused a scandal at the time. [187] After the Albigensian crusade he applied four times

---

[181] J. Linskill, *Raimbaut de Vaqueiras*, No. I, vs. 66. The reference was noted by Schultz-Gora, Z. r. Ph. XII (1888), 544.

[182] "Aimericum et Lupum fratres nostros" in the act of submission by Roger-Bernard to the church and King of France, June, 1229 (*Histoire de Languedoc*, Vol. VIII, cols. 903-906.

[183] Martin-Chabot, III, 100, 259, 269, 277.

[184] *Ibid.*, III, 101, n. 7. See also P. Meyer, *Croisade contre les Albigeois*, II, 367, n. 2.

[185] *Histoire de Languedoc*, Vol. VIII, col. 767. In this too may be seen a sign of his illegitimacy. Rather than redraw the internal boundaries of the County of Foix, his father gave him interests in existing properties.

[186] *Ibid.*, VI, 564; Andraud, p. 106.

[187] The social ostracism of Na Loba becoause she loved the Count of Foix "de drudaria" is recounted in the "razo" of Raimon de Miraval and

for recognition by the church, but was refused. He had four children, three daughters and a son, founding the line from which were descended the lords of Rabat. He died before 1262.[188] The context in which he is mentioned, Mercadier and Margarit, neither of whom was noble, is a further indication that Raimon Vidal is referring to the illegitimate Lobat de Foix.

Na Mahieu de Pallars (vs. 915)

There is not indication that such a person was ever Countess of either Pallars jussà or Pallars sobirà, nor is there any record of such a person known as "de Pallars" connected with the family of the counts.[189] Mathilda, daughter of Bernart de Cumenge and Marie de Montpellier, married Sans de la Barta;[190] she is connected with Pallars in that her uncle, Bernart's younger brother Roger de Cumenge, married Guilleuma Countess of Pallars and daughter of Artau IV and Guilleuma. The connection is too slight to give a sure identification.

---

commented on by R. Lejeune, "Ce qu' il faut croire des 'Biographies' provençales," *Le Moyen Age*, XLIX (1939), 233-249 (see p. 240). Lejeune advances the theory that Loubat de Pennautier, Loba's brother, is the one mentioned by Raimon Vidal. It is possible that Barral of Marseilles knew the Pennautiers as they lived in the same part of Provence; hence the reference to "en Lobat" by Raimbaut de Vaqueiras may be to Lobat de Pennautier, not his nephew. The absence of any mention of a place of origin however seems sufficient reason to classify the reference with the others. Beyond the fact that Lobat de Pennautier was the brother of a well-known sister there is no information concerning him, and it is therefore assumed that Raimon Vidal's reference is to the better-known Lop de Foix. The use of the diminutive "Lobat" in verse compared to the "Lop" or "Lupus" of official documents is hardly surprising. The figure of Loubat de Pennautier is vague enough. According to L. de Santi ("La Louve de Pennautier," *Revue des Pyrénées*, XVI [1904], 359-69), Loubat de Pennautier and Raimon de Pennautier, father of Na Loba, are one and the same.

[188] *Histoire de Languedoc*, VII, Part. II, cols. 336, 340, 341, 351. Lop de Foix is mentioned in the list of heretics "Inquesta de Albigensibus" although he repeatedly reaffirmed his loyalty to the church.

[189] No mention in Ramon d'Abadal i de Vinyals, *Catalunya Carolingia*: Vol. III, *Els Comtats de Pallars i Ribagorça*, or in Ferran Valls-Taberner, "Els Comtats de Pallars i Ribagorça a partir del segle XI," *Estudis universitaris catalans*, IX (1915-1916), 40-101, reprinted in *Obras selectas de Fernando Valls-Taberner*, Vol. IV, *Estudios de historia medieval* (Barcelona: Consejo superior de investigaciones científicas, Escuela de Estudios medievales, 1961), pp. 125-205.

[190] Miret i Sans, *Itinerari de Jaume I*, p. 13 et seq.

INDEX OF NAMES 163

The Guilleuma who married Roger de Cumenge was Countess in her own right, uniting Pallars jussà and Pallars sobirà. She lived until at least 1250, having spent her last twenty years in a convent.[191] While both she and her mother were important enough to be well known, neither was celebrated by any troubadour so far as is known, and problems of scribal error and scansion make the identification highly improbable, even though it is possible that one of them may have used Mahieu as a second name, a practice not uncommon at the time.

Malfet (vs. 799)

See *Abril issia*, vs. 799, n.

Margarito de Brindisi ("En Margarit") (vs. 581)

A famous Sicilian admiral, serving under William II of Sicily and Tancred. The first incident in his career to attract the attention of historians occurred in 1186 when he was sent by William II to help Isaac Comnenus, Emperor of Cyprus in his revolt against the Byzantine emperor, Isaac Angelus. Margarit routed the Byzantine navy which had come to capture Cyprus, destroying seventy of their ships in the harbor.[192] Two years later, on the eve of the third crusade, he was sent from Tyre by Conrad of Montferrat to the aid of the kingdom of Jerusalem with a force of sixty ships and 200 knights. Tripoli was at that time besieged by Saladin, with little prospect of relief. When Margarit's flotilla appeared it was not at first recognized, and the garrison remained for a time in doubt, but when the crusaders' banner was hoisted from the poop of the admiral's ship, a great cry went up and the inhabitants rushed to the shore to welcome him.[193] As a result of these reinforcements Saladin

---

[191] Valls-Taberner, "Els comtes de Pallars," *Obras selectas*, pp. 199 and 201.

[192] Nicetas Choniates, *Historia* (De Isaaco Angelo, lib. I sec. 5), ed I. Bekker, *Corpus Scriptorum Historiae Byzantinae, Vol. XXII* (Bonn: E. Weber, 1835), pp. 483-84.

[193] *Iacobi de Uitriaco Acconensis Episcopi Historia Hierosolimitana*, ed. Jacques Bongars, *Gesta Dei per Francos* (Hanover: J. Aubrius, 1611), pp. 1155-56; Sicard of Cremona, *Chronicon*, R. I. S. VII, p. 530; *Chronica Anonima*, ed. J.-L.-A. Huillard-Bréholles, *Historia Diplomatica Friderici Secundi*, I, Part. II, 890-91; *Continuation of William of Tyre*, Bk. XXIV,

was forced to raise the siege and withdraw his troops to Merkab, held by the Knights Hospitallers, where the process was repeated. At Laodicea the inhabitants were not disposed to fight anybody, but Margarit interceded on their behalf with Saladin, offering to help him against the neighboring kingdoms, and finally threatening him with the third crusade, according to an eyewitness.[194] In addition to bringing what help he could to the cities besieged by Saladin's armies he swept the eastern Mediterranean clear of Moslem corsairs[195] and captured the islands of Scarpanto, Cefalonia, and Zanta.[196] It was even thought that he had captured Jaffa and Djibalah, killing 5,000 Turks and capturing eight emirs, according to the letter sent to Phillip Augustus by his ambassadors at the Court of Byzantium.[197]

After the death of William II and the accession of Tancred,[198] Margarit was living in Messina when Richard the Lion-heart came to the town with his army. Margarit was one of the influential people who went to conduct him to Tancred. A few days later a riot broke out between the English and the Sicilians. Margarit was a member of the committee set up to restore order, but during negotiations Richard left in a rage and captured the town, leaving it to be pillaged by his troops. Margarit escaped by night with his family and moveable possessions,[199] leaving his house to be seized

---

chaps. 5, 7, 11 in *Recueil des historiens des croisades*: *Historiens occidentaux* (Paris: Académie des Inscriptions et Belles-Lettres, 1859), II, 114, 115, 119-21. The *Continuation* refers to a "Vert chevalier" who had an interview with Saladin at Tripoli, probably confusing the incident with Margarit's interview with Saladin at Laodicea.

[194] Imad ad-Din, in Abu Shama's *Book of the Two Gardens*: *Recueil des historiens des croisades*: *Historiens orientaux*, IV, 362-63. Imad ad-Din, whose testimony was probably biased (Michele Amari, *Storia dei Musulmani di Sicilia* [2d. ed. rev.; Catania: Romeo Prampolini, 1939], pp. 537-38) says that Margarit's attitude was humble and that his presence did more harm than good to the defenders of the town since he, like they, was short of provisions.

[195] Bongars, p. 1156.

[196] *Gesta Regis Henrici Secundi*, ed. W. Stubbs, R. B. M. A. S. XLIX, Part II, 54 and 199.

[197] Ralph de Diceto, *Opera Historica*, ed. W. Stubbs, R. B. M. A. S. LXVIII, II, 58-59; *Gesta Regis Henrici Secundi*, p. 51.

[198] Margarit was made Count of Malta shortly after Tancred's accession, according to C. A. Garufi, "Margarito di Brindisi conte di Malta," *Miscellanea di archeologia, storia e filologia dedicata al professore Antonio Salinas* (Palermo: 1907), p. 277.

[199] *Gesta Regis Henrici Secundi*, p. 138.

by the English king. After peace was restored between Richard and Tancred, Richard gave Margarit's house back to him.[200]

In 1191 the newly-crowned emperor, Henry VI, aided by the Pisans and Genoese, attacked the kingdom of Sicily and laid siege to Naples. Under the command of Richard d'Acerra the Norman garrison maintained a steadfast defense assisted by the Sicilian command of the sea;[201] presumably the Sicilian navy was commanded by Margarit. A miniature shows some of the garrison on board a ship firing arrows at a group of German knights galloping along the shore.[202] Because of sickness, bad sanitation, desertion, and the resistance offered by the garrison, the position of the besiegers grew worse until, when Henry VI himself fell ill, the siege was raised. The Pisan fleet of thirty-three vessels, which had been blockaded by Margarit in Castellamare, fled under cover of night, missing the Genoese fleet which had just arrived. The Genoese, on learning of the emperor's withdrawal, "dolentes ad mortem," went to Ischia and thence to Palmarola and Montecercelli where they encountered Margarit with a force of seventy-two galleys, two "sagettes" and two "scuriates." Challenged by Margarit, the Genoese fleet of twenty-two ships prepared for battle, but Margarit turned his back and went to Ischia. The Genoese sailed to Civita Vecchia and thence to San Germano where they were authorized by Henry VI to return home.[203] While the chronicler states that Margarit ran away ("dedit terga") on meeting the Genoese fleet, such an action is scarcely credible in an admiral until then so bold, and from whom the Pisans, if not the Genoese, had recently fled. It seems more likely that it was the Genoese who broke off the engagement, finding themselves heavily outnumbered, and that an indecisive naval battle was converted into a moral victory by a biased chronicler.

During the siege of Naples, Henry VI had sent Empress Constance to Salerno, which had gone over to his side. When the siege was raised and Henry fell ill the rumor of his death spread in

---

[200] Diceto, p. 86; Roger of Hoveden, *Chronica*, ed. W. Stubbs, *R. B. M. A. S.* LI, Part II, 66; *Gesta Regis Henrici Secundi*, p. 128.

[201] Ferdinand Chalandon, *Histoire de la domination normande en Italie et en Sicile* (2 vols.; Paris: A. Picard, 1907), II, 443-57.

[202] The miniature, found in a MS. of Peter d'Eboli (*Carmen de Rebus Siculis*) is described by Chalandon, II, 455, n. 1.

[203] Caffari, *Continuatorium Annales Genuenses, R. I. S.* VI, 365.

Salerno. A crowd surrounded the palace of Terracina where Constance was staying and made her prisoner. [204] She was sent to Tancred at Messina, conducted there by Margarit. [205]

With the death of Tancred in 1194 and the inability of Queen Sibyl to handle affairs of state, Henry VI saw a new opportunity to make an attempt on the Sicilian kingdom. The possessions on the mainland fell without a struggle. Markward of Anweiler, commanding the Pisan, Genoese, and English fleets, undertook the conquest of the island itself with conspicuous success. Sibyl took refuge in Palermo, whose harbor castle was under the direction of Margarit [206] and where she could hope to make some resistance. On the approach of Henry however, the inhabitants of Palermo surrendered the town to him, whereupon Sibyl fled. Since there was no point in resisting any further, Margarit handed over the castle to Henry. Henry rewarded Margarit by making him Duke of Durazzo and Prince of Tarrento, and gave him the princedom of the sea. [207] The honors thus given were no more than an illusion, however, for four days after his coronation on Christmas day, Henry arrested the royal family and a numer of the principal nobles, among whom was Margarit. They were sent to Germany and imprisoned. [208] After the revolts of 1196 and 1197, Henry made sure that the Sicilian leaders would not threaten his position even in prison. Margarit was blinded and castrated. [209]

What became of Margarit during the next three years is not known. In 1200, he came to Paris with a scheme in which he pro-

---

[204] Chalandon, pp. 457-58.

[205] Sicard of Cremona, p. 615; Ptolemy of Lucca, *Historia Ecclesiastica, R. I. S. XI,* col. 1275. At this time Margarit was "victoriae regii stolii admiratus," according to a document of 1192 in the Archivos de la Cava, L 35 (quoted by Chalandon, II, 416, n. 4).

[206] Chalandon, II, 485.

[207] Roger of Hoveden, *Opera historica,* III, 269. It is not clear if the "principatum maris" was a purely honorific title or carried some authority with it; Markward of Anweiler was Admiral of Henry's combined fleet, but the Pisan, Genoese, and English sections were each commanded separately (Chalandon, II, 480). It is likely that the Sicilian fleet remained under the personal command of Margarit.

[208] Ptolemy of Lucca, Vol. XI, col. 1117. The information concerning Margarit is derived from a miniature in the MS. of Peter of Eboli (Chalandon, II, 487, and n. 5). Roger of Hoveden, however, places the capture of Margarit in 1197 (*Opera historica,* IV, 27).

[209] Roger of Hoveden, *Opera historica,* IV, 27.

posed to make Phillip Augustus Holy Roman Emperor, or Emperor of Byzantium, whichever he chose. The fact that Phillip Augustus consented to such a plan indicates that, mutilated though he was, Margarit still had much power and influence. With the consent of the king of France, Margarit raised supplies of horses, arms, wagons, and provisions, and sent word to the ports under his control that all galleys should converge on his headquarters at Brindisi. The plan was never put into effect, for, preceding Phillip to Rome, Margarit was there assassinated by a servant whom he had mistreated. [210]

In all the sources consulted, no mention has been found of the low birth of Margarit. Ptolemy of Lucca, however, refers to him as "de genere Regio Siculorum." [211] It is possible that Raimon Vidal may have been mistaken, confusing Margarit with Maione, his predecessor as admiral of the Sicilian fleet. Both held the same title, both served under William II, and the vague similarity of names may have also contributed to a confusion. Maione's father had sold oil at Bari, a fact which was known, and he was despised for it. [212] The evidence of Raimon Vidal himself, however, seems preferable to that of Ptolemy of Lucca; Raimon Vidal lived closer to the event, while Ptolemy, living long after, merely collected legendary tradition. For these reasons his opinion is discounted by Garufi. [213] Furthermore, the ceaseless warfare waged by the feudal nobility on land, harmful though it was in its effects, rarely if ever earned for the nobles the epithet of "routier" in contemporary chronicles; the name of "pirate," so freely bestowed on Margarit by the chroniclers, may therefore be taken as an indication that he was of low birth.

Testimonies to his reputation show contempt, fear, and admiration. Sicard of Cremona [214] refers to him as "quidam pirata" and Nicetas Choniates as "a very powerful pirate," [215] while Roger of

---

[210] *Ibid.*, p. 121.
[211] Ptolemy of Lucca, Vol. XI, col. 1275.
[212] Hugh Falcand, *Historia Sicula*, R. I. S., VII, p. 266: "... cujus pater oleum Bari vendere consueverat (sic enim dicebatur)." It is of interest to note that Hugh Falcand was in a position exactly contrary to that of Raimon Vidal on the subject of heredity: "Nam de semine tyranni nihil unquam nisi tyrannicum procreari, impioque patre genitos paternae quoque futuros impietatis haeredos."
[213] Garufi, p. 273.
[214] Sicard of Cremona, p. 615.
[215] Choniates, p. 484: πειρατῶν κράτιστος

Hoveden calls him "prince of pirates."[216] Ptolemy of Lucca refers to him as "Margaritus Epirotarum rex" and "regem Epirotarum sive Achaiae," quite erroneously. He has misread his source, which must have been "piratarum rex," and included the "sive Achaiae" as his own explanation.[217] A more flattering opinion is held by Marino Sanudo, who calls him a "powerful pirate,"[218] and in the *Historia Hierosolimitana* he is called "vir admodum strenuus," "rex maris," and "alter Neptunus."[219] But the greatest tribute to him of all was ascribed to an enemy; at Tripoli Saladin is reported to have said: "Iste sunt galee illius qui est leo marinus et nulla contra eum resistere potest."[220]

Mataplana (vs. 639)

The site of the castle of Mataplana today reveals no more than a few ruins, rear to which is the old sixteenth century farm of Mataplana, and the chapel of Sant Joan de Mataplana. The deed by which Elvira de Pallars endowed the chapel in 1356 reads: "juxta castrum nostrum de Mataplana." The chapel itself is near Gombreny, which in turn is some ten kilometers northwest of Ripoll.[221]

Maurelhas (vs. 840)

Located in the canton of Ceret, Pyrénées-Orientales. The modern form of the name is Maurellàs (Fr. Maureillas). Examples of the name collected by P. Aebischer are: 982 "in Maurelianos" (Archives cap. d'Urgell, Cartulari f. 148 v, d. 442); 1395 "castell de Maurellans (Alart, DGH. 46); 1435 "Maurilianis" (Alart, DGH. 86).[222] An En B*ernat* de Maurelans was a scribe in the "escrivania" of Perpinyà, documented 1310.[223] The form "Maurelans" is noted twice

---

[216] Roger of Hoveden, *Opera historica,* III, 161.
[217] Ptolemy of Lucca, Vol. XI, cols. 1117 and 1275.
[218] Bongars, II, 194.
[219] *Ibid.,* p. 1155.
[220] *Chronica Anonima,* I, 891.
[221] Juan Serra Vilaró, *Baronies de Pinos i Mataplana,* I, 309.
[222] Paul Aebischer, *Études de toponymie catalane* (Barcelona: Imprenta Elzeviriana, 1926), pp. 107-08.
[223] Pierre Vidal, "Documents sur la langue catalane," *Revue des langues romanes,* Second Series, II (1876), 67.

in 1316, in a list of towns in Rosselló to be taxed,[224] and again in 1317.[225]

It is highly doubtful that the Raimundo de Maureia mentioned in a lawsuit with the Abbott of S. Joan was connected with the town since the final -n would still be preserved; Moreia is more likely here to correspond to the hamlet of Morea in Pallars jussà.

En Mercadier (vs. 580)

He and Margarit are used by Raimon Vidal as examples of men who were noble by their deeds but not by birth.

Mercadier, a famous leader of "routiers," was a professional soldier who spent most of his time in the service of Richard the Lion-heart, whose friend and companion he became, fighting with him in the long wars against Phillip Augustus of France.

In 1183 he laid waste the land of Archambaut de Comborne around Limoges, returning to Périgord after the expedition. Ten days later the "routiers" under Mercadier, Constantin de Born (brother of Bertran de Born) and Radulf de Castelnau besieged the castle of Pompadour, destroyed the churches of Loberissac, Baissac, and Corsona, and held their captives to ransom.[226] At the end of February in the following year Mercadier sacked the town of Issoudun in Berry; he captured the castle, manned it with his troops, and held it for Richard.[227]

During the time when Richard was on crusade he sent letters of credit dated August 3, 1191, on Marcadier's behalf to a Pisan merchant. It is probable therefore that Mercadier accompanied his sovereign to Palestine.[228] On Richard's return from captivity Mercadier again assisted him against Phillip.

---

[224] Bofarull, *Colección*, XII (Census of Pere III, el Cerimoniós, 1359), p. 115.

[225] Pierre Vidal, *Revue des langues romanes*, 4th Series, I, 61 and 67.

[226] Gaufredi Prioris Vosiensis, *Pars Altera Chronici Lemovicensis, Recueil*, XVIII, p. 220.

[227] *Les Gestes de Philippe-Auguste* (*Extraits des chroniques de St. Denis*), *Recueil*, XVII, p. 382; Rigordus, *De Gestis Philippi Augusti, Francorum Regis*, *Recueil* XVII, p. 42; Guillelmus Armoricus, *De Gestis Philippi Augusti*, *Recueil* XVII, p. 72; Gaufredi Prioris Vosiensis, p. 220.

[228] M. Powicke, *The Loss of Normandy, 1189-1204* 2nd ed. rev. (Manchester: Manchester University Press, 1961), p. 232, n. 138.

In 1194, Richard routed the French army near Vendôme, capturing many of Phillip's men, his treasury, and royal chapel. Phillip himself was forced to flee, but turned aside from the high road to hear mass. Richard, "breathing threats," missed the turning and rode far in the wrong direction until his horse foundered, when Mercadier lent him another. Not finding Phillip, Richard returned to Vendôme. [229]

In 1198, a truce was established between Richard and Phillip. As a result Richard dispersed his forces. Phillip found the chance too good to miss, and invaded Normandy at the head of a large army. On receiving Richard's appeal for help, Mercadier at once came with his "routiers" and heavily defeated Phillip near Gisors. In full flight, the French knights were galloping over the bridge of Gisors when it broke. About twenty were drowned by the weight of their armor, and Phillip himself was nearly lost. [230] Richard then laid waste the Vexin with his mercenaries and destroyed the castle of Courcelles. [231]

---

[229] Roger of Hoveden, *Chronica*, LI, Part II, 256; Walter of Coventry, *Memoriale, R. B. M. A. S.* LVIII, Part II, p. 65.

[230] Roger of Hoveden, *Chronica*, LI, Part II, 256; Walter of Coventry, Part II, p. 127. Richard related the incident in a letter in which he mentions that Mercadier captured thirty knights. The letter is given by Roger of Hoveden, *Annalium Parte Posteriori, Recueil* XVII, p. 589. Peter of Langtoft recounted the incident in his versified *Chronicle, R. B. M. A. S.* XLVII, Part II, p. 120:

> " 'Or sus, sire ray de Fraunce!' Markadé ly dist,
> 'tes brays sunt moyllez, tu honys tun habyt ...
> Le ray Richard comaunde ke Phelippe sayt salvez.
> Mathy de Mount Moryz, baroun renomez,
> Sir Alayn de Ruscy, sur Fulke de Griffez
> of lur chevalerye, sunt pris et menez;
> Markady prist XX de tuz les melz vanez.
> Or est le ray Richard de Angeon returnez;
> en garde a Markadé les prisouns sunt lyverez."

The chronicle of Peter of Langtoft was translated into English by Robert of Brunne. The additional details that he gives are not necessarily accurate, but show that Mercadier's reputation extended into another language, country, and period:

> "A knyght, a bourdour, kyng Richard hade,
> a doughty man in stoure, his name was Markade.
> He sauh kyng philip als he lay in the water,
> 'Sir kyng, rise up and skip, for thou hast wette thy hater.
> Thou fisshes not worthe a leke, rise up and go thy ways,
> for thou hast wette thy breke, schent is thy hernays.' "

[231] Rigordus, *Recueil* XVII, 42.

It must have been after this incident that a bridge was named in Mercadier's honor, "le pont Makadé," which cost £25 to build, according to the accounts of Chateau Gaillard. [232]

In May occurred Mercadier's most famous exploit. While Richard was engaged in Normandy, Mercadier and John Lackland raided the countryside around Beauvais. The Bishop of Beauvais, Philippe de Dreux, rode out against them accompanied by his deacon and William de Merlou and his son, and many knights and infantry. The Bishop, who was an enemy of Richard's and was not known for saintliness, was captured with most of his knights and brought in triumph to Richard. On presenting his prisoners Mercadier said: "Pris vus ai le cantathur e le respondethur." [233] Richard ordered them to be imprisoned as they were, in their armor. There followed long negotiations by the Pope on their behalf, but they were not released until after Richard's death.

On the death of Alan de Dinan, Richard sent Mercadier into Brittany with a large army where, according to the chronicler, "there was a great war and the death of many men." [234]

In the same year (1198) Baldwin, Count of Flanders, tried to recapture the places taken from him by Phillip. Richard aided him by sending Mercadier with his troops, who ravaged the land around Abbeville and plundered the French merchants who had come to the fair. On returning to Normandy, Mercadier attacked the enemies of Richard there, pillaging and holding prisoners to ransom. [235]

In 1199 a five-year truce was signed by Richard and Phillip, but was declared void by Richard after Phillip had fortified some castles

---

[232] Powicke, p. 206.
[233] Matthew Paris, *Historia Anglorum*, R. B. M. A. S. XLIV, Part II, p. 59. According to Matthew of Westminster, *Flores Historiarum*, R. B. M. A. S. XCV, Part. II, p. 115, he said: "Sus, Richard, sus, jo te ai mené le cantatur de Balvais." The capture is reported by Roger of Hoveden, *Chronica*, Part IV, p. 16; Walter of Coventry, Part II, p. 104; Roger of Wendover, *The Flowers of History*, R. B. M. A. S. LXXXIV, Part I, p. 245; Ralph de Diceto, *Ymagines Historiarum*, R. B. M. A. S. LXVIII, p. 152; Bartholomew Cotton, *Historia Anglicana*, R. B. M. A. S. XVI, p. 89; Guillelmus Armoricus, *Philippidos, Recueil* XVII, Liber V, vs. 334, p. 178; Guillelmus Armoricus, *De Gestis Philippi Augusti*, XVII, 72; *Ex Chronico Anonymi Laudunensis Canonici, Recueil* XVIII, pp. 710-711; *Les Gestes de Philippe-Auguste (Extraits des chroniqueurs de St. Denis*, XVII, 382.
[234] *Ex Breve Chronica Abbatiae Panispontis, Recueil* XVIII, p. 332.
[235] Roger of Hoveden, *Annalium Pars Posterior*, p. 590.

in contravention of the truce, and when four of his knights laid an ambush for Mercadier. [236]

Besieging the castle of Châlus in April, Richard and Mercadier were making the rounds of the fortifications one evening when Richard was struck in the shoulder by a bolt from a crossbow. Under cover of darkness the king returned to his tent where Mercadier's own physician tended the wound. He could draw out the shaft but not the head, which he had to remove in an operation from which Richard never recovered. When the castle was captured, the crossbowman who had shot the arrow was brought to Richard's tent. Richard forgave him and ordered him to be set free, but Mercadier had him seized again and flayed alive after Richard's death. [237]

The problem of the succession to the throne caused a division in the Plantagenet empire. An uprising in Anjou was quelled by Mercadier and Eleanor of Acquitaine, Richard's mother. [238]

In Gascony the population fled the fields to take refuge in the walled towns. Archbishop Hélie of Bordeaux invited Mercadier and his troops into the country and declared that he would maintain peace with their help. Thus reassured, the Gascons returned to their homes and their fields; but then the "routiers" began to ride, pillaging as they went, and returning to the castle of the Archbishop's nephew which they used as a base of operations. [239]

Shortly thereafter a marriage was arranged between Louis, Phillip's son, and Blanche of Castile. Eleanor of Acquitaine went to accompany her granddaughter on her journey across France, and Mercadier rode to meet them. At Bordeaux, where the party had stopped to celebrate Easter, Mercadier was assassinated by a servant of Brandin, seneschal of Gascony. [240]

---

[236] Roger of Hoveden, *Chronica*, Part. IV, p. 80; Walter of Coventry, Part II, p. 139.

[237] Roger of Hoveden, *Chronica*, Part. IV, pp. 82-83; Walter of Coventry, Part II, p. 142.

[238] Roger of Hoveden, *Chronica*, Part IV, p. 88; Walter of Coventry, Part II, p. 144; Roger of Wendover, p. 286; Matthew Paris, *Chronica Major*, R. B. M. A. S. LVII, Part II, p. 454.

[239] Innocent III, *Epistolae, Recueil* XIX, pp. 448-450.

[240] Roger of Hoveden, *Chronica*, Part. IV, p. 114; Walter of Coventry, Part II, p. 159; *Chronique de St. Martial*, ed. Henri Duplès-Agier (Paris: Firmin-Didot, 1874), p. 67; Ralph of Coggeshale, *Ex Chronico Anglicano, Recueil* XVIII, p. 85. Brandin was a "routier" in the service of John Lackland who made him a seneschal.

If the chroniclers were the only source of information, our knowledge of Mercadier's character would go no further than what we know of other "routiers," and the concept of his nobility would be limited to the honorific particle "En" given to him by Raimon Vidal. There is, however, a deed dated 1194 in which Mercadier grants to the monks of Cedouin a tithe of the fishing industry that he had set up near his castle of Bigoroque in the Dordogne. The deed shows that the castle, which had belonged to Ademar de Bainac, dead without issue, had been given to Mercadier by Richard as a gesture of thanks for his services. It shows too that although Mercadier did not receive a title of nobility (he describes himself as "famulus" of Richard where ordinarily titles of nobility would be given), he became a part of the landed society, with the rights and privileges which the possession of land conveyed. It is of interest too that Mercadier, whose business was war, should have accepted the responsibilities of his position as a landowner and developed the fishing industry on his estate, going to some pains to do so. The most important aspects of this document, however, are the insights it affords into his relationship with Richard, and his own character. Of the friendship between himself and the king he says:

> ...I, Mercadier, servant of Richard, illustrious and glorious king of England, duke of Normandy and Aquitaine, count of Anjou and Poitou, having served in the camp of my lord king with as much faithfulness as effort, having always conformed to his will and hastened to fulfill his commands, I thereby became accepted by him and dear to him, and I was commander of his army...

The words are those of a man whose chief pride lay in his loyal service and which, as it were, takes the place of the social rank which he did not have.[241]

---

[241] Part of the deed is given in *Recueil* XVIII, 710-711, n. *e*: "Notum sit tam praesentibus quam futuris, quod ego Merchaderius, domini Richardi illustris et gloriosi Regis Angliae, Ducis Normanniae et Aquitaniae, Comitis Andegavorum et Pictavinensium, famulus, cum in castris ejusdem domini Regis tam fideliter quam strenue militarem, et a voluntate illius non discordarer et quae praecipiebat implendo properarem, et ob hoc tanto Regis acceptus eram et carus, et eram dux exercitus ejus...."

Miquel de Luesia (vs. 816)

One of the nobility of Aragon, Miquel de Luesia inherited the title and possessions of Luesia, near Egea de los Caballeros, Saragossa province,[242] in 1192.[243] He was a member of Alfons' court[244] but of only minor influence since his name appears toward the end of the list of witnesses in documents that he signed. In the court of Pere, his position was still a minor one.[245] From June, 1199 to August, 1207, his name does not appear. During this period however he increased in authority and reputation, for in March, 1211, at Lleida his signature is second after those of the interested parties, and in front of Blasco Romeu, Ramon Folc, Ramon de Montcada, R. de Cervera, and Galseran de Pinos.[246] By October of the same year he had become majordomo of Aragon.[247] During most of 1212 he was continually with the royal court. He commanded an army corps at the battle of Las Navas de Tolosa,[248] afterwards continuing his work of administration until the following year, when he accompanied Pere into Provence and died at the battle of Muret defending the person of the king.[249]

He was probably a patron of Peire Vidal, for he is mentioned as one of the knights who visited the poet with Alfons,[250] and Peire Vidal addressed a poem to him:

> En Luzi' a tal Miquel
> que.m val mais que cel del cel.[251]

---

[242] Identified by Milá y Fontanals, *De los trovadores*, p. 340, n. 9, correcting p. 126 (Luciá).

[243] In a document of December, 1191, is found "Eximenus de Lusia (regnante) in Lusia." Caruana, "Itinerario," p. 199. Miquel de Luesia first appears in 1190, signing a document in the *Cartulari de Poblet*, No. 30, 1, 14.

[244] *LFM* I, 434, No. 413 (the pact between Pons de Cabrera and Alfons).

[245] *Ibid.*, I, 31, No. 21 (September, 1192); p. 257, No. 243 (September, 1192); p. 439, No. 416 (June, 1199); II, 287, No. 801 (February, 1197).

[246] Baudon de Mony, II, 68.

[247] Miret i Sans, "Itinerari de Pedro II," p. 28.

[248] He is mentioned as one of the "nobles y grandes omes de Aragón" by Alfonso X (*Primera crónica general de España*, II, 690b).

[249] *Gesta Comitum Barcinonensium*, p. 54; Jaume I, I, 27. His presence at the council of war just before the battle is mentioned in Martin-Chabot, II, 25.

[250] Boutière and Schutz, p. 368; Favati, p. 276.

[251] Peire Vidal, *Liriche* (ed. Avalle), II, 316, vss. 77-78 of "Be.m pac d'ivern e d'estiu." Avalle dates the poem at 1174-80 with the "tornada"

Monelhs (vs. 840)

Today known as Monells, in Gerona province.

En el siglo XII tuvieron tanta importancia sus mercaderes, que el rey don Jaime ordenó en 1234 que la medida de granos de Monells fuese tenido como patrón en todo el obispado de Gerona. El ser entonces Monells población libre y en la cual no se detenía a nadie, influyó mucho para que concurrieran a sus ferias y mercados gran cantidad de mercaderes. [252]

The town is not mentioned in the census of Pere el Cerimoniós, which is understandable since the census was for taxation purposes, and as a free town Monells would not be taxed. Until 1226 at least, however, the revenues from the market were the property of the Bishop of Gerona, as can be seen from a document of that year. [253]

Berenger, Bernard, and Raimon de Mulnellis (Munillis, Mulneis, Molnels, Molnells) lived in the latter half of the twelfth century. The relationship between the three cannot be established with certainty; perhaps they were brothers. The signatures of Berenguer and Raimon are found on the same documents, [254] and of Bernard and Raimon on others. [255] There are documents with the signature of one alone. [256]

Pinos (vs. 799)

See *Abril issia*, vs. 799, n.

---

preceding that dedicated to Miquel de Luesia added in 1184 (p. 309). The poem thus is the earliest reference to Miquel that we possess.

[252] *Diccionario Geográfico de España*, Vol. XII (1960).

[253] Monsalvatje y Fossas, *Colección deplomática del condado de Besalú*, II, 104-106.

[254] Bofarull, *Colección*, IV, 291. No. 116, June 1160 (reprinted in *LFM* I, 274, No. 254); Bofarull, *Colección*, IV, 297 No. 119 July, 1160.

[255] *Ibid.*, IV, 302, No. 121, September, 1160; IV, 359, No. 149 (no date).

[256] Berenger: *ibid.*, IV, 310, No. 123, July 17, 1161 (reprinted in *LFM*, I, 353, No. 330). Bernard: Bofarull, *Colección*, IV, 308, No. 122, February 1161. Raimon: *LFM* II, 290, No. 804, November 19, 1159; I, 286, No. 261; p. 287, No. 262, both on October 13, 1178; Villanueva, V, 268, 271.

Pons de Cervera (vs. 837)

In 1148 Pons de Cervera carried off Almodis, the sister of Raimon Berenguer IV. In reparation he made over to Raimon Berenguer the family castle of Castellfullit de Riubregós.[257] He is probably the same as the Pons de Cervera who, seven years later, witnessed a document at Poblet with his brother Raimon.[258] A Guilhem de Cervera was the son of one of the two, and in turn was father to Raimon, Guilhem, and Pons. Guilhem, Raimon and Guilhem "junior" appear in a document of December, 1178, while Guilhem and his son Raimon on January 1st, 1179, reached an agreement with Alfons concerning Lleida, Candasnos, Jabut and Cervera.[259] The younger Guilhem fought at Muret, according to Boades (p. 313.) Pons appears for the first time in company with his brother in 1180.[260] The greatest mention of Pons de Cervera is in 1187, when he was arbiter in a dispute between Ramon, Abbott of Amer, and Mirón, Lord of Hostoles.[261]

Pons de Vernet (vs. 793)

Mention of Pons de Vernet is first made in 1197 at Perpignan, where Pere I gave him and others the rights to some property.[262] In 1200 Pons de Vernet gave the town of Ortolanes to Pere I,

---

[257] *LFM* I, 195-96, Nos. 184, 185. The document itself is missing.
[258] *Cartulari de Poblet*, No. 227.
[259] Caruana, "Itinerario," pp. 111-112.
[260] *Cartulari de Poblet*, No. 233.
[261] Monsalvatje y Fossas, *Condado de Besalú*, p. 40. Interim mention is found in the *LlBSC* for 1181 (No. 246) and in the *LFM*, II, 137-38 (Nos. 630, 631), 1183. Other members of the family were Pere de Cervera (Miret i Sans, *Itinerari de Jaume* I, p. 62), and Berenguer de Cervera (*ibid.*).
[262] *LFM*, II, 286-87. It is impossible to determine who his parents were from the evidence available. A "Poncius de Verneto" is named as arbiter in a dispute in 1140 (*ibid.*, II, 241-242); Raimon de Vernet gave the tower of Vernet to the Templars in 1175 (Miret i Sans, "Guerau de Cabrera," *Estudis universitaris catalans*, IV, 308), while "Ermengaud de Vernetto" is found in a document of 1188 (Baudon de Mony, II, 35. Perhaps Poncius de Verneto was the grandfather and Raimon de Vernet the father. Both names occur again in the history of the family. A "Pere de Vernet" fought at Muret (Bernat Boades, p. 313).

receiving it again as a fief.[263] In 1211 he witnessed a document in Roselló.[264]

The name Pons de Vernet occurs again in Desclot's chronicle[265] as a member of Nunyo Sanç's contingent for the conquest of Majorca. In the same list figures the name of Arnau de Vernet. In a document dated June 7, 1249, signed at San Cugat, the name Raimon de Vernet appears; he was the son of Arnau.[266] The name of Pons, together with Raimon and Arnau, appears on another document of the same day. After 1249, the signature of Pons is no longer found; he probably died thereafter. That of Arnau occurs twice, in 1260 at Lleida and 1264 at Barcelona, in which he is described as a "militar."[267] Conjecture on such slender evidence is hazardous, but the best explanation seems to be that Pons was the elder brother of Arnau (Desclot mentions his name first), and that he died before his brother, after 1249. It is not improbable therefore that the Pons de Vernet of the period 1197-1211 and he of the period 1229-1249 are one and the same.

Pons Hug II and Hug IV d'Empuries (vs. 824)

The biographies by Francisco Monsalvatje y Fossas[268] make no claim to being complete. With a similar reservation some additional facts can be presented.

Pons Hug II (governed from 1173 to 1200) was at Blomac, Carcassès, in June 1188, and at Gerona in August of the same year.[269] In 1191-2 he ran the risk of being dragged into the conflict between Arnau de Castellbo and Alfons, according to the enigmatic sixth stanza of Guilhem de Berguedan's "sirventes" "Be.m volria q'om saupes dir."[270] In 1194 he was at Lleida, according to a document of the *"Llibre Blanch" de Santas Creus.*[271]

---

[263] *LFM*, II, 285.
[264] Miret i Sans, "Itinerari de Pere I," p. 19.
[265] Desclot, IV, 92.
[266] "Ego Arnaldus de Verneto dono et concedo tibi Raimundo de Verneto, filio meo...."
[267] Miret i Sans, *Itinerari de Jaume I*, pp. 305, 362.
[268] Monsalvatje y Fossas, *Los Condes de Ampurias vindicados*, pp. 98-110.
[269] Miret i Sans, *Itinerari de Alfonso I, Boletín de la Real Academia de Buenas Letras* (1904), p. 446.
[270] Martín de Riquer, *El trovador Guilhem de Berguedan y las luchas feudales de su tiempo* (Castellón: 1953), pp. 29-30.
[271] *LIBSC*, No. 372, p. 373.

Hug IV was at the battles of Las Navas de Tolosa [272] and Muret, [273] but it his part in the expedition to Majorca that has attracted the attention of historians. Both Desclot and the author of the chronicle of Jaume I show his influence in recommending the project to the Catalan nobility. According to the chronicler of Jaume I he said:

> "Aço.us dire yo ans de la resposta que.us deuen fer los vostres nobles: si homens del mon an mala fama, nos si la havem bona, ço es, que la soliem haver, e vos sots vengut entre nos con nostre senyor natural; e es mester que vos fassats tals obres ab nostra aiuda, que.l pretz que havem perdut que.l cobram; e en esta manera lo cobravem si vos prenets .l. regne de sarrains ab aiuda de nos, que sia dins mar; e tota la mala fama que nos havem tolrem de nos, e sera.l meylor feyt que crestians faessen .C. anys ha. E val mes que nos muyrem e que cobrem lo bon prets que soliem haver e la bonea que solia haver nostre linyatge e nos, que viure en esta mala fama en que son. Per que.us dic que en totes guises del mon, per mon conseyl se faria aquest feyt." E a aquesta paraula que.l comte d'Ampuries ach dita, s'acordaren tuyt. [274]

Similar in its bold tone and in the reference to past glory is the speech that Desclot attributes to him:

> Senyor en rey: so que vós avets comensat ne sembla gens que de vos sia mogut, segons los dies que vós avets, mas fèts atreyt al bon linyatge d'on vós sóts exit. Per què yo, sènyer, ne són molt alegre cor tan bé comensats. E seguir-vos he ab .LXXX. cavalers e ab .XX. balesters a caval e ab .M. sirvents; e donar-lur he bona soa e fer-lur he lur obs tro que dessà siam tornats. [275]

Desclot has apparently combined into one single speech what Hug d'Empuries may have said on two different occasions, for the offer of specific troops was made on the following day according to

---

[272] Alfonso X, II, 690 b.
[273] Bernat Boades, p. 313.
[274] Jaume I, I, 124, 126.
[275] Desclot, II, 77.

the chronicle of Jaume I,[276] in which he promised sixty knights. A more reliable source is two documents in the Archives of Aragon listing the forces contributed by the Catalan nobility according to which Hug d'Empuries contributed seventy knights, and servants.[277]

At the siege of Majorca the Count of Empuries and Nunyo Sanç, with 200 knights and 2,000 infantry, routed 2,000 Saracens and captured their baggage.[278] As the siege was prolonged, Hug IV had an underground chamber dug, large enough for himself and 200 knights, and from there dug a mine under the walls of the town, as a result of which a large section of the wall gave way.[279] He dug two other mines, one on the western side of the town which undermined the wall and tower (December, 1229).[280]

The following Easter, Guillem de Montcada fell ill and died, and was quickly followed by several other members of the family. Hug d'Empuries took this for an evil omen and he too died.[281]

The Count and Countess of Provence (vs. 626)

Raimon Berenguer V (1209-1245) and Beatrice. For his relationships with the troubadours see, *inter alia*, I. Cluzel, "Princes et troubadours," *Boletín de la Real Academia de Buenas Letras*, XXVII (1957), 335-48.

---

[276] "Seyor, aquest feyt que vos volets començar no.1 poria hom sobreloar, car el mostra sa bonea que ha, car be ne pot esdevenir. E promet vos que.y hire ab LX cavalers armats. E iassia que Deus m'aja fet comte d'Ampurias, En G. de Muntcada es lo meylor hom de nostre linyatge, e.l pus noble, car el es seyor de Bearn e de Muntcada, que te per vos, e de Castel Viy, que es son alou; e atorch les paraules que el ha dites. E en aquel compte dels .CCCC. cavalers met aquels .LX. meus, car tot nostre linyatge los vos hi levaria; e d'aquela part que promesa es a el e als altres, que donets a mi per los homens de caval e de peu que jo.y menare, car tots los cavalers que nos ni.ls altres hi haurem tots iran ab cavals armats." (Jaume I, II, 10). (The sense is reproduced in the *Libre dels feyts d'armes*, p. 323.

[277] "S. Ugonis comitis Empuriarum septuaginta milites et servientes quos potere." The first is dated December 23, 1228, the second September 18, 1229. Both are quoted by H. Delpech, *La Bataille de Muret et la tactique de la cavalerie au XIIIe siècle* (Paris-Toulouse: Picard, 1878), pp. 143-44.

[278] Desclot, II, 113.

[279] *Ibid.*, II, 116-17; Jaume I, II, 52.

[280] Desclot, II, 123-26.

[281] "E el comte d'Ampuries, quan viu la mort d'aquestes .III. dix que tots aquels qui eran del linyatge de Muntcada hi haurien a murir, e sempre fo malalt, e no malaveja sino .VIII. dies, e a cap dels .VIII. dies el muri." (Jaume I, II, 70).

Raimon de Vilademuls (vs. 831)

First appears as a signatory to the treaty between Alfons and Raimon V, Count of Toulouse, in 1171. On March 17, 1176, he was witness to a document at Perpignan, [282] and on April 18 of the same year he witnessed the treaty between Raimon V of Toulouse and Alfons concerning the county of Provence, signed on the island of Guernica. [283] In October, 1176, he was at Celano, near Digne in Provence, October 1178 at Perpignan, and in October 1179 was at Béziers, and at Carcassonne in November. At Perpignan, March 1181, he witnessed another document, [284] and was at Carcassonne on May 14, 1188, where he was witness with his brother Berenguer, Bishop of Tarragona, to the concession in fief by Alfons of the Carcassès, Razès, Termenois, and Lauragais to Raimon Roger, Count of Foix. [285] In July, 1190, Raimon de Vilademuls was granted the castle of Pals for life by Alfons, the deed of concession being signed at Balaguer. [286] In April, 1191, he was at Montsoriu and in June, 1192, at Perpignan, where he signed three documents. [287] In 1197, he was one of the signatories to the decree of Pere I against heretics, and also signed the amnesty of 1198. In June of the same year he witnessed the pact between Pere I and Guerau de Cabrera. [288] He died in 1199.

The above record indicates an influential and powerful man who for more than twenty years accompanied the royal court as a counselor.

Raimon de Vilademuls' brother Berenguer, Bishop of Tarragona, was assassinated by Guillem Ramon de Montcada, February 16, 1194.

On his death in 1199 his estates were inherited by his only child Maria, who married Hug IV d'Empuries (q.v.). In 1226, the estate and title, with the exception of La Roca del Comte in Roselló which

---

[282] Caruana, "Itineraria," p. 89.
[283] *LFM*, II, 362-4.
[284] Caruana, "Itinerario," p. 131.
[285] Baudon de Mony, II, 35.
[286] Caruana, "Itinerario," p. 186.
[287] *Ibid.*, pp. 193, 201.
[288] F. Monsalvatje y Fossas, *Los Castillos del condado de Besalú* (Olot: Bonet, 1919), pp. 164-65.

was retained by Maria and Hug d'Empuries, passed into the possession of the house of Rocabertí.[289]
Vilademuls lies between Figueres, Besalú, and Gerona.

Raimon Galseran de Pinós (vs. 798)

The grandfather of Raimon Galseran was Galseran I de Pinós, who married Estefania,[290] and was one of the executors of the will of Raimon Berenguer III.[291] According to legend,[292] the Admiral Galseran de Pinós was captured by the king of Granada who held him and his companions for a ransom of 100,000 gold "dobles," 100 pieces of brocade, 100 white horses, 100 cows, and 100 maidens. His son Galseran II married Berengaria; their son was Raimon Galseran. The signatures of all three are found in a document of August 30, 1177.[293] The date of birth of Raimon Galseran can thus be guessed approximately as 1157.

Galseran II is documented from 1172 to 1194.[294] He was present at the signing of the treaty ending the war between Alfons and Raimon of Toulouse, which took place at Guernica between Beaucaire and Tarascon in February, 1185.[295] He was also a partisan of Guillem Ramon de Montcada, encouraging him in his quarrel with the bishop of Tarragona.[296]

---

[289] *Ibid.*
[290] Serra Vilaro, I, 93.
[291] *LFM*, I, 527.
[292] Mentioned by Francisco M. Rosell in the Introduction of his edition of the *Liber Feudorum Maior*, p. xxv, referring to Martín de Riquer, *La leyenda de Galceran de Pinós y el tributo de las cien doncellas* (Barcelona, 1944).
[293] *LlBSC*, No. 199.
[294] *Cartulari de Poblet*, p. 335, 1. 28 (June 5, 1172); Miret i Sans, *Itinerari de Alfonso I* (February, 1176 at Anglesola, June 30, 1177 at Lleida); *LlBSC* has "Galseran de Pinos" for May 2, 1173 (Nos. 162 and 163), but it may have been Galseran I; after 1177, it may be assumed that the "Galseran" was Galseran II. The dates are September 13, 1180 (No. 236), October 14, 1185 (No. 278), September 7 and 8, 1188 (Nos. 314 and 315), December 1190 (Nos. 342 and 343) and August 29, 1194 (No. 378). See also Baudon de Mony, II, 37.
[295] Miret i Sans, *Itinerari de Alfonso I*; Emile Léonard, *Catalogue des actes des comtes de Toulouse — Raymond V (1149-1194)* (Paris: Picard, 1932), p. 77, n. 112.
[296] Coll i Alentorn, p. 121, quoting Pere Tomic, *Històries e conquestes*, chap. XXXVI; also Monsalvatje y Fossas, *Condado de Besalú*, p. 164, quoting Feliu de la Pena.

During his father's lifetime Raimon Galseran appears to have omitted the "de Pinós" from his legal signature, [297] which appears again on September 6, 1188. In 1185 he is signed "filius Raimundus," omitting the "Galseran" in accordance with the practice noted by Miret i Sans; [298] in the second document his signature appears after that of his father. These, together with the references contained in the "Vidas" (see below), permit identification of "Raimon Galseran de Pinós" [299] with the "Raimon Galseran" who signed the following documents: *LFM*: 1181-82 at Huesca (I, 495, No. 466), 1183 at Vich (I, 480, No. 456), 1199 at Barcelona (I, 438, No. 416); at Bonanat in March, 1208 (Bofarull, *Colección,* VIII, 111, No. 40); in February, 1210 or 1211 he witnessed the betrothal of Jaume I and Aurembaix, daughter of Ermengau d'Urgell; [300] in 1217 he witnessed the peace treaty between Viscount Guerau de Cabrera and Jaume I (Miret i Sans, *Itinerari de Jaume I,* I, 21). Also listed in the *Itinerari de Jaume I* are the dates 1217 at Sixera (p. 23), at Lleida twice in 1218 (pp. 24, 575), at Gerona in 1222 (p. 39) and at Lleida 1223 (p. 45). The importance of these documents is that the signature in each case either immediately precedes or follows that of Uc de Mataplana. Since the baronies of Pinós and Mataplana were contiguous and both were important this can be taken as an indication that the "Raimon Galseran" who signed the documents is Raimon Galseran de Pinós.

Raimon Galseran de Pinós was one of the Catalan nobles who accompanied Alfons on his visit to Peire Vidal in 1195. [301] He was a friend of Bertran de Born, who addressed to him the "sirventes" "Quan la novela flors par e·l verjan": [302]

---

[297] *LFM*, II, 120.
[298] Miret i Sans, "Notes per la biografia del trovador Guerau de Cabrera," *Estudis universitaris catalans,* Vol. IV (1910). However, Bernat Boades simply notes "Galceran de Pinos" as being present at the battle of Muret (p. 313).
[299] Miret i Sans, "Itinerari de Pere I"; March 6, 11, 21, 1211 (3 docs.) at Lleida; October 11, 1212 at Tamarit; November 13 at Alagón, November 22 at Saragossa in the year 1212.
[300] *Ibid.*
[301] Boutière and Schutz, p. 368.
[302] Stimming, *Bertran de Born,* No. XIV, vss. 49-50, p. 92.

> Sirventes, vai a·n Raimon Gauceran
> lai a Pinos, en ma razo l'espel
> quar tan aut son siei dich e siei deman
> de lieis que te Cabrera e fo d'Urgel

The relationship between Raimon Galseran and the Countess of Urgell is explained by the "razo":[303]

> E cant el (Bertran de Born) ac fait son sirventes, el lo mandet a.n Raimon Jauzeran, qu'era del comtat d'Urgel, seingner de Pinous, valens hom e larcs e cortes e gentils, e non era nuls hom en Cataloingna que valgues lui per la persona; et entendia se en Na Marquesa, qu'era filla del comte d'Urgel e moiller d'En Girout de Cabrieras...

The "razo" is correct up to a point, for Marquesa, daughter of Ermengau VII (de Valencia), married Pons de Cabrera. Guerau de Cabrera was their son (see "Count and Countess of Urgell," "Guillem de Cardona").[304] He was the object of a sarcastic "sirventes" written by Guilhem de Berguedan, "Be·m volria q'om saupes dir."[305]

The possessions of the family were numerous and included the castles of Sant Martí, Queralt and Miralles,[306] Pinós, Gósol, Querforadat, Vallmanya, Alo, Espà and Saldes,[307] Prats, Manresana, Tàrrega, Alguaire, Albesa, Gavarrós, Bagà, Brocà, Gisclareny, Lavança, Fórnols, Josa, Cava, Ansovell, Sant Jaume, Banat, Vilanova, Urg, Gaya, Villeg, and Taltaull,[308] though not all were possesed by the family entirely, being held in conjunction with or under other feudatories, and probably not all at the same time. The list is impressive, however, and reveals a family of considerable importance.

---

[303] Boutière and Schutz, p. 137. See also I. Frank, "Pons de la Guardia, troubadour catalan du XIIe siècle," *Boletín de la Real Academia de Barcelona*, XXII (1949), 247.
[304] Monfar y Sors, pp. 438-39.
[305] ed. M. de Riquer, *El Trovador Guilhem de Berguedan*, pp. 30-31.
[306] *LFM*, II, 59, No. 544.
[307] *Ibid.*, II, 60, No. 545.
[308] Serra Vilaro, I, 100-103.

The Count of Toulouse (vs. 864)

Probably Raimon V of Toulouse (1194-1222) who married Sança, daughter of Alfons. His father Raimon married Elionor, also a daughter of Alfons. [309]

Uc de Mataplana (vs. 642)

Several members of the family lived during the period 1165-1265. Two were troubadours.

1. Uc de Mataplana, author of the "sirventes" directed against Raimon de Miraval, "D'un sirventes m'es pres talans," [310] married to Sancha. He died at the end of 1213 as a result of wounds incurred during the battle of Muret. [311]

2. His son married Jussiana. Milá y Fontanals asserts that she was Jussiana "de Basso," [312] however Miret i Sans pointed out that Jussiana de Bas married Pere de Cervera. [313] He died in 1229 at the siege of Majorca. "Ego, Hugo de Mataplana et domina Jusiana uxor mea ..." from a document dated January, 1227. [314]

3. His son Uguet, also at Majorca according to Milá y Fontanals. Either Uguet or his son was a student at the University of Bologna in 1268-69. It was probably he who exchanged "coblas" with Blacasset [315] ("En Blacasset, eu sui de nog") [316] and who was the patron of Raimon Vidal.

---

[309] Desclot, II, 6, n. 4.
[310] Andraud, pp. 139-40.
[311] Milá y Fontanals, *De los trovadores*, p. 323.
[312] *Ibid.*, p. 323.
[313] Miret i Sans, *Los Vescomtes de Bas en la illa de Sardenya*, quoted by Comas, p. 87.
[314] No. 339 (Jaime I), Archivo de la Corona de Aragón.
[315] Still alive in 1279.
[316] Milá y Fontanals, *De los trovadores*, p. 331. The evidence for Uc de Mataplana and his elder brother Pons studying at Bologna is contained in M. Sarti and M. Fattorini, *De Claris Archigymnasii Bononiensis Professoribusque a saeculo XI usque ad saeculum XIV* (2 vols.; Bologna, 1888-1896), II, 310; and in *Chartularium Studii Bononiensis* (Bologna, 1927 and 1936, Vols. VII, VIII, and X). Both are quoted by Adriana Caboni, "Le Poesie di Uc de Mataplana," *Cultura Neolatina*, I (1940), 216-221.

The Count and Countess of Urgell (vss. 802, 917)

The history of the Counts of Urgell has been written extensively enough not to need elaboration.[317] Two counts lived within the period referred to by Raimon Vidal; he may have intended either to be understood by the reader.

Ermengau VII inherited the county in 1154 and spent most of his life in the service of Fernando of Leon. He married Dolça, sister of Alfons. He died in 1184 in an ambush near Behena, returning from a successful raid into the Moorish kingdom of Valencia.[318]

Dolça was celebrated by Raimbaut d'Aurenga, who addressed a poem to her.[319] She outlived her husband by many years, and was still alive in 1212.[320]

Ermengau VIII became Count in 1184 on the death of his father. He married Elvira, Countess of Subirats, who was mentioned by Aimeric de Sarlat,[321] Aimeric de Belenoi,[322] and Aimeric de Peguilhan.[323]

---

[317] Monfar y Sors, chaps. liii-lv; Miret i Sans, *Estudis universitaris catalans*, IV (1910), 229-331.

[318] Monfar y Sors suggested that the expedition may have been pacific, and that he had been arranging an exchange of prisoners. The circumstances of his death have been discussed. The *Gesta comitum Barcinonensium* says that he was killed by Christians (p. 43); Zurita (Lib. II, cap. XL, Vol. I, Saragossa 1610 fol. 84) implies that he was killed by Moors: "... se juntaron diversas companias de ginetes y gente de guerra del reyno de Valencia y de todos los lugares circunvezinos, y fueron muertos el conde y su hermano," which is accepted by Riquer (*Z. r. Ph.* LXXI [1955], 16) though in the Latin index Zurita returned to the opinion of the *Gesta* (quoted by Monfar y Sors, p. 416).

[319] Pattison, No. XVII, p. 123. The "Vida" relating their love without ever having seen each other is erroneous, for it says that the Countess of Urgell was "Lombarda" (or a Lombard), "filla del marques de Busca." The "Vida" quotes another poem which is dedicated to the "comtessa valen, lai en Urgel."

[320] In October of that year Pere gave her the castle and town of Menargues, with income in Balaguer and Albesa, according to a document mentioned by Miret i Sans, "Itinerari de Pere I," *Butlletí de la Reial Acadèmia de Bones Lletres*, IV (107-08), 34.

[321] Aimeri de Sarlat, "Fis e leials, e senes to enguan," Raynouard, *Choix*, III, 387: "Pros comtessa, lo noms de Sobeiratz Es luenh auzitz per totz et enansatz, Per qu'ieu no.m part de vostra senhoria, Ni o farai aitan com vius estia."

[322] C. Appel, *Das Leben und die Lieder des Trobadors Peire Rogier* (Berlin: Reimer, 1882). The poem, attributed to Peire Rogier, is rejected by

One of the characteristics of the ladies mentioned by Raimon Vidal is their generosity in building and endowing religious institutions (vss. 922-23). Ermengau VII and Dolça founded the Premostratensian monastery of Santa Maria de Bellpuig, and the church of San Pere with a Benedictine monastery in the village of Pons.[324] Ermengau and Elvira endowed the church of Our Lady of Gualter, near Pons. In 1203 he, with Pere I, laid the foundation stone of the new cathedral of Lleida. Although the cathedral was not completed until 1278 the undertaking of so vast a project would have attracted considerable attention. He also built part of the choir of Poblet and was buried there in 1203.[325] As for Elvira, she continued the work of building and endowment after his death. Monfar y Sors[326] asserts that he saw in the monastery of Poblet an inscription testifying to her generosity and relating that, in 1213, she bought a farm from the monastery and then gave it back to the monks. She founded the monastery of Sant Hilari in Lleida and was buried there in 1220, bequeathing to it the proceeds from the sale of her jewels.[327]

While both Ermengau VII and Dolça, and Ermengau VIII and Elvira, appear to have been very generous at a time when generosity to the church was normal, the work of Ermengau VIII and Elvira, directed toward large and well-known institutions such as Poblet and the cathedral of Lleida, probably attracted more attention than that of Ermengau's father and mother, and that consequently Elvira may have been the "contessa de Urgelh" that Raimon Vidal had in mind.

Appel, whose edition is on pp. 83-84. "La contessa de Sobiratz" is mentioned in vs. 57.
[323] Bergert, p. 43.
[324] Monfar y Sors, p. 406.
[325] *Ibid.*, p. 430.
[326] *Ibid.*, pp. 444-45.
[327] *Ibid.*, p. 445.

ABBREVIATIONS

Bofarull, *Colección*

    Prosper Bofarull y Mascaró ed. *Colección de documentos inéditos del Archivo general de la Corona de Aragón* (Barcelona: D. J. E. Monfort, 1876).

Caruana

    J. Caruana, ed. "Itinerario de Alfonso II de Aragón," *Estudios de edad media de la corona de Aragón*, vol. VII (Saragossa: Consejo Superior de Investigaciones Científicas, 1962), pp. 72-298.

DCVB

    Antoni M. Alcover and Francesc de B. Moll, *Diccionari català-valencià-balear*. 10 vols. (Palma de Mallorca: Imp. Alcover, 1930-62).

Du Cange

    Charles Du Fresne Du Cange, *Glossarium mediae et infimae latinitatis*. 10 vols. 7th. ed. revised (Niort: L. Favre, 1883-87).

FEW

    Walter von Wartburg, *Französisches Etymologisches Wörterburch* (Tübingen: Mohr, 1948-).

Godefroy

    Frédéric E. Godefroy, *Dictionnaire de l'ancienne langue française et de tous ses dialectes du IXe au XVe siècle*. 10 vols. (Paris: Vieweg, 1880-1902. Reprint New York, 1961.)

Histoire de Languedoc

    Claude de Vic and Joseph Vaissete, *Histoire générale de Languedoc*. 15 vols. 2nd. ed. revised. (Toulouse: Privat, 1872-92).

LFM

    Francisco M. Rosell, ed., *Liber Feudorum Maior*. 2 vols. (Barcelona: Consejo Superior de Investigaciones Científicas: Sección de estudios medievales, 1945-47).

LIBSC

Federico U. Martorell, ed., "*Llibre Blanch*" *de Santas Creus* (Barcelona: Consejo Superior de Investigaciones Científicas; Sección de estudios medievales, 1947).

Mistral

Frédéric Mistral, *Lou Trésor dóu Felibrige*. 3rd. ed. 2 vols. (Aix-en-Provence: Rollet, 1968).

Levy, Pet. Dict.

Emil Levy, *Petit dictionnaire provençal-français*. 3rd. ed. (Heidelberg: Winter, 1961).

Levy, PSW

Emil Levy, *Provenzalisches Supplement-Wörterbuch*. 8 vols. (Leipzig: O. R. Reisland, 1894-1924).

Raynouard, *Choix*

François J. M. Raynouard, *Choix des poésies originales des troubadours*. 6 vols. (Paris: F. Didot, 1816-1821).

Raynouard, Lexique

François J. M. Raynouard, *Lexique roman*. 6 vols. (Paris: Sylvestre, 1836-1845. Reprinted, Heidelberg: Winter, 1953).

RBMAS

Rerum Brittanicarum Medii Aevi Scriptores, 99 vols. (London: Public Record Office, 1858-1911).

Recueil

Recueil des historiens des Gaules et de la France, 24 vols. (Paris: V. Palmé, 1840-1904).

RIS

Lodovico Antonio Muratori, *Rerum Italicarum Scriptores* 31. vols. (Milan: Soc. Palatinae, 1723).

Tobler-Lommatsch

Adolph Tobler and Erhard Lommatsch, *Altfranzösisches Wörterbuch* (Wiesbaden: Steiner, 1925-).

Z. r. Ph.

Zeitschrift für romanische Philologie

BIBLIOGRAPHY

D'ABADAL I DE VINYALS, RAMON. *Catalunya carolingia*. Vol. III: Els Comtats de Pallars; Ribagorça. Barcelona: Institut d'Estudis Catalans, 1955.

ABU SHAMA. *Livre des deux jardins*, in *Recueil des historiens des croisades: Historiens orientaux*. Vols. IV and V. Paris: Académie des inscriptions et belles-lettres, 1898.

AEBISCHER, PAUL. *Études de toponymie catalane*. Barcelona: Imp. Elzeviriana, 1926.

ALCOVER, ANTONIO AND MOLL, FRANCISCO DE B. *Diccionari Català-Valencià-Balear*. 10 vols. Palma de Mallorca: Imp. Alcover, 1930-62.

ALFONSO X. *Primera crónica general de España*. Edited by R. Menéndez Pidal. 2 vols. Madrid: Bailly-Balliere, 1955.

ANDRAUD, PAUL. *La vie et l'œuvre du troubadour Raimon de Miraval: Étude sur la littérature et la société méridionales à la veille de la guerre des Albigeois*. Paris: E. Bouillon, 1902.

ANGLADE, JOSEPH. *Onomastique des troubadours*. Montpellier; Publications spéciales de la Société des Langues romanes, 1915.

———. "Les Troubadours provençaux en Biscaye," *Revista de filología española*, XV (1928), 343-353.

APPEL, CARL. *Bernart de Ventadorn: Seine Lieder*. Halle: M. Niemeyer, 1915.

———. *Das Leben und die Lieder des Trobadors Peire Rogier*. Berlin: G. Reimer, 1882.

———. *Provenzalische Chrestomathie*. 6th ed. revised. Leipzig: O. R. Reisland, 1930.

———. *Provenzalische Lautlehre*. Leipzig: O. R. Reisland, 1918.

ASTON, STANLEY C. *Peirol, Troubadour of Auvergne*. Cambridge: Cambridge University Press, 1953.

———. "The Name of the Troubadour Dalfin d'Alvernhe," *French and Provençal Lexicography*, Ohio 1964, pp. 140-163.

BARRAU DIHIGO, LLUIS, and MASSÓ TORRENTS, JAUME (eds.). *Gesta comitatum barcinonensium*. Barcelona: Institut d'Estudis catalans, 1925.

BARTHOLOMEW COTTON. *Historia Anglicana*. Vol. XVI of *Rerum Britannicarum Medii Aevi Scriptores*. London: Public Records Office, 1869.

BARTSCH, KARL. *Denkmäler der provenzalischen Literatur*. Vol. XXXIX of *Bibliothek des litterarischen Vereins*. Stuttgart: Bibliothek des Litterarischen Vereins, 1856.

———. *Provenzalisches Lesebuch*. Elberfeld: R. L. Friderichs, 1855.

BAUDON DE MONY, CHARLES. *Relations politiques des comtes de Foix avec la Catalogne*. 2 vols. Paris: A. Picard, 1896.

BEC, PIERRE. *Les Saluts d'amour du troubadour Arnaud de Mareuil.* Toulouse: E. Privat, 1961.

BERGERT, FRITZ. Die von den Trobadors genannten oder gefeierten Damen: *Beihefte zur Zeitschrift für romanische Philologie,* vol. XLVI. Halle: Zeitschrift für romanische Philologie, 1913.

BERNAT BOADES. *Libre dels feyts d'armes de Catalunya.* Barcelona: Biblioteca catalana, 1878.

BERNAT DESCLOT. *Crònica,* ed. M. Coll i Alentorn. 5 vols. Barcelona: Barcino, 1949-51.

BERTONI, GIULIO. *Il canzoniere provenzale di Bernart Amoros.* Fribourg: Université de Fribourg, 1911.

———. *I Trovatori d'Italia* (biografie, testi, traduzioni, note). Modena: U. Orlandini, 1915.

BOFARULL Y MASCARO, PROSPER. *Colección de documentos inéditos del Archivo general de la Corona de Aragón.* Barcelona: D. J. E. Monfort, 1876.

BOHS, WILHELM. "'Abrils issi' e Mais intrava,' Lehrgedicht von Raimon Vidal von Bezaudun," *Romanische Forschungen,* XV (1904), 204-316.

BONGARS, JACQUES (ed.). *Iacobi de Vitriaco Acconensis Episcopi Historia Hierosolomitana,* in *Gesta Dei per Francos.* Hanover: J. Aubrius, 1611.

BOUTIÈRE, JEAN, AND SCHUTZ, ALEXANDER H. *Biographies des troubadours.* 2nd rev. ed. Paris: Nizet, 1964.

CAFFARI. *Continuatorium Annales Genuenses.* Edited by Lodovico A. Muratori. Vol. VI of *Rerum Italiarum Scriptores.* Milan: Società Palatina, 1725.

Cartulari de Poblet. Edited by Eduard Toda and others. Barcelona: Institut d'Estudis Catalans, 1938.

CARUANA, J. "Itinerario de Alfonso II de Aragón," *Estudios de edad media de la corona de Aragón,* vol. VII, pp. 72-298.

CATEL, CHARLES DE. *Histoire des comtes de Toulouse.* Toulouse: P. Bosc, 1623.

CHALANDON, FERDINAND. *Histoire de la domination normande en Italie et en Sicile.* 2 vols. Paris: A. Picard, 1907.

CHARDIN, TEILHARD DE. "La première charte des coutumes de Montferrand," *Annales du Midi,* III (1891), 283-309.

CHAYTOR, HENRY J. *Savaric de Mauléon.* Cambridge: Cambridge University Press, 1939.

Chronica Anonima. Vol. I, Part II of *Historia Diplomatica Friderici Secundi* Edited by Jean-Louis-Alphonse Huillard-Bréholles. Paris: H. Plon, 1852.

CLUZEL, IRÉNÉE. "Princes et troubadours de la maison royale de Barcelone-Aragon," *Boletín de la Real Academia de Buenas Letras,* XXVII (1957-58), 321-73.

COLL I ALENTORN, MIQUEL. *La llegenda de Guillem Ramon de Montcada.* Barcelona: Ayma, 1957.

COMAS I PUJOLS, ANTONI. "Raimon Vidal." Unpublished dissertation, University of Barcelona, 1956.

Continuation of William of Tyre. Vol. II of *Recueil des historiens des croisades: Historiens occidentaux.* Paris: Académie des Inscriptions et Belles-Lettres, 1859.

CORNICELIUS, MAX. "So fe e·l temps c'om era iays," *Novelle von Raimon Vidal.* Berlin: Fock, 1888.

COROMINAS, JOAN. "De gramàtica històrica catalana: A propòsit de dos llibres," *Studia philologica et literaria in honorem L. Spitzer*. Berne: Francke, 1958, pp. 123-148.
———. *Diccionario crítico etimológico de la lengua castellana*. 4 vols. Berne: Francke, 1954.
———. "Notes etimologiques," *Butlletí de dialectologia catalana*, XIX (1931), 1942.
———. "The Old Catalan Rhymed Legends of the Old Seville Bible," *Hispanic Review* XXVII (1959), 361-383.
Cortes de Aragón, Valencia y Cataluña. Vol. I, Part I. Madrid; 1896.
COULET, JULES. *Le troubadour Guilhem de Montanhagol*. Toulouse: E. Privat, 1898.
CRESCINI, VINCENZO. *Manuale per l'avviamento agli studi provenzali*. 3rd. ed. revised. Milan: E. Hoeppli, 1926.
———. *Manualetto provenzale*. Verona-Padua: Drucker, 1892.
———. "Per il testo d'una delle canzoni di Bernart de Ventadorn," *Homenaje a Menéndez Pidal*. Vol. II. Madrid: Hernando, 1925.
DEJEANNE, JEAN-MARIE L. "Les 'coblas' de Bernart-Arnaut d'Armagnac et de Dame Lombarda, *Annales du Midi*, XVIII (1906), 63-68.
DELPECH, HENRI. *La bataille de Muret et la tactique de la cavalerie au XIIIe siècle*. Paris-Toulouse: Picard, 1878.
DENIS PYRAMUS. *La Vie Seint Edmund le rei*. ed. H. Kjellmann. Göteborg: 1935.
Diccionario geográfico de España. 17 vols. Madrid: Prensa Gráfica, 1956-62.
DU CANGE, CHARLES DU FRESNE. *Glossarium mediae et infimae latinitatis*. 10 vols.; 7th ed. revised. Niort: L. Favre, 1883-87.
DUPLÈS-AGIER, HENRI (ed.). *Chronique de Saint Martial*. Paris: Firmin-Didot, 1874.
ERNST, WILLY. "Die Lieder des provenzalischen Trobadors Guiraut von Calanzo," *Romanische Forschungen*, XLIV (1930), 255-406.
Ex Breve Chronica Abbatiae Panispontis, in vol. XVIII of *Recueil des historiens des Gaules et de la France*. Paris: V. Palmé, 1879.
Ex Chronica Anonimi Laudunensis Canonici, in Vol. XVIII of *Recueil des historiens des Gaules et de la France*. Paris: V. Palmé, 1879.
FOURNIER, PAUL. *Le Royaume d'Arles et de Vienne*. Paris: Picard, 1891.
FOURNIER, PIERRE-FRANÇOIS. "Le nom du troubadour Dauphin d'Auvergne," *Bibliothèque de l'École des Chartes*, XLI (1930), 66-99.
FRANK, ISTVAN. "Pons de la Guardia, troubadour catalan du XIIe siècle," *Boletín de la Real Academia de Buenas Letras de Barcelona*, XXII (1949), 229-328.
GARUFI, CARLO A. "Margarito di Brindisi conte di Malta," *Miscellanea di archeologia, storia e filologia dedicata al professore Antonino Salinas*. Palermo: 1907, pp. 273-82.
Gaufredi Prioris Vosiensis. Pars Altera Chronici Lemovicensis in Vol. XVIII of *Recueil des historiens des Gaules et de la France*. Paris: V. Palmé, 1879.
Gesta Regis Henrici Secundi. Edited by W. Stubbs. *Rerum Brittanicarum Medii Aevi Scriptores*. Vol. XLIX, Part II. London: Public Record Office, 1867.
Gestes de Philippe-Auguste (Extraits des chroniques de Saint Denis) in Vol. XVII of *Recueil des historiens des Gaules et de la France*. Paris: V. Palmé, 1878.

Godefroy, Frédéric E. *Dictionnaire de l'ancienne langue française et de tous ses dialectes du IXe au XVe siècle.* 10 vols. Paris: Vieweg, 1880-1902. Reprint New York, 1961.
González, Julio. *El Reino de Castilla en la época de Alfonso VIII.* 3 vols. Madrid: Escuela de Estudios medievales, 1960.
Gröber, Gustav. *Grundriss der romanischen Philologie.* Strasbourg: Karl J. Trübner, 1897.
Guillelmus Bretonus Armoricus. De Gestis Philippi Augusti in Vol. XVII of *Recueil des historiens des Gaules et de la France.* Paris: V. Palmé, 1878.
———. Philippidos, in Vol. XVII of *Recueil des historiens des Gaules et de la France.* Paris: V. Palmé, 1878.
Herzog, Emile. "Besprechungen," *Zeitschrift für romanische Philologie,* XXXI (1907), 378-81.
Higounet, Charles. *Le comté de Comminges de ses origines à son annexation à la couronne.* 2 vols. Toulouse, Paris; E. Privat, 1949.
Hill, Raymond T., and Bergin, Thomas G. *Anthology of the Provençal Troubadours.* Yale Romanic Studies No. XVII. New Haven: Yale University Press, 1941.
Hugh Falcand. *Historia Sicula,* in Vol. VII of *Rerum Italiarum Scriptores.* Milan: Società Palatina, 1725.
Innocent III. *Epistolae,* in Vol. XIX of *Recueil des historiens des Gaules et de la France.* Paris: V. Palmé, 1880.
Jaume I. *Cronica.* Edited and translated by J. M. de Casacuberta, 5 vols. Barcelona: Editorial Barcino, 1926-60.
Jeanroy, A. and J.-J. Salverda de Grave. *Poésies de Uc de Saint-Cire.* Toulouse: Privat, 1913.
Jeanroy, Alfred. "Comptes rendues," *Romania,* XXXIII (1904), 612-15.
———. "Les femmes poètes dans la littérature provençale aux XIIe et XIIIe siècles," *Mélanges de philologie offerts à Salverda de Grave.* Batavia: J. B. Wolters, 1933.
———. *Jongleurs et troubadours gascons des XIIe et XIIIe siècles.* Paris: Champion, 1923.
———. *La poésie lyrique des troubadours.* 2 vols. Paris: Didier, 1934.
Juan Ruiz. *Libro de buen amor.* Edited by J. Corominas. Madrid: Gredos, 1967.
Kolsen, Adolf. *Guiraut von Bornelh, der Meister der Trobadors.* Berlin: V. Vogt, 1894.
———. *Sämtliche Lieder des Trobadors Guiraut de Bornelh.* 2 vols. Halle: M. Niemeyer, 1907-35.
Lavaud, René, ed. *Poésies complètes du troubadour Peire Cardenal.* Toulouse: E. Privat, 1957.
Lejeune, Rita. "Le date de l'Ensenhamen d'Arnaut-Guillem de Marsan," *Studi Medievali,* New Series, XII (1939), 160-71.
Léonard, Émile. *Catalogue des actes des comtes de Toulouse — Raymond V (1149-1194).* Paris: A. Picard, 1932.
Levy, Emil. "Anhang," *Romanische Forschungen,* XV (1904), 315-16.
———. "Besprechungen," *Literaturblatt für germanische und romanische Philologie,* Vol. X (1889), cols. 57-60.
———. *Petit Dictionnaire provençal-français.* 3rd ed. Heidelberg: Carl Winter, 1961.
———. *Provenzalisches Supplement-Wörterbuch.* 8 vols. Leipzig: O. R. Reisland, 1894-1924.

LEWENT, KURT. *Zum Text des Lieder des Guiraut de Bornelh*. Florence: L. S. Olschki, 1938.
Liber Feudorum Maior. Edited by Francisco M. Rosell. 2 vols. Barcelona: Consejo Superior de Investigaciones Científicas: Sección de Estudios medievales, 1945-47.
LINSKILL, JOSEPH. *The Poems of the Troubadour Raimbaut de Vaqueiras*. The Hague: Mouton, 1964.
"*Llibre Blanch*" *de Santas Creus*. Edited by Federico U. Martorell. Barcelona: Consejo Superior de Investigaciones Científicas, 1947.
MARCA, PIERRE DE. *Histoire de Béarn*. Paris: Vve. J. Camusat, 1640.
MARSHALL, J. H., ed., *The* Donatz Proensals *of Uc Faidit*. Oxford: Oxford U. P., 1969.
MARTIN-CHABOT, EUGÈNE. *La Chanson de la croisade albigeoise*. 3 vols. Paris: Champion, 1931-61.
MASSÓ TORRENTS, JAUME. "La Canço provençal en la literatura catalana," *Miscel·lania Prat de la Riba*. Barcelona: Alpha, 1932.
MATTHEW PARIS. Historia Anglorum. Vol. XLIV of *Rerum Britannicarum Medii Aevi Scriptores*. London: Public Record Office, 1874.
MATTHEW OF WESTMINSTER. Flores Historiarum. Vol. XCV, Part II of *Rerum Britannicarum Medii Aevi Scriptores*. London: Public Record Office, 1890.
MELLI, EVIO. "I *salut* e l'epistolografia medievale," *Convivium* IV (1962), 385-98.
MEYER, PAUL. *Chanson de la croisade contre les albigeois*. 2 vols. Paris: Renouard, 1875-79.
MILÁ Y FONTANALS, MANUEL. "Antiguos tratados de Gaya Ciencia," *Obras completas*, Vol. III. Barcelona: A Verdaguer, 1890.
———. *De los trovadores en España*. Vol. II of *Obras completas*. Barcelona: A. Verdaguer, 1889.
MIRET I SANS, JOAQUIN. "La casa de Montcada en el vizcondado de Bearn," *Buttletí de la Reial Academia de Bones Lletres de Barcelona*, Vol. I. (1903).
———. *Itinerari de Alfonso I*. Barcelona: Institut d'Estudis Catalans, n.d.
———. *Itinerari de Jaume I*, "*El Conqueridor*." Barcelona: Institut d'Estudis Catalans, 1918.
———. "Itinerari de Pere I," *Butlletí de la Reial Academia de Bones Lletres de Barcelona*, Vol. I (1904).
———. "Notes per la biografia del trovador Guerau de Cabrera," *Estudis universitaris catalans*, IV (1910), 229-331.
MISTRAL, FRÉDÉRIC. *Lou Tresor dóu Felibrige*. 3rd ed. Aix-en-Provence: 1968.
MONFAR Y SORS, DIEGO. *Historia de los condes de Urgell*. Edited by P. Bofarull y Mascaro. Barcelona: J. E. Montfort, 1853.
MONSALVATJE Y FOSSAS, FRANCISCO. *Los castillos del condado de Besalú*. 2 vols. Olot: J. Bonet, 1919.
———. *Colección diplomática del condado de Besalú*. 2 vols. Olot: J. Bonet, 1919.
———. *Los condes de Ampurias vindicados*. Olot: J. Bonet, 1917.
NAUDIETH, FRITZ. "Der Trobador Guillem Magret," *Beihefte zur Zeitschrift für romanische Philologie*, LII (1914), 79-114.
NICETAS CHONIATES. Historia. Edited by Immanuel Bekker. Vol. XXIII of *Corpus Scriptorum Historiae Byzantinae*. Bonn: E. Weber, 1835.

NICOLAS DE BRAY. Gesta Ludovici Octavi. Edited by André Duchesne. Vol. V of *Historiae Francorum Scriptores*. Paris: Cramoisy, 1649.
PARDUCCI, AMOS. *Costumi ornati: Studi sugli insegnamenti di cortigiani medievali*. Bologna: Zanichelli, 1927.
———. "La 'lettera d'amore' nell'antico provenzale," *Studi medievali*, New Series, XV (1942), 69-110.
PARIS, GASTON. "Un lai d'amours," *Romania*, VII (1878), 407-415.
PATTISON, WALTER T. *The Life and Works of the Troubadour Raimbaut d'Orange*. Minneapolis: University of Minnesota Press, 1952.
PEIRE D'ALVERNHA. *Liriche*. Edited by Alberto del Monte. Turin: Loescher-Chiantore, 1955.
PEIRE VIDAL. Liriche. Edited by D'Arco Silvio Avalle. *Documenti di Filologia* No. IV. 2 vols. Milan and Naples; Riccardo Ricciardi, 1960.
PETER OF LANGTOFT. Chronicle. Edited by T. Wright. Vols. XLVII-XLVIII of *Rerum Britannicarum Medii Aevi Scriptores*. London: Public Record Office, 1866-68.
PETRI VALLIUM SARNAII. *Hystoria Albigensis*. Edited by Pascal Guébin and Ernest Lyon. 3 vols. Paris: Champion, 1926-39.
POWICKE, M. *The Loss of Normandy, 1189-1204*. 2nd revised. ed. Manchester: Manchester University Press, 1961.
PTOLEMY OF LUCCA. Historia Ecclesiastica. Vol. XL of *Rerum Italiarum Scriptores*. Edited by Lodovico A. Muratori. Milan: Società Palatina, 1725.
PUJOL, PERE. *Documents en vulgar dels segles XI, XII & XIII procedents del bisbat de la seu d'Urgell*. Barcelona: Palau de la Diputació, 1913.
RALPH OF COGGESHALE. Ex Chronico Anglicano. Vol. XVIII of *Recueil des historiens des Gaules et de la France*. Paris: V. Palmé, 1879.
RALPH OF DICETO. Opera Historica. Vol. LXVIII of *Rerum Britannicarum Medii Aevi Scriptores*. London: Public Records Office, 1876.
RAYNOUARD, FRANÇOIS J. M. *Choix des poésies originales des troubadours*. 6 vols. Paris: F. Didot, 1816-1821.
———. *Lexique Roman*. 6 vols. Paris: Silvestre, 1836-1845. Reprinted, Heidelberg: Winter, 1953.
RICKETTS, PETER. *Les poésies de Guilhem de Montanhagol: Troubadour provençal du XIIIe siècle*. Toronto: Pontifical Institute of Mediaeval Studies, 1964.
RIGAUT DE BARBEZIEUX. *Liriche*. Edited by Alberto Varvaro. Bari: Adriatica editrice, 1960.
RIGORDUS. De Gestis Philippi Augusti, Francorum Regis. Vol. XVII of *Recueil des historiens des Gaules et de la France*. Paris: V. Palmé, 1878.
RIQUER, MARTIN DE. "Las poesías de Guilhem de Berguedan contra Pons de Mataplana," *Zeitschrift für romanische Philologie*, LXXI (1955), 1-32.
———. *El Trobador Guilhem de Berguedan y las luchas feudales de su tiempo*. Castellón: 1953.
———. "Los problemas del roman provenzal de Jaufré," *Recueil de travaux offert à Clovis Brunel*. 2 vols. Geneva: Droz, 1955. Vol. II, pp. 435-61.
ROCHEGUDE, HENRI PASCAL. *Le Parnasse occitanien*. Toulouse: Bénichot 1819.
ROGER OF HOVEDEN. Annalium Pars Posteriori. Vol. XVII of *Recueil des historiens des Gaules et de la France*. Paris: V. Palmé, 1878.
———. Chronica. Vol. LI of *Rerum Britannicarum Medii Aevi Scriptores*. London: Public Record Office, 1868.

ROGER OF WENDOVER. The Flowers of History. Vol. LXXXIV of *Rerum Britannicarum Medii Aevi Scriptores*. London: Public Record Office, 1886.
ROHLFS, GERHARD. *Le Gascon: Études de philologie pyrénéenne*. Halle: Niemeyer, 1935.
RONJAT, JULES. *Grammaire historique des parlers provençaux modernes*. 4 vols. Montpellier: Société des Langues romanes, 1930-41.
SALAZAR Y CASTRO, LUIS. *Historia genealógica de la casa de Lara*. 4 vols. Madrid: Imprenta real, 1694-97.
SANTI, LOUIS DE. "La Louve de Pennautier," *Revue des Pyrénées*, XVI (1904), 359-69.
SCHULTZ-GORA, OSKAR. Review of M. Cornicelius, So fo e·l temps c'om era iays, *Zeitschrift für romanische Philologie*, XII (1888), 544.
———. "Der Trobador P. B. L. T.," *Zeitschrift für romanische Philologie*, LI (1931), 591-602.
SHEPARD, WILLIAM P. and CHAMBERS, FRANK M. *The Poems of Aimeric de Peguilhan*. Evanston: Northwestern University Press, 1950.
SICARD OF CREMONA. Chronicon. Vol. VII of *Rerum Italiarum Scriptores*. Edited by Lodovico A. Muratori. Milan: Società Palatina, 1725.
SOLDEVILA ZUBIBURU, FERRAN. *Historia de Catalunya*. 3 vols. Barcelona: Alpha, 1962.
SOLTAU, OTTO. *Blacatz, ein Dichter und Dichterfreund der Provence*. Berlin: Ebering, 1898.
———. "Die Werke des Troubadours Blacatz," *Zeitschrift für romanische Philologie*, XXII (1899), 201-48.
SORDELLO. *Le Poesie*. Edited by Marco Boni. Bologna: Libreria Antiquaria Palmaverde, 1954.
STENGEL, EDMUND. *Die beiden ältesten provenzalischen Grammatiken: Lo Donatz proensals und Las Rasos de Trobar*. Marburg: Elwert, 1878.
STICHEL, KARL. *Beiträge zur Lexikographie des altprovenzalische Verbums*. Marburg: Elwert, 1890.
STIMMING, ALBERT. *Bertran de Born, sein Leben und sein Werke*. Halle: Niemeyer, 1879.
STROŃSKI, STANISLAUS. "Quelques protecteurs des troubadours," *Annales du Midi*, XVIII (1906), 473-93.
THOMAS, ANTOINE. *Bertran de Born*. Toulouse: E. Privat, 1888.
TOBLER, ADOLPH, and LOMMATSCH, ERHARD. *Altfranzösiches Wörterbuch*. Wiesbaden: Steiner, 1925-.
UGOLINI, FRANCESCO. "Il canzoniere inedito di Cerveri di Girona," *Atti della R. Academia dei Lincei*, Series VI, Vol. V (1936).
USSEGLIO, LEOPOLDO. *I Marchesi di Monferrato in Italia ed in Oriente durante i secoli XII e XIII*. 2 vols. Casale Monferrato: Miglietta, 1926.
VALLS-TABERNER, FERRAN. "Els comtats de Pallars i Ribagorça a partir del segle XI," *Estudis universitaris catalans*, IX (1915-16), 40-101. Reprinted in *Obras selectas de Fernando Valls-Taberner*. Vol. IV, Estudios de historia medieval. Barcelona: Consejo Superior de Investigaciones Científicas, Escuela de estudios medievales, 1961. Pp. 125-205.
VIC, CLAUDE DE, and VAISSETE, JOSEPH. *Histoire générale de Languedoc*. 15 vols. 2nd ed. revised. Toulouse: Privat, 1872-92.
VIDAL, PIERRE. "Documents sur la langue catalane," *Revue des langues romanes*. Second Series, Vol. II (1876).

Vilaro, Juan Serra. *Baronies de Pinos i Mataplana*. 2 vols. Barcelona: Balmes, 1930.
Villanueva, Joaquín Lorenzo. *Viage literario a las iglesias de España*. Madrid: Imprenta Real, 1806. Vol. V.
Walter of Coventry. Memoriale. Vol. LVIII of *Rerum Britannicarum Medii Aevi Scriptores*. London: Public Record Office, 1872.
Wartburg, Walter von. Französisches Etymologisches Wörterbuch. Tübingen: Mohr, 1948-.

www.ingramcontent.com/pod-product-compliance
Lightning Source LLC
Chambersburg PA
CBHW030236240426
43663CB00037B/1171